Second Takes

THE SUNY SERIES

HORIZONS of CINEMA

MURRAY POMERANCE | EDITOR

Second Takes

Critical Approaches to the Film Sequel

Edited by

Carolyn Jess-Cooke

and

Constantine Verevis

SUNY PRESS

Cover image: *Pirates of the Caribbean: At World's End* (Gore Verbinski, 2007). Courtesy Walt Disney/The Kobal Collection/Mountain, Peter.

Published by
State University of New York Press, Albany

For information, contact State University of New York Press, Albany, NY
www.sunypress.edu

Production by Eileen Meehan
Marketing by Anne M. Valentine

Library of Congress Cataloging-in-Publication Data

Second takes : critical approaches to the film sequel / edited by
    Carolyn Jess-Cooke and Constantine Verevis.
        p. cm. — (SUNY series, horizons of cinema)
    Includes bibliographical references and index.
    ISBN 978-1-4384-3029-4 (hardcover : alk. paper)
    ISBN 978-1-4384-3030-0 (pbk. : alk. paper)
    1. Film sequels. I. Jess-Cooke, Carolyn, 1978– II. Verevis, Constantine.

PN1995.9.S29S84 2010
791.43'75—dc22   2009022995

10 9 8 7 6 5 4 3 2 1

For my husband Jared, my daughter Melody,
and my son Phoenix, with much love
—CJC

For Julie, Zoi, Mia (and the M&Ms:
Manny & Maxie, Milli & Monti)
—CV

Contents

Illustrations

Acknowledgments

The editors would like to thank the following people for their relevant assistance and stimulating conversations that greatly aided the production of this book: David Hancock, Christopher Land, Sanjay Sood, Evita Cooke, Claire Perkins, Deane Williams, and Noel King. At SUNY Press, James Peltz and Murray Pomerance have acted as supportive and encouraging editors from the commencement of the project, and they are to be warmly thanked for their heartening feedback and sharp editorial vision at various stages of the project. Thanks also to the School of English, Communications and Performance Studies at Monash University for furnishing the book with images. Finally, a special thanks to our contributors: working with each one of you has been a genuine pleasure.

Introduction

CAROLYN JESS-COOKE AND CONSTANTINE VEREVIS

TONIGHT'S SCHEDULE FOR A LOCAL cinema reads as follows:

Die Hard 4.0 (15)
Directed by: Len Wiseman
Starring: Bruce Willis, Timothy Olyphant, Maggie Q
11:00 13:50 17:10 20:10 21:20

Fantastic Four: Rise of the Silver Surfer (PG)
Directed by: Tim Story
Starring: Ioan Gruffudd, Jessica Alba, Chris Evans
11:00 13:20 15:30

Harry Potter and the Order of the Phoenix (12A)
Directed by: David Yates
Starring: Daniel Radcliffe, Emma Watson, Rupert Grint
10:30 11:00 11:30 12:00 13:00 13:30 14:00 14:30 15:00 16:00 16:30 17:00 17:30 18:00 19:00 19:30 20:00 20:30 21:00

Hostel Part II (18)
Directed by: Eli Roth
Starring: Bijou Phillips, Lauren German, Roger Bart
21:30

Ocean's Thirteen (PG)
Directed by: Steven Soderbergh
Starring: George Clooney, Brad Pitt, Matt Damon
20:50

Pirates of the Caribbean: At World's End (12A)
Directed by: Gore Verbinski
Starring: Johnny Depp, Orlando Bloom, Keira Knightley
17:50

Shrek the Third (U)
Directed by: Chris Miller
Starring: Mike Myers, Eddie Murphy, Cameron Diaz
11:10 11:40 12:20 12:50 13:40 14:40 15:10 15:40 16:10 16:50 17:20 18:10 18:40 19:10 19:50 20:20[1]

1

S TRIKINGLY, EVERY FILM LISTED here is a sequel. This being summer of 2007, it is not unusual for sequels to hold a strong cinematic presence—but *every screening*? And, looking at film releases sched-duled for the coming months, the horizon is filled with sequels. Previous months have been very similar: *Hannibal Rising* (Peter Webber, 2007) took $82 million worldwide at the box office—not bad for a fourth installment—while *Spider-Man 3* (Sam Raimi, 2007) has taken almost $1 billion worldwide since its release just three months ago.[2] A recent article in the *New York Times* puts this into perspective: "In the last five years, only about 20 percent of the films with more than $200 million in domestic ticket sales were purely original in concept, rather than a sequel or an adaptation of some pre-existing material" (Cieply). What is the significance of this, we ask, and why is sequel production increasing when critics have been lamenting about the sequel's dismal impact on originality since cinema began? What can the various "takes" on sequelization these films offer tell us about the sequel's relation to the text(s) from which it departs? More important, what does this sequel-dominated remit suggest about contemporary film production? What are the forces governing this resurgence of sequelization?

A closer examination of the films listed here provides some clues. First on the menu is *Die Hard 4.0* (Len Wiseman, 2007), which sees Bruce Willis retake the lead as action tough-nut John McClane (at 52 years old, no less) nineteen years after the first *Die Hard* (John McTiernan, 1988).

Figure I.1. *Live Free or Die Hard* (aka *Die Hard 4.0*; Len Wiseman, 2007). Courtesy 20th Century Fox/The Kobal Collection/Masi, Frank.

Willis has personally endorsed this venture as "better than the first one," whereas *The Guardian* stumbles to call it a sequel "(quatrequel? tetrequel?)" (qtd. in Sciretta; see also Bradshaw). Both discussions signal the film's unequivocal derivation of previous texts, that the film is *always in relation* to its heritage and that both its meaning and entertainment value ultimately derive from a negotiation of the first three Die Hard episodes (1988, 1990, 1995). The term "sequel" is thus invested with notions of "better-ness" and retrospectivity, but is additionally thrown into question by sequels that are not "part twos." In this regard, discussing *Fantastic Four: Rise of the Silver Surfer* (Tom Story, 2007) and *Hostel Part II* (Eli Roth, 2007) as "first" sequels seems appropriate, whereas *Shrek the Third* (Chris Miller, 2007) and *Ocean's Thirteen* (Steven Soderbergh, 2007) offer what has come to be known as the "threequel," or third film installment, which does not close the series (like the final part of a trilogy) but which does not really take it anywhere either (see Hendrix). "Threequels" are gap-fillers, apparently, or textual bridges that keep fans interested and merchandize sales up. Purportedly, and as its title suggests, *Pirates of the Caribbean: At World's End* (Gore Verbinksi, 2007) *is* the conclusion of a multibillion-dollar trilogy, although the enormous range of *Pirates'* tie-ins sweeping across the globe is enough to suggest that this film's textual boundaries take the concept of sequelization (or indeed "threequelization") to a whole new level.[3] It is likewise with *Harry Potter and the Order of the Phoenix* (David Yates, 2007), the fifth film in the series, the release of which preempts by one week the release of the last book in the *Harry Potter* series. Again, the hailstorm of textual aftermaths and merchandize tie-ins surrounding, preceding, and informing this film makes differentiating between book and film, film and sequel, sequel and merchandize very difficult.

From this relatively small list of films emerges a wide range of textual categories, cues, and connections that challenge any existing theory of intertextuality or even, as Gérard Genette puts it, *transtextuality*, his definition of "everything that brings [one text] into relation (manifest or hidden) with other texts" (*Architext* 81). This list also challenges previous notions of the film sequel as a "part two" or continuation of a previous "original," insofar as the term "sequel" comes to mean, in some cases, the continuation of a continuation, whereas the concept of "originality" is swiftly unmoored from its safe corner in the harbor of literary (and film) theory and set adrift amid the squalls of narrative recycling. If this list is anything to go by, things have gotten a lot more complicated in critiquing textuality.

This book confronts the complications film sequels and their discursive aftermath(s) pose. Taking a range of sequels as case studies, the following chapters propose dynamic new critical approaches to emergent shifts across the spectrum of textual relations. Vigorously contending with the sequel's industrial, aesthetic, cultural, political, and theoretical contexts, these chapters open new vistas on the exciting landscape of textual transposition. As one of few books dedicated to the subject of film sequelization,[4] this collection discusses the sequel's investments in repetition, difference, continuation, and retroactivity, and particularly those attitudes and approaches toward the sequel that see it as a kind of figurehead of Hollywood's commercial imperatives.

For indeed the sequel—like the cinematic remake—has been largely disparaged throughout cinema's history as a textual leech, a formulaic financial format, and the assassin of "originality" (see Berliner; Castle; Greenberg; Hoberman; Verevis). Claire Perkins provides the example of the trailer for the 2006 Melbourne International Film Festival (MIFF), and the way it valorizes the novelty and cultural value of its programming by contrasting it to the assumed dearth of originality in contemporary Hollywood:

> [The MIFF trailer] features a scruffy, bespectacled teenager sandwiched between two suited Hollywood executive-types in the back of a limousine. As the car moves through a neon-lit streetscape, the execs use a non-question initially directed at the kid—"OK, so your script is a sequel, right?"—to launch into a breathless exchange concerning the relative economic benefits of sequels, prequels and post-sequel prequels before deciding between themselves that a sequel remake (which they term a "sequel-sequel") is the way to go with this project, and turning again to the kid to ask him how much he wants for the trilogy or—better—the tetralogy, reassuring themselves and him that "he can stretch . . . he'll stretch . . . we'll stretch it . . . yeah, yeah." The scene fades to black over their final mumblings, and the tagline for MIFF 2006 comes up: "It's a long way from Hollywood." (14)

In a similar way a spate of recent commentaries use terms such as "hackneyed," "avaricious," "unnecessary," and even "sucky" to discuss the sequel and project sequelization as a purely capitalist endeavor with terrifying outcomes for originality (see Coates; Nelson; Sullivan).[5]

Yet before we continue to rant about originality, we should really consider whether it ever really existed in the first place. Sequelization, we argue, operates not only as a secondary film venture but, as many highly self-reflexive and resolutely metareferential sequels denote, as a deconstructive framework within which such sweeping generalizations and fundamentally problematic terms such as "originality" and "intertextuality" can be unpacked and repositioned in the new contexts within which contemporary film is produced. Closer examination of sequel criticism reveals the real argument often *not* to be about sequelization, but about a variety of Hollywood activities and reception practices under the cloak of a dubious "villain." Indeed, most of the articles and reports that decry the sequel in such terms tend to cite it as a "recent" cinematic virus that has reached a peak, and in many ways it appears that the term "sequel" is employed—often mistakenly—to describe a whole range of imitative, derivative, appropriational, and remaking activities, as well as to define various processes of exchange between film studios and audiences (see Friend, "Copy Cats"; Silverman; Simonet). In short, the sequel's discursive circulations are overloaded with accusations and definitions that otherwise demand closer scrutiny.

This book unpacks the cynicism and misinformed definitions surrounding sequelization and goes on to examine its more critical registers. We have titled this book *Second Takes* in recognition of the ways in which the sequel recapitulates features of an "original," but additionally offers something new to its source. In contradistinction to the remake, the sequel does not prioritize the repetition of an original, but rather advances an exploration of alternatives, differences, and reenactments that are discretely charged with the various ways in which we may reread, remember, or return to a source. Concomitant with the gamut of merchandizing tie-ins, cross-media platforms, and film franchises that inform contemporary Hollywood cinema, the sequel is primarily a site within which communal spectatorship and paratextual discourses may be circulated, and by which the experience of an "original" may be extended, revisited, and heightened.

From such critical registers the collection's first chapter departs. Constantine Verevis's chapter examines the strategies of multiplication and serialization that inform multifilm franchises and series. Seeking ultimately to overcome the limitations of purely taxonomic definitions that seek to differentiate sequels from remakes, series, and sagas, the film sequel is interrogated here as a function of a network of commercial interests, textual strategies, and critical vocabularies. By looking to the ways in which this network is played out in George A. Romero's (living) Dead trilogy—*Night of the Living Dead* (1968), *Dawn of the Dead* (1978), *Day of the Dead* (1985)—and its various off-shoots, including Romero's recent *Land of the Dead* (2005) and *Diary of the Dead* (2007), Verevis argues for the inseparability of the sequel's commercial, textual, and critical imperatives, at the same time calling for an overturning of the historical prioritization of an "original" text, offering the political and authorial modes at the heart of sequelization as much more compelling critical frameworks.

Such discussions of the sequel's various categories and textual relations outlined in Verevis's chapter are expanded on in Jennifer Forrest's chapter, in which she defines the idea of a "true" sequel as distinct from other forms of film serialization. Looking principally to a group of films from the Hollywood studio era, Forrest proposes discrete differences between the series and the true sequel. Negotiated through the example of *Four Daughters* (Michael Curtiz, 1938) and its sequels—*Four Wives* (Michael Curtiz, 1939) and *Four Mothers* (William Keighley, 1941)—Forrest's definitions prove vital for an analysis of contemporary industry practices that increase the audience for a product (sequels that are in reality a series) by appealing deceptively to a more sophisticated spectator—one that is conditioned to consume film "originals." Telling the difference, Forrest argues, is not always in the studios' interests.

Textual transpositions—whether between sequels and serials or originals and sequels—are, first and foremost, understood as industrial products. Yet Thomas Leitch's chapter adds a new form of textual transposition to the mix—"sequel-ready" fiction—which highlights the "marriage" that has taken place in recent years between literature and media, or rather the conditions by which this union has taken place. Although literary adaptation has been a dominant cinematic force since its inception, one may argue that the course of appropriation has not been entirely smooth. In the case of Helen Fielding's novel *Bridget Jones* (prefigured in Fielding's columns for the *Independent*) and its filmic incarnations—*Bridget Jones's Diary* (Sharon Maquire, 2001) and *Bridget Jones: The Edge of Reason* (Beeban Kidron, 2004)—Leitch argues that the source text contains those elements that are necessary for an easy filmic transaction and, more important, for an apparently "natural" stream of sequels to emerge. By examining the matrix between the narrative dynamics that make fictional texts peculiarly hospitable to sequels and the cultural, social, and indeed sexual shifts that produce these texts, Leitch demonstrates movements between text and screen that orient the concept of "sequel" firmly within the "original."

Both the considerations of sequelization as distinct from serialization and the sequel as connective tissue across a textual collective as Forrest and Leitch explored are readdressed in R. Barton Palmer's chapter. Here Palmer notes the methods by which an "original" is constructed as such specifically by those "part twos" and derivations that offer retrospectively interpretive contexts. In turn, the sequel is constructed as a mechanism of reorientation within several related texts. As demonstrated by *The Godfather* and its *Parts II & III* (Francis Ford Coppola, 1972, 1974, 1990), Palmer's notion of reorientation seeks to address the forces binding the Godfather texts together. The sequel is identified as a method by which we can more fully understand and explore this collectivity, in the same moment as the singularity of each film is maintained and redefined through the sequel's textual imperatives. Palmer's considerations of "before" and "after" additionally inform his analyses of the films as he identifies the process of "sequeling" at the films' commercial and textual levels to be a key factor in the texts' narratological and aesthetic operations. From this vantage point, a broader perspective is shed on the process of sequelization in terms of the treatment of beginnings and endings that are encountered throughout adaptational successions.

Considerations of "beforeness" and "afterwardsness" are additionally explored elsewhere in the collection throughout their spectatorial and hermeneutic contexts. Calling on the Warner Brothers' Batman film franchise—in particular *Batman Begins* (Christopher Nolan, 2005), Paul Sutton's chapter explores the notion of the *prequel*, drawing on the notion of "afterwardsness" as a way to approach the prequel's theoretical, cultural, and economic boundaries. Despite its semantic registers of "beforeness," Sutton notes that the prequel is most often made after an "original," and, accordingly, negotiations of "before" and "after" underscore the prequel. Yet far from remaining as an internal logic, the prequel's skewed temporality spills over into its external operations. The guiding light of this chapter is the idea of "afterwardsness" as an expression of the reconstructive and re-creative nature of spectatorship. This process of spectatorship, Sutton argues, re-creates or remakes the films it "remembers," while at the same time enabling the "autotranslation" of the viewing subject. The prequel emerges from this study as a categorical process that takes place *outside* of the modes of film production and within the boundaries of audience reception.

Among the most critical issues informing the film sequel are its imbrications in cross-cultural dialogues. Daniel Herbert's chapter notes the important cultural interactions circulating among Japan, South Korea, and Hollywood, throughout the remaking and sequelization of Koji Suzuki's novel *Ring* in a cycle of films that includes *Ringu* (Hideo Nakata, 1998), *Rasen* (Jôji Iida, 1999), and *The Ring* (Gore Verbinski, 2002). Cohering within a "macro-regional" textual geography, these films—which evoke an entire wave of Hollywood remakes of Asian films that has become a significant trend within the global cultural industries—function to thread together connections and expose tensions between the cultures from which the texts derive. Herbert artfully composes a metaphor, geographic as well as economic and cultural: namely that of *The Ring* Intertext *as* the Pacific Rim. His chapter not only demonstrates the ways in which these interactions circulate among *The Ring* cycle's aesthetic strategies, transnational identities, and technological erasures, but also reminds us that sequelization is by no means a phenomenon limited to Hollywood filmmaking.

Simon McEnteggart's chapter looks to cultural anxieties within the sequel in relation to the superhero subgenre, with a specific emphasis on films of the first decade of the twenty-first century and of the post-9/11 landscape. Whereas superhero films are often regarded cynically as filmic ventures aimed at a specific fan-base, McEnteggart argues that the superhero sequel registers cultural anxieties during the era of production. As an example, *Superman: The Movie* (Richard Donner, 1978) vocalizes concerns regarding the post-1960's decline in religious ideology and the "invisible threat" of the cold war throughout the narrative. In turn, its sequels focus on an actual attack by the cold war ideology on American ideals and institutions (*Superman II*, 1980), the anxieties regarding the advancement of technology, corrupt bureaucracy, and masculine duality (*Superman III*, 1983), and the fears involving nuclear power (*Superman IV: The Quest for Peace*, 1987). Whereas superhero films made prior to 9/11 typically contain internal battles of "good versus evil," McEnteggart argues that sequels created in the post-9/11 period—*Superman Returns* (Bryan Singer, 2006), *Blade II* (Guillermo del Toro, 2002), *X-Men 2* (Bryan Singer, 2003), and *Spider-Man 2* (Sam Raimi, 2003)—feature greater external threats posed by the "other" and are symbolic of the "war on terror" that President George W. Bush proposed. In examining superhero sequels, valuable theoretical frameworks regarding cultural and historical anxieties are revealed, as well as the evolving state of political awareness in popular culture texts.

Interrogating a different aspect of US filmmaking, Claire Perkins considers cultural difference in terms of the processes of exchange and dialogue established between two historical periods and their attendant cultural resonances. By considering several recent films, such as *The Royal Tenenbaums* (Wes Anderson, 2001), *Lost in Translation* (Sofia Coppola, 2003), and *The Squid and the Whale* (Noah Baumbach, 2005), Perkins juxtaposes this "smart" cinema with the commercial system of the Hollywood blockbuster. Perkins proceeds to reveal the American "smart" film as a sequel to the "New Hollywood" of the late 1960s and early 1970s, primarily in terms of its method of repeating themes of alienation—typified in Jerry Schatzberg's 1971 film, *Scarecrow*—and by substituting irony and nihilism for the nostalgia and anger (or activism) of the earlier period. By arguing that "smart" cinema signals a kind of cultural transition (facilitating the creation of a "new image" in commercial filmmaking), Perkins further suggests the sequel as a type of critical lens through which to rethink the formal and political crises of the first "New Hollywood."

Hollywood's self-appropriation and canonization is the subject of Joyce Goggin's chapter. As Goggin sees it, the original, the remake, and the sequel serve as showcases for popular stars rather than as sites of adaptation for any revered artistic antecedent. By investigating the Ocean's films—*Ocean's Eleven* (Lewis Milestone, 1960) and its Steven Soderbergh directed remake (*Ocean's Eleven*, 2001) and sequels (*Ocean's Twelve*, 2004, and *Ocean's Thirteen*, 2007)—Goggin considers autoreflexivity in these films as the promotion of the famous stars who act in them. The sequel's commercial dimension is further considered in the light of the Las Vegas context, in which the narrative emphasis on gambling, stealing, and materialism is seen to serve as a uniquely referential portrait of the sequel's economic purposes. The "nowness" on which the Ocean's series banks is therefore constituted by the temporality of the gambler, and the logic of "presentness" extends to the films' trademark, self-conscious humor (predicated on the stars' awareness of their own popularity at the time of production). These films not only construct a kind of "nowness" through the hype of Las Vegas, gambling, and pop-cultural icons, but also return to themselves for source material, thereby bringing the past repeatedly into the present.

Turning to the film-television interface, Ina Rae Hark explores the dynamics of resurrection inherent in the sequel phenomenon by looking to *Serenity*, the 2005 feature film sequel to Joss Whedon's hybrid science fiction/Western television series *Firefly*, cancelled by the FOX network after only eleven episodes had been broadcast in 2002. Universal approved the follow-up film in part because it served as a loss leader to persuade Whedon to sign a picture development deal with the studio, but the studio also held out the possibility of a series of film sequels if *Serenity* became a box-office success. Whedon thus had to craft a film that provided fitting closure for fans of the truncated series—the "decent burial" of the chapter's title—yet one that also left open the possibility of "resurrection." Hark's chapter draws on fan discourse to demonstrate the ways in which *Serenity* and *Firefly* deal with death, loss, and mourning, and how they provide a unique perspective on the metatextual bereavement process that sequels to past television programs invariably enact.

Nicholas Rombes speculates on how new and emerging digital mediums and interfaces—ranging from DVDs, to video cell phones, to the video iPod—are reshaping traditional notions of the sequel. As this chapter observes, imagining "before" and "after" is becoming increasingly difficult as the ubiquity of communication technologies and media interfaces means that narratives are in a continually "present" state. During the classic cinema era viewers had relatively little control over, or physical interaction with, the screen. Sequels were released and viewed according to the wishes of the studios. Today, however, what does it mean to release a sequel when audiences exercise a much greater degree of control not only over the film cycle that includes sequels, but also over the temporal dimensions of individual films themselves? Furthermore, the numerous bonus features, added material, and alternate endings and footage included in DVDs today contribute to the dissolution of the sequel.

Finally, the sequel's role in an ever-increasing landscape of media convergence and franchising is considered in Carolyn Jess-Cooke's chapter. With a focus on the *Pirates of the Caribbean* (Gore Verbinski, 2003, 2005, 2007) films, merchandizing, and related media outputs, this chapter looks to the forms of consumer participation across the franchise as what she calls "sequelized" spectatorship. Sequelized spectatorship is considered in terms of the many forms of interaction and participation with which the Pirates's spectator engages, which include a long list of secondary spectatorial encounters, as well as role-playing, secondary performance, and generational correspondence. The primary method by which the franchise achieves this, Jess-Cooke argues, is by creating another kind of sequel: that is, a sequel to the ideological and cultural architecture of the film's production house, the Walt Disney Company. Operating as a process of ideological exchange and perpetuation, the sequel thus enables the retransmission of Disney values throughout the *Pirates* franchise, while the qualities of community and synergy attributed to piracy across its textual history rereads the Walt Disney Company as an institution for the community, or one in which a sense of belonging and collaboration can be located. Citing Disney's collaborative structures as a means by which its films and media platforms are perpetuated across generations, the chapter posits sequelized spectatorship as the way in which the text invites the spectator to rewrite it across multiple media arenas, activities, physical territories, and generational boundaries.

Notes

1. See <http://www.cineworld.co.uk/reservation/ChoixResa.jgi?DATE=200 70713&CINEMA=53>. Accessed 12 July 2007.

2. The exact figure is $886,140,575. See <http://www.boxofficemojo.com/ movies/?id=spiderman3.htm>. Accessed 20 July 2007.

3. Since the time of writing (2007), a fourth installment—*Pirates of the Caribbean 4*—has been projected for release in 2011.

4. Others include Budra and Schellenberg, eds., *Part Two: Reflections on the Sequel*; Drew, *Motion Picture Series and Sequels: A Reference Guide*; Husband, *Sequels: An Annotated Guide to Novels in Series*; Jess-Cooke, *Film Sequels: Theory and Practice from Hollywood to Bollywood*; Nowlan and Nowlan, *Cinema Sequels and Remakes, 1903–1987*.

5. See also <http://www.comixtreme.com/forums/archive/index.php/t-15344. html>. Accessed 22 July 2007.

1

CONSTANTINE VEREVIS

Redefining the Sequel

The Case of the (Living) Dead

I N HIS ESSAY "INNOVATION and Repetition," Umberto Eco outlines several types of *serial repetition* that characterize the universe of (post)modern mass media. These categories are: the *retake, remake, series, saga,* and *intertextual dialogue,* or dialogism (166–73). Eco's typology of media repetition provides a useful point of entry to a discussion of *film seriality*—retakes, remakes, and series—but Eco's categories (and his examples) are not without difficulty and overlap. As Leonardo Quaresima points out (with reference to film remakes), these serial phenomena are "both well-known and immediately recognisable [terms] commonly used in everyday language and film publicity campaigns alike, [but they are phenomena] whose status is undefined" (75). This chapter takes a particular interest in the category of the retake—or *sequel*—but seeks to overcome the limitations of purely taxonomic definitions, both those that describe the retake as a commercially minded decision to "recycle the characters of a previously successful story in order to exploit them, by telling what happened to them after the end of their first adventure" (Eco 167), as well as those that outline the various textual subcategories of the sequel: *direct continuation sequel, in-name-only sequel, fake sequel, virtual remake,* and so on (see Thonen). Moving beyond these approaches, this

11

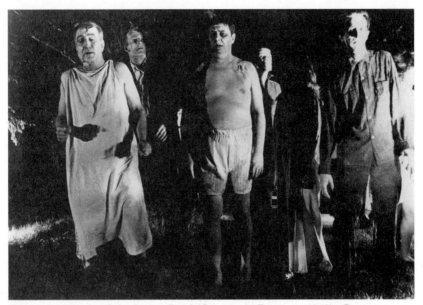

Figure 1.1. *Night of the Living Dead* (George A. Romero, 1968). Courtesy Image Ten/The Kobal Collection.

chapter interrogates the film sequel as a complex situation: a function of a *network* of commercial interests, textual strategies, critical vocabularies, and historical contexts. This understanding of the sequel will be advanced through the example of George A. Romero's Dead trilogy—*Night of the Living Dead* (1968), *Dawn of the Dead* (1979), *Day of the Dead* (1985)—and the terrible progeny that ultimately lead to his fourth and fifth zombie features, *Land of the Dead* (2005) and *Diary of the Dead* (2007).[1]

With his feature film debut—*Night of the Living Dead*—George Romero is credited with having transformed the modern horror film and (more particularly) the zombie mythology of the 1930s and early 1940s, known principally from Hollywood films such as *White Zombie* (Victor Halperin, 1932), *Revolt of the Zombies* (Victor Halperin, 1936), and *I Walked with a Zombie* (Jacques Tourneur, 1943). Outside of nineteenth-century Caribbean travel literature, the North American public was mainly unfamiliar with voodoo (or *voudoun*) rites and zombie folklore until the publication of William Seabrook's autobiographical account of his travels in Haiti, *The Magic Island* (1929). The first signs of the influence of Seabrook's travelogue and of the arrival of the zombie figure in American popular culture was Kenneth Webb's 1932 production of *Zombie* for the New York stage (Bishop 198–99; Russell 9–17). In the

same year, and at the crest of the American horror film boom, direc-
tor-producer team Victor and Edward Halperin took the essentials of
Seabrook's research into zombie mythology—"the Haitian setting, the
sugar cane fields and voodoo trappings"—to devise the astutely marketed *White Zombie* for Universal Pictures (Russell 22). Subsequent
films—including *Revolt of the Zombies*, the Halperin brothers' "unofficial
sequel" to *White Zombie* (28)—were interested in the ghoulish figure of
the zombie but, with the notable exception of *I Walked with a Zombie*,
not necessarily in its attendant Caribbean heritage and voodoo history.
Voodoo thrillers such as *Zombies of Mora Tau* (aka *The Dead that Walk*,
Edward L. Cahn, 1957) continued into the next decade but the 1950s
is considered a transitional period for the zombie genre with its core
"issues of voodoo, race and colonial anxiety [gradually] supplanted by
fears of invasion, of brainwashing and mass apocalypse" (47). Through
the 1950s—in films such as *Creature with the Atom Brain* (Edward L.
Cahn, 1955), *Invasion of the Body Snatchers* (Don Siegel, 1956), and *Invisible Invaders* (Edward L. Cahn, 1959)—zombies and *zombification* become
the perfect vehicle for encapsulating cold war "anxieties about the loss
of individuality, political subversion and brainwashing" (52). If this cycle
of films anticipates Romero's broad revision of the zombie film genre,
then the most direct precursor to the *Dead* films (especially in so far as
it challenges the distinction between the living and the dead, between *us*
and *them*) is *The Last Man on Earth* (Ubaldo Ragona and Sidney Salkow,
1964), an Italian-American adaptation of Richard Matheson's 1954 vam-
pire-apocalypse novel *I Am Legend* (62–64).[2]

Romero has consistently acknowledged that he drew inspiration
from the premise of Matheson's *I Am Legend*—the story of one last
human in a desolate world populated by plague-spawned, zombie-like
vampires—to sketch a (never published) three-part short story that
became the genesis of the *Dead* series (see Fischer 638; Gagne 24; Hickenlooper 346; McCarty 61; Waller 275; Yakir 60). Commonly referred
to as "Anubis," Romero's story is described "as an allegory about what
happens when an incoming revolutionary society [in this case, the living
dead] replaces an existing social order" (Gagne 24). In the first part of
"Anubis" a group of people takes refuge in a farmhouse as the recently
deceased inexplicably rise from the grave to feed on the flesh and blood
of the living: "In Part I [the zombies] appear, but operative society seems
to be staying on top of it, even though there's a lot of chaos. . . . It's Part
I that we turned into *Night of the Living Dead*: the new society appears
and attacks every aspect of our society. . . . People don't really know
how to deal with it. . . . The scientific society has absolutely no answers"
(Romero qtd. in Yakir 60).

The second episode, which takes up the story some six months later, finds that the zombie phenomenon has become widespread and uncontrollable to the extent that "there [is now] an equal balance [of power], with the outcome [for established society] undecided" (60). Attempting to contain the plague, a posse of heavily armed military personnel moves through a contaminated area exterminating the living dead, but as it does so the team accidentally leaves behind a cache of weapons. A group of zombies discovers the arms, and (as in *Dawn of the Dead*) there is the first glimmer of recognition and remembrance. The third movement (the basis for the original screenplay of *Day of the Dead*)[3] is set some years after the initial outbreak. The balance of numbers has shifted, and now a different militia—an army of the living dead—pursues a lone, wounded human across a desolate landscape. Of the final installment, Romero says: "in the Third Part, it [is] the zombies who are operative. I have this vision of a layered society where the humans are little dictators, down in bomb shelters, and they fight their wars using zombies as soldiers. . . . It's a return to what the zombie was in the beginning [namely, a slave in a class struggle]" (60). While the films of the Romero trilogy turned out to be very different, the progression of the phenomenon—its *serialization*—and principal thematic concerns are basically in evidence at the source (see Gagne 25).

Night of the Living Dead has been called one of "a select wax-works of films whose names alone unspool their images" (Doherty 20). Initially a modest commercial success on the drive-in circuit, *Night of the Living Dead* was rereleased theatrically in 1970, and it began to build its cult status as a midnight movie. The US critical response to Romero's film—typified by notorious reviews in *Variety* and the *Chicago Sun-Times*—was mostly hostile (see Gagne 36), but good press and strong box-office returns in Europe paved the way for its critical reevaluation, including Robin Wood's describing *Night of the Living Dead* (and the Dead trilogy) as "one of the most remarkable and audacious achievements of modern American cinema" ("Woman's Nightmare" 45). As Wood (and others) have pointed out, *Night of the Living Dead*'s enduring reputation and widespread influence resides not only in its excessive visceral jolts and frustration of genre conventions, but also in the overturning of dominant cultural norms and unmasking of tensions in patriarchal and domestic relationships (Wood, "Apocalypse Now" 91). More evidently, and well before Romero seriously considered an "official" sequel to his cult hit, "*Night of the Living Dead*—like all commercially successful genre films—was imitated, borrowed from, and exploited [*serialized*] by other storytellers" (Waller 297). Kim Newman says: "the most obvious and immediate effect of the success of *Night of the Living Dead* was a sudden epidemic of inferior [low-budget] flesh-eating zombie films" (*Nightmare Movies* 6). Most notable of these was Benjamin Clark's *Children Shouldn't Play with Dead Things* (1972), a film that follows a theater troupe of hippies to a lonely Florida burial island where their midnight incantation and ersatz ritual inadvertently awakens the dead. As in *Night of the Living Dead*, the various players take refuge in a deserted house where they are besieged by the blood-thirsty zombies. The actors desperately fight off the ghouls, but ultimately all are consumed before (in an ending that anticipates the start of Lucio Fulci's *Zombi 2*) the living dead board a small boat and float back toward the mainland (Newman, *Nightmare Movies* 7; Russell 71–72).

In Spain, where *Night of the Living Dead* was particularly well received, Romero's film was revised in Jorge Grau's Spanish-Italian coproduction (filmed in England), *The Living Dead at the Manchester Morgue* (*Fin de Semana para los Muertos*, aka *Let Sleeping Corpses Lie*, 1974). Described as a film "so close to Romero's *Night of the Living Dead* as to be almost a crib" (Glaessner 78; see Waller 297–98), *The Living Dead at the Manchester Morgue* follows two characters, George and Edna, who are accidentally thrown together during an ill-fated weekend in the British countryside. Together the couple discovers the beginnings of a zombie plague—apparently caused by the high-pitched hum of agricultural machinery—but are unable to secure from local authorities any assistance in their attempt to confine its spread. At the Southgate Hospital morgue—a locus of zombie activity—George tries to save Edna from the swelling horde of the undead, but on discovering that she has already become a zombie pushes her into a treatment room, set alight in the chaos. As described by Jamie Russell, there is (at the moment of Edna's engulfment in the flames) a certain ambiguity—a moment of *identification*—that anticipates the increasingly sympathetic treatment of zombies across Romero's later body of work (83). George survives the conflagration at the morgue but—when later shot dead (in a reprise of the ending of *Night of the Living Dead*) by the bigoted Sergeant McCormick—returns as a zombified hero to take his revenge on the police officer and the bankrupt value system he represents. These generic revisions—in particular the overly *political* message of Grau's ecologically driven zombie plague and the film's challenge to "values of authority, heroism and religious faith"—anticipate the trajectory of the Dead trilogy, with *The Living Dead at the Manchester Morgue* "bridging the gap between Romero's *Night of the Living Dead* and his later *Dawn of the Dead*" (81).

According to Paul Gagne, Romero's "desire to find a metaphorical 'underbelly' comparable to that in *Night of the Living Dead* [was] one of the main reasons" for taking several years to develop the *Dawn of the Dead* sequel (87). The inspiration for expanding the zombie concept beyond his first feature reportedly came around 1975 when Romero was introduced to the huge Monroeville shopping mall (southeast of Pittsburgh), a closed environment that suggested itself as the perfect setting for the "equal-balance" part of the trilogy (see Gagne 83; Manders 38–39; Yakir 60). Soon after his visit, Romero began writing a screenplay, "darker and bleaker" than that of *Night of the Living Dead*, which "centred around this couple, a guy and a pregnant woman, who were living up in [the] crawlspace [of the mall to escape the zombie hordes]. He was like a hunter-gatherer going down into the mall for supplies and food" (qtd. in Gagne 83). Romero went on to widen the idea—in the finished screenplay, four survivors take refuge in a shopping mall where they create an ideal of consumer living—into *Dawn of the Dead*'s overt critique of a 1970s rampant culture of consumption. At the same time, Romero's interest in the second installment of the *Dead* series appears to have been initiated as much by *commercial* imperatives as it was by an interest in serializing the allegorical message of *Night of the Living Dead* across subsequent decades. Although Romero's first film had performed solidly, the Image Ten consortium (a limited partnership established to produce the film) had received only a modest return on the substantial revenue generated by the property. One reason for this was the fact that a copyright line had been inadvertently left off the film's credits in a series of late changes of title from *Night of the Flesh Eaters* to *Night of Anubis*, both of which were finally rejected in favor of *Night of the Living Dead*. The oversight led to the distribution of countless black market prints (and unauthorized video cassettes), and Romero has stated that the release of a colorized version of *Night of the Living Dead* and then an authorized remake—the Tom Savini directed *Night of the Living Dead* (1990)—were "purely financial" decisions by the producers of the original film to license the property and recoup lost earnings (Frasher 19; Gagne 39).[4]

Second (and more significantly), although Romero was responsible for the initial "Anubis" story, the screenplay for *Night of the Living Dead* was a collaboration between Romero and John Russo of the Image Ten consortium. Romero and Russo (along with others at Image Ten) retained ownership of the *Night of the Living Dead* property, but a falling out of the cowriters ultimately led to the development of two separate pathways to sequelization. Russo was the first to react, developing the story of the living dead initially through a literary "remake"—a novelization of *Night of the Living Dead* (1974)—which was followed with a story sequel, *Return of the Living Dead* (1978; Waller 297). Around the time that Russo's second book was published, Romero announced his plan to produce not only a film sequel (*Dawn of the Dead*), but also to project a Dead trilogy along the lines of "Anubis." But because Romero and Russo had coauthored the *Night of the Living Dead* screenplay, there was some dispute over who legally owned the film sequel rights. A formal agreement was worked out in 1978 when the Laurel Group (the company Romero and Richard Rubinstein had formed to produce *Martin*, 1976) sold *Dawn of the Dead* to United Film Distribution whereby Romero was given the right to produce and distribute his sequel and Russo the permission to develop his *Return of the Living Dead* story (and subsequent screenplay) into a film. The significance afforded to the titles of the films in communicating a set of public expectations around the serialization of the property is indicated by the fact that the Laurel Group had already moved against a Chicago film distributor that had tried—in an instance of *faux* sequelization—to rerelease *Messiah of Evil* (aka *Dead People*, aka *Revenge of the Screaming Dead*, Willard Huyck, 1973) as *Return of the Living Dead* (Gagne 166). Although the Motion Picture Association of America ultimately ruled that Romero did not have exclusive rights to the use of the title "Living Dead," it was determined under the agreement that (the proposed) *Return of the Living Dead* could not be promoted as an "official" sequel to Romero's *Night* (Gagne 166; Peachment 19).

Numerous commentators have observed that the repetitions of *Dawn of the Dead* (and the later *Day of the Dead* and *Land of the Dead*) effectively blur the "threshold between that of a genre film, a sequel, and a remake" (Sutherland 68). Gregory Waller, for instance, describes *Dawn of the Dead* as "a continuation and an elaboration" of *Night*, at once "a reconsideration of the major themes and assumptions of the earlier film [*a remake*], and an informed, ambitious, innovative expansion of the story of the living and un-dead [*a sequel*]" (298). In another example, Tim Lucas refers to *Dawn of the Dead* as a "non *sequitur* sequel to . . . *Night of the Living Dead*" for the fact it does not recycle characters from the first film but "shows how a different group of people react when the recently dead revive to satiate their hunger for warm, living flesh" (41). At a level of generality, the Romero zombie films—in particular the trilogy—*do* seem to repeat (or remake) the same basic plot in which a group of survivors takes refuge in a safe environment (a deserted house, a shopping mall, an underground bunker, a walled city) that it protects from the zombie hordes until finally the haven is overrun. More specifically, Wood argues that *Night* and *Dawn of the Dead* are based on the same triangular structure in which the central group of survivors is threatened by *both* the living dead *and* a strongly masculinized group: the rednecks in *Night*, the motorcycle gang in *Dawn*. In the later *Day of the Dead* this structure is extended so that a small group is endangered (on the one hand) by the zombies, and (on the other) by the military *and* the scientists, the latter of which together stand for the corrupt superstructure of US patriarchal authority and the masculine-rationalist ideology that underpins it (Wood, "Woman's Nightmare" 46). But at the same time, Wood insists that Romero *never repeats himself*, stating (elsewhere) that the first two installments of the trilogy not only work *together* to redefine the zombie genre but are very *distinct* from one another: "*Dawn of the Dead* is much more than the elaborate re-make it has been taken for" ("Apocalypse Now" 91). Specifically, Wood refers to the several ways in which *Dawn of the Dead* (and Romero's subsequent *Day of the Dead*) extend—or *serialize*—the narrative, historical, and political allegory of *Night of the Living Dead*.

The most obvious textual marker of the *narrative* serialization of the Romero zombie trilogy is the "diurnal progress of their respective titles"—night, dawn, and day—which signals the advancement and escalation of the zombie plague (Sutherland 68). At the end of *Night of the Living Dead*, the nightmare of corpses returning to feed off the flesh of the living—a calamity apparently caused by radiation from a returning Venus probe—seems to have dissipated as quickly as it began. But the film's uneasy resolution—not just the fact that the sole survivor of the night (the black hero, Ben) is gunned down by the redneck posse, but also that establishment values (love, heroism, family) have proven so ineffectual in the face of the crisis—suggests that the containment of the plague is more apparent than real. *Dawn of the Dead* begins with the heroine Fran, a Pittsburgh television station employee, sleeping against a red control booth wall. She awakens with a start to find the studio in chaos, with confused attempts to transmit information—news bulletins of the type seen in the besieged farmhouse of *Night*—about the escalating zombie crisis. The opening sequences of *Dawn*—the disorganized and frantic activity at the television station and (next) an equally chaotic and desperate scene in which state troopers attempt to clear a tenement building of the living dead—work as traditional exposition scenes, communicating information (eliminating the need for any *direct* knowledge of the previous installment) and emphasizing how rapidly the institutions of society can disintegrate (Gagne 86; Waller 298–99). The major part of *Dawn of the Dead* follows the fortunes of four survivors—Fran and her boyfriend Stephen, and two troopers, Roger and Peter—who flee the city carnage in a helicopter only to discover masses of shambling zombies roaming the countryside. Below them, a scene of military convoys and redneck posses hunting down, and making sport of, the zombies unfolds. As Ed Lowry and Louis Black point out, this extermination game "might be the closing moments of *Night of the Living Dead*," but where the earlier film implied that the threat had been contained, *Dawn of the Dead* sequelizes the event "to suggest that the [zombie] threat has already succeeded in destroying civilization as we know it" (17).

Dawn of the Dead is not a "conventional" or *direct* sequel but rather—like a historical *saga* (Eco 169–70)—focuses on the efforts of a (later) group of people who battle to survive as the epidemic (unleashed some time earlier) escalates out of control. In this respect *Dawn of the Dead* follows the second part of "Anubis" (in which the balance of things is at a point where the outcome is undecided), but *Dawn* serializes another important aspect of that installment: *the development of a zombie consciousness.* The early scenes of *Dawn of the Dead*—in which armed posses hunt down the undead—not only demonstrate the rapid break down of civil order but also begin to complicate the distinction between victim and villain (see Waller 300). Reflecting on *Dawn of the Dead* and its relation to the other films of the trilogy (and beyond), Romero says that the progression—the sequelization—of the zombie revolution is its *central point*:

> In my mind, the zombies have always been evolving. . . . Even in *Dawn* I was trying to show some zombies with "personalities"—a soft-ball player, a nun . . . that poor guy on the escalator, just trying

Figure 1.2. *Dawn of the Dead* (George A. Romero, 1978). Courtesy United Film/The Kobal Collection.

to get by. I was trying to give them some sympathy. And at the very end, when Peter is escaping and a zombie grabs his gun, he makes a decision that it is a better gun than the one he has. In other words, I have tried to make them progress. Bub [the slightly "domesticated" zombie in *Day of the Dead*] to me is [a] classic Karloff [character], a sympathetic monster. (qtd. in D'Agnolo-Vallan 24)

When the four protagonists of *Dawn of the Dead* land their helicopter on the roof of the suburban mall that will become their refuge (and ultimately their prison), they observe that the zombies are irresistibly drawn to the shopping center because they dimly remember that it once played a major part in their lives. As Steven Shaviro points out, "[the zombies] seem most fully human when they are wandering the aisles and escalators of the mall like dazed but ecstatic shoppers" (92). Once evicted by the survivors, the swelling number of zombies in the car park and at the entrances to the mall is evidence of their determination to penetrate the sealed environment and reclaim their "materialistic past" (Iaccino 154–55). In a telling scene—and in answer to Fran's question: "Who the hell are they [the living dead]?"—Peter observes: "They're us, that's all." Throughout the film, we see evidence of conditioned behavior, and toward the end, when Stephen falls prey to the zombies, he "remembers" the false wall that his friends erected to conceal the entrance to their hideout and leads the other zombies to the refuge. As Fran and Peter make their escape to the helicopter one of the zombies wrestles a rifle from Peter and stares curiously at the weapon. More than any other single action, this gesture—the remembrance of the firearm—anticipates the third installment in the series.

Drawing on the third stage of "Anubis," Romero devised an initial script treatment for *Day of the Dead* that takes the zombie revolution to the point where the undead have vastly outnumbered humanity and gained intelligence enough to perform basic tasks.[5] Set some five years after the plague has begun, the story tells of a new world order where the populace is divided into social castes: the civilian masses, living in squalid conditions above ground; teams of scientists living underground and working at ways to condition the zombies; a military faction devoted to shaping the zombies into an army of the living dead; and the corrupt, former politicians who control the military operation and live in comfort deep in the compound (Gagne 147–48; Williams, *Knight* 129–30). Newman describes the script for (the unrealized) *Day of the Dead* as one that depicts "a future world where living and dead have come to terms, and trained zombies fight wars on behalf of human masters who live in walled city states. . . . Facetiously announced as *Zombies in the*

White House [the never realized version of *Day of the Dead* ends] with the establishment in the ruins of the old society of an ambiguously utopian new normality" ("*Day of the Dead*" 267). Unable to secure funding for his ambitious scenario, Romero was forced to reduce the scope of *Day of the Dead* substantially, but nevertheless advanced his third installment in the direction of establishing ever-greater similarities between the living and the nonliving. The completed *Day of the Dead* begins (where *Dawn* left off) with a civilian-military expedition—consisting of scientist Sarah and her three male colleagues—landing its helicopter in a Florida street and then, on finding masses of zombies (and no sign of survivors), returning to its underground military base. In the facility (overseen by the ruthless autocrat, Captain Rhodes), the eccentric Dr. Logan (nicknamed "Frankenstein") employs a variety of conditioning techniques in the interest of training and controlling the zombies. Logan's pet project is a domesticated zombie, affectionately known as "Bub," who has been educated to remember socially conditioned instinctive behavior, to recognize objects, and to perform simple tasks. But when Rhodes discovers that Logan has trained Bub by feeding him human flesh carved from the remains of fallen soldiers, he summarily executes the scientist. Discovering Logan's body, Bub moves from feelings of deep sorrow to ones of vengeful anger. In the final scenes of the film, Bub discovers a cabinet of weapons and leads the living dead (who have overrun the compound) in an impressive "zombie coup" against Rhodes and his men (Iaccino 157; Rowe, "Man of 1,000 Zombies" 67). At the end of *Day* (in a reprisal of *Dawn*) only Sarah, John, and their friend McDermott escape the bunker, making their way by helicopter to a remote tropical island to begin anew.

The increasing power and intelligence of the living dead (and the associated reemergence of the class struggle) across Romero's zombie trilogy relates to another overarching aspect of its serialization: namely, its *political* dimension. Romero says that, at the time he decided on a follow up to *Night of the Living Dead*, he had also "gotten the idea that it would be nice to do one of these [zombie films] for every decade and try to reflect the attitude of the times" (qtd. in M. Simpson 60). *Night of the Living Dead* in particular is described as a film that "seized the *zeitgeist* by the throat": a film that presents a hopeless world where nothing matters, and in this way reflects the social upheavals and breakdown of civil order that occurred during the turbulent period of the 1960s (Doherty 20). Although the social allegory of *Night* was not initially commented on, there has (in the decades since its release) been a proliferation of social and cultural interpretations. In an early evaluation, R. H. W. Dillard sees *Night of the Living Dead* as a film whose assault on government, family, and individuality "undercuts [the most] cherished values of our whole civilization," a film whose *real horror* is not a result of "inspiring a fear of the dead or even a fear of the ordinary world" but rather a consequence of "its refusal to resolve those fears in any way that does not sacrifice human dignity and human value" (27–28). Others have variously seen the film as a comment on US involvement in the Vietnam War (Higashi), a metaphor for the black experience in America (Lightning), a depiction of the radical futurelessness of the nuclear age (Caputi), and as a critique of capitalist-consumer society: "Romero's zombies stand in for those work-ers and consumers who, since the flash-point year of 1968 . . . have been thrown on the scrap heap. Economically extinct, socially displaced, they return to devour those who have survived them" (Beard 30). Wood, in particular, has taken up the latter approach, insisting that *Night of the Liv-ing Dead* (and the trilogy as a whole) must be seen historically "in terms of Romero's [*serialized*] responses to changes in American society and ideology" ("Woman's Nightmare" 45). For Wood, each one of the films is, in its own unique way, "an assault on the structures and assumptions of patriarchal capitalism": *Night* is centered around the 1960s nuclear family and its inner tensions; *Dawn* is focused on 1970s consumerism and dominant couple relationships (both heterosexual and male-buddy); and *Day* is centrally concerned with (militaristic and scientific) structures of 1980s masculine-rationalist ideology (45–46).

Although Romero maintains that he missed the opportunity to extend the political commentary of the Dead trilogy into the 1990s, he did contribute a screenplay to the Tom Savini-directed remake, *Night of the Living Dead* (1990). Some critics insist that Savini's version fails to impress—and fit into the Romero cycle and mythos—exactly because it does not take the opportunity to draw parallels between the zombie as surplus human capacity and conscious fears (of the decade) about mass unemployment (Beard 30). Against this view, others contend that whatever the *commercial* imperatives behind the *Night* remake, Romero's authorship is exactly expressed through the remake's implication of social plague and serialization of the trilogy's *politics of gender*. Notably, Barry Keith Grant argues that where the depiction of the catatonic Barbara in the original *Night of the Living Dead* seems to support "sexist assump-tions about female passivity, irrationality and emotional vulnerability," the remake transforms Barbara into "an active, assertive character . . . a narrative agent [and a survivor]" (65). In this assessment, Romero emerges as a writer-director with a particular interest in gender rep-resentation, one who serializes his principal female character: from the original Barbara, "in a state of limbo on the outskirts of women's libera-tion," through Fran's intermediate depiction of the "untrained survivor," and on to Sarah as "a woman of the 1980s [and] natural leader" (Gagne 90). Accordingly (and even though the Savini version mostly follows the narrative invention of the original), Barbara not only survives (second time around), but does so by exhibiting a "clear-headed, unsentimental resourcefulness" lacking in the film's male characters (Grant 69). Following the escape trajectory mapped by her predecessors Fran and Sarah, the new Barbara survives "by deducing [that] the correct strategy in response to the zombie attacks [is] neither to defend the house . . . nor to retreat to the cellar . . . but to flee. . . . She acts more effectively, in other words, free of the territoriality associated in the film with masculinism" (67). Barbara's respite is, however, only short-lived, for what she discovers on rejoining the living is that her fellow humans—who sadistically ridicule the zombies and use them for target practice—are no different to (indeed, probably worse than) the zombies. The final scene of the torture of zombies and the passing overhead of a private helicopter not only foreshadows the (already completed) *Dawn* sequel,[6] but encapsulates the trilogy's movement from initially presenting the undead as a monstrous threat to recognizing "hysterical masculinity" as the greater danger (74; see Iaccino 153; Perez 59).

The historical and political dimensions of the Romero written and/ or directed Dead films—*Night, Dawn, Day,* and (the next) *Night*—contribute to an understanding of their serialization, but these films are more evidently marked as (official) sequels/remakes by the promotional strategies that characterize each of the successive installments. In this understanding of the film sequel, the logic of the phenomenon resides in the commercial (and sometimes critical) success and value of an earlier (original) film, and the reciprocal interest the sequel generates in the previous installment (or installments) of the "franchise."[7] In continental Europe, Romero's *Night of the Living Dead* was followed by a unique edit of *Dawn of Dead,* overseen by coproducer Dario Argento and released under the alternative title, *Zombi* (Gagne 97; Marcus). The immediate commercial success of *Zombi* saw it quickly followed by Lucio Fulci's *Zombi 2* (aka *Zombie Flesheaters*), the first one of several Italian zombie films to use a numerical suffix to promote itself as a semisequel and exploit the market's eagerness for more graphic scenes of the dead returning to consume the living. The film follows a newspaper reporter and young woman (in search of her missing scientist father) to a Caribbean island where the pair discover a zombie epidemic—evidently caused by voodoo rites—that culminates in the rise of the island's maggot-eaten zombie conquistadors. Despite its title, Fulci's film bears little (if any) direct narrative resemblance to *Zombi,* and (as Russell points out) it appears equally inspired by contemporaneous Italian cannibal films and earlier Caribbean-set zombie movies as it does by the Romero-Argento film: "when Argento wrote that *Dawn of the Dead* [*Zombi*] was his creation [Fulci reminded him] that zombies were around even before [such films as] *I Walked with a Zombie*, [and that] zombies belong to Haiti and Cuba, not to Dario Argento" (142). This defense of Fulci's own ("original") contribution to the zombie film genre seems further supported by the suggestion that *Zombi 2*'s graphic depiction of decaying zombies, and specifically of the undead shambling though the island's desolate palmy streets, anticipates Romero's later *Day of the Dead* (see "Rev. of *Zombie*" 75). Ultimately, while *Zombi 2* (at least) initially seeks to locate its commercial identity in the Romero-Argento sequel, the film and its offspring—notably, Fulci's later "zombie trilogy" (1980–1981) and the "nonsequel" of *Zombi 3* (1988)—serialize only a loose set of *generic* features and attributes belonging to a larger zombie canon.

The question of false or *indirect* sequelization is perhaps even more evident in the case of *Return of the Living Dead*, the film that grew out of Russo's paperback of the same title. Following some years in development, Russo's original treatment for a sequel to *Night of the Living Dead* made its way to Orion Pictures where it was substantially rewritten before production began in 1984. According to Gagne, Russo's initial script—which "wanted to retain the gutsy feeling of starkness and reality from *Night*"—was set some ten years after the events of the first film: "the plague is gone but not forgotten, and certain precautions are still being taken by religious groups and cults" (166). By contrast, the Orion Pictures version, which Dan O'Bannon rewrote and directed, transforms the material into a horror-comedy hybrid, retaining only a single direct plot link to *Night of the Living Dead*. O'Bannon says the studio had little interest in the *Return of the Living Dead* property unless it retained its title—its "most exploitable element"—but that issues of intellectual property (*authorship*) and Romero's ongoing concern over the legality of the enterprise motivated him to change details from the original Russo script and directly address its relation to *Night of the Living Dead*: "I knew audiences . . . would want to know what the connection was between the two films. I wanted to get it out of the way and give them a good initial laugh. If I hadn't done that I would have been in serious trouble with the people who would figure I had just ripped-off Romero, or would try and place it somewhere in his trilogy" (qtd. in Jones, "Dan O'Bannon" 19). *Return of the Living Dead* establishes a type of continuity when Frank, a manager of a medical supply warehouse, tells his assistant Freddie the "real story" behind *Night of the Living Dead*. The film, Frank explains, was based on a true incident that took place at a Pittsburgh veteran's hospital where an accidental chemical spill led to the reanimation of dead bodies: "they told the guy who made the movie that if he told the true story, they'd sue his ass off, so he changed all the facts around." Taking Freddie to the basement to show him the airtight gas containers in which the now dormant corpses have been stored, Frank accidentally unleashes another (near unstoppable) zombie plague. From this point, the film at once resembles *Night*—it follows the attempt of a restricted number of characters to survive the overnight ordeal—but also radically departs from Romero's mythos, featuring zombies who talk, run, and will not be stopped by a blow to the head. Although Romero took steps to ensure that *Return of the Living Dead* would not clash with the near contemporaneous release of *Day of the Dead*, the title of O'Bannon's "illegitimate sequel" nonetheless led to confusion among industry and public alike, and is thought to have limited the financial success of the official Romero chapter (Gagne 167; see Biodrowski; Peachment).

Return of the Living Dead was a substantial commercial success—generating its own run of "official sequels": the "virtual remake" of *Return of the Living Dead Part II* (Ken Wiederhorn, 1988) and *Return of the Living Dead 3* (Brian Yuzna, 1993)—but the ongoing touchstone for zombie films continued to be the Romero-authored trilogy. Shinji Mikami cited *Night of the Living Dead* (along with Fulci's *Zombi 2*) as a starting point for the "survival horror" of his Resident Evil PlayStation video game, one commentator noting that the interface "lifted wholesale the camera angles and action sequences from Romero's classic zombie flicks such as *Dawn of the Dead*" (Russell 172). Romero was in turn briefly considered as director for the feature film version of the *Resident Evil* franchise that had already generated three video-game sequels and a series of books. The resultant 2002 feature (directed by Paul Anderson) retains some of the popular zombie characters from the game (notably the zombie Doberman dogs), but operates as a *prequel* to the "narrative," depicting the events leading up to the transformation of the fictional Raccoon City from ordinary American town to living dead necropolis. The "manic zombie mayhem" that ensues from a laboratory outbreak of the corpse reanimating virus focuses on attempts by a small band of survivors to escape the compound, and (like the video game) has been described as a "scene-for-scene copy" of *Dawn of the Dead* but (tellingly) one that "fails to situate *Resident Evil* zombies within any larger social [*political*] context" (Foundas 24). Most significantly, the mainstream commercial success of *Resident Evil*—and its (direct narrative) sequel *Resident Evil: Apocalypse* (Alexander Witt, 2004)—was to contribute to industry confidence in big-budget zombie films, notably the Zack Snyder directed (authorized) remake of *Dawn of Dead* (2004).[8] Recognized as a "commercial title that [had] permeated pop culture in a way that [was] disproportionate to the

success of the original film," *Dawn of the Dead* provided a presold property ready for generic revision (Jones, "New Dawn" 36). While retaining
the shopping mall setting as a temporary refuge for its (expanded) group
of survivors, the *Dawn* remake ultimately borrows little from the Romero
mythos (and sociopolitical subtext), and (like *Resident Evil*) imagines its
zombies not as sympathetic souls, but as terrifying and powerful killing
machines (Jones, "New Dawn"; Wheaton).

Universal Picture's *Dawn of the Dead* remake is the single film most
often credited as catalyst for the revival of the "legendary Dead franchise," enabling Romero to broker a $15 million-plus deal with Univer-
sal for the (long in development) fourth installment, *Land of the Dead*
(Chang 58; Rae 46; Rowe, "Land of the Dead" 53). However, in critical
accounts, these economic imperatives most often take second place to a
description of the political and *authorial* serialization of the Dead films:
"The *Dead* cycle—the fulgurating black and white of *Night of the Living
Dead*, the bloody comic-book humour of *Dawn of the Dead*, the radical
nihilism of *Day of the Dead*—represents something . . . *personal, obsessive
and fundamental to [Romero's] oeuvre*. [. . .] It is, in Romero's words, 'the
place where I can show most how I see the world' " (D'Agnolo-Vallan
23, emphasis added). *Land of the Dead* thus advances (*serializes*) Romero's personal, critical, and (frequently) subversive look at the respective
decade in which each Dead installment is located, in this case presenting a fortified city as an (obvious) allegory for the United States, living
with—but not facing up to—the realities of global terrorism. Described
as "virtually Karl Marx's *Das Kapital* on the multiplex screen" (Martin)
and "a cartoon of Bush II-era cruel America" (Newman, "Land" 76),
Land of the Dead focuses on a Pittsburgh-like city—a city between two riv-
ers, protected by water—controlled by the corrupt technocrat Kaufman
who has constructed a luxurious walled community—the lavish high-rise
development of Fiddler's Green—for himself and a privileged group of
survivors. At the base of Kaufman's palace-fortress is a squalid encamp-
ment of less fortunate survivors, including mercenaries (Riley, Charlie,
and—later—Slack) who forage for supplies in the outside world in a
heavily armored vehicle, named Dead Reckoning. Across the water—in
the land of the dead—the excursions of the marauding (often vicious)
humans attract the attention of Big Daddy, an evolved zombie who leads
an army of the dead in an attempt to reclaim what is rightfully theirs
from the blinkered and unsustainable society of Fiddler's Green.

Land of the Dead begins with a title—"Some Time Ago"—and an
explanatory montage sequence of degraded sound and image that Meghan
Sutherland describes as "an impressionistic primer on the events of night,
dawn, and day that lead up to the 'land' we find before us" (67). A second
title card—"Today"—gives way to a scene of stale, shambling corpses that

establishes that the zombies have been undead for many years and that society—as we know it—ended long ago. In contrast to their digitally rebooted kin (in *Dawn of the Dead* redux, *Resident Evil*, *28 Days Later* [Danny Boyle, 2002], and the like) these are slow-moving zombies but evidently ones that are continuing to evolve, the opening scene revealing a trio of decaying musicians who manage an approximate tune. Later in the opening, *Land of the Dead* introduces the zombie "hero" Big Daddy, an "everyman" former gas station attendant who seems at the point of moving beyond the undead's tendency to repeat only simple tasks to regain real intelligence. Watching Big Daddy from a concealed vantage point, the living "hero" Riley observes: "[The zombies are] trying to be us. They used to be us. [They are] learning to be us again." Romero adds: "Big Daddy is not instantly as sympathetic as [*Dawn of the Dead*'s] Bub. He is [a revolutionary figure like] Zapata . . . I have always felt less attraction for the humans. I may have a protagonist [like Riley] who is thinking a bit more clearly than all the others, but the humans have always been less sympathetic to me" (qtd. in D'Agnolo-Vallan 24). At the end of *Land of the Dead*, the action heroes (and lead players)—Riley and his offsiders, Charlie and Slack—escape the besieged city but Big Daddy dispatches the villain Kaufman and leads the zombie slaves to freedom. In this—the most optimistic ending of the *Dead* series—Romero appears to have fashioned a more conventional genre film and (according to commentators) for the first time "purpose built" an ending to anticipate a commercial sequel with some of the same characters (Jones, "Dead Reckoning" 66). But the sequelization of *Land of the Dead* resides principally in Romero's *authorship*, his "unique signature" and "sociological commentary" (Rae):

> [*Land of the Dead*] continues the same themes [as the trilogy] of people not communicating, things falling apart internally and people not dealing with it. . . . That's the theme that runs through all of this. . . . The idea of building a society of glass, and not caring about what's going on around you—wearing blinders. (Romero qtd. in Rowe, "Land of the Dead" 51)

> I tried to set up a little depiction of what America is like today. . . . I always see the zombies as an external force . . . and in a distant way the zombies represent what we, the global community, should really be thinking about: something like . . . power to the people. (Romero qtd. in D'Agnolo-Vallan 24)

Just before Romero returned with *Land of the Dead*, Simon Pegg and Edgar Wright, the British actor-writer-director team responsible for

Spaced (1999–2001), took up the idea that the Dead trilogy is a *series* of reports on isolated incidents (in the larger story of the end of civilization) to envision the "rom-zom-com" (romantic-zombie-comedy) of *Shaun of the Dead* (Edgar Wright, 2004). In a "reverential" handling of Romero's oeuvre, Wright and Pegg say they wanted to "treat the zombie genre with respect":

> We didn't want to make fun of the zombies, we wanted to keep them real and serious but then transplant our comedy and romance into it. In a way the zombies are an exacerbation of the human problems in the film rather than what the film is actually about. . . . We always kind of imagined that [*Shaun of the Dead*] is part of the Romero universe. . . . If *Dawn of the Dead* and what's happening in Pittsburgh is the big story then, our film is what's going on in the background. (qtd. in Williams, "Real Scream" 5)

Shaun of the Dead thus preserves not only the narrative invention—a group of survivors takes refuge in a local pub from a horde of shambling zombies—but also the *mythos* of a Romero zombie film, giving it a local and contemporary sociopolitical "subtext" by situating zombification in the everyday drudgery and routine of north London life. Across the body of *Shaun of the Dead*—in such episodes at that in which Shaun and his friends practice at being zombies in order to move undetected through a horde of the living dead—the filmmakers literalize the now famous *Dawn of the Dead* line—"they're us [and we're them]"—and serialize Romero's imperative that the zombie film allegorize the *state (and shame) of the nation*. In recognition of this gesture, Romero in turn "authorized" Pegg and Wright's deferential treatment of the Dead trilogy by inviting the pair to cameo as zombies in a *Land of the Dead* club sequence. Finally, in placing *Shaun of the Dawn* within the historical tradition (*mythos*) of Romero's "Anubis" and Dead trilogy—the attenuated spine of the contemporary zombie cinema—Pegg and Wright not only pay a debt of influence, but also underline the authorial and political dimension at the core of the *sequelization* of the Dead.

Notes

1. *George Romero's Diary of the Dead* (2007) was in production at the time of writing (2007).

2. At the time of writing (2007) a Francis Lawrence directed remake of *I am Legend* was in production.

3. The screenplay is available as a DVD extra on the Divimax Special Edition of *Day of the Dead*.

4. See also Walter Marcus's account of the Anchor Bay DVD 30th Anniversary Limited Edition of *Night of the Living Dead*—extended with new material, including an epilogue with Debbie Rochon—as a (similar) attempt to recoup lost profits, in this case by Image Ten investors John Russo and Russell Streiner.

5. At the time of writing (2007) a Steve Miner directed remake of *Day of the Dead* was in production.

6. Szebin says: "On Savini's *Night of the Living Dead*, the fine line that separates sequel and remake is slightly blurred. . . . The action of the original film ends about 65 minutes into the new version, with the remainder of the story taking a new direction" (9).

7. This (cumulative) value is clearly communicated in a promotional item—such as the theatrical trailer for Romero's *Day of the Dead*—which draws attention to the progression of the Dead series and the *authorial vision* of its creator.

8. Romero's film had, in a sense, already been "officially remade" as a panel-for-panel redraw in Steve Nile's graphic novel version, *Dawn of the Dead* (IDW Publishing, 2004). Chris Ryall later contributed a *Land of the Dead* graphic novel to the same IDW series (2005).

2

JENNIFER FORREST

Of "True" Sequels

The Four Daughters Movies, or the Series That Wasn't

A CCORDING TO THE COMMON wisdom, sequels, series, genre films, remakes, and spin-offs operate in the same territory: they revisit familiar material or formulas, and they appeal primarily to popular audiences. They also generally enjoy a degraded status compared to their more esteemed colleagues, originals. In a 2002 *New York Times* article, Michiko Kakutani bemoaned the "recycling mania" that has seemingly greatly "accelerated" in recent years (1). As prevalent as this practice seems today, however, not only has it been a staple of studio production from the industry's inception, its frequency also significantly pales in comparison to that of the Classic Hollywood period when studios got the maximum use of their properties as well as of their contract employees (see Simonet). While references to a "recycling mania" strive to reduce all instances of revisited material to the same deplorable activity, sequels, series, genre films, and remakes possess their own distinct characteristics and reflect different industry practices.

The most discussed, and often most reviled, among recycled productions during the 1990s were remakes, especially US versions of

Figure 2.1. *Four Mothers* (William Keighley, 1941). Courtesy Warner Bros/
The Kobal Collection.

critically successful foreign films. However, unlike when they are readaptations of classic literary works, remakes generally do not result in
multiple films. Two notable exceptions to the limited number of remakes
to which a same source text or film can give birth exist. First, producer
Bryan Foy claimed to have "used the plot of *Tiger Shark* (1932) suc-
cessfully in ten other films by changing the title, the locale of the story,
and the names of the characters" (Macgowan 344). It is no wonder that
Foy, who was nicknamed the "Keeper of the Bs," worked at Warner
Brothers, where, as Douglas Gomery notes: "Stories were used over and
over again" (115). Almost as impressive in numbers were the six versions
of George S. Kaufman's play *The Butter and Egg Man* (1925), also at
Warner Brothers.

   In the first decade of the twenty-first century the media has shifted
its focus from predatorial remakes to sequels and series, which are under-
standably the most visible of the types of recycled materials produced in
Hollywood, and which lend themselves to seemingly endless variations
on a theme and a formula. In today's descriptions of films, distinguish-
ing between sequels and series is often difficult, first, because critics use
the words virtually interchangeably, and second, because studios usually

identify both sequels and series by repeating the title of the initial film and/or affixing a number identifying each film's place in a production sequence. The difference between the two, however, goes beyond the technical definition of (1) a sequel (usually only one film) featuring the same characters and continuing the story of a previous film;[1] and (2) a series (usually a minimum of three films) presenting recurring characters in unrelated episodes.[2] Contrary to Kakutani's classification of the two within the same industry recycling practice, studios intentionally design sequels and series for different audiences. During the Classic Hollywood period, series films were almost exclusively B-unit productions and targeted primarily the popular audiences of second-run theaters. Although the dismantling of the old studio system with the US government's successful Paramount antitrust prosecution did not kill series production, series no longer fell solely into the B-film category—they can, and often do, boast big-name stars and blockbuster budgets. They also continue to appeal to a spectator looking for entertainment rather than for films presenting greater aesthetic aspirations or psychological challenges. The entertainment-seeking spectator knows how to analyze the taglines that indicate a "false" sequel—a film that may lead to a series—and the "true" sequel—a film that functions as a companion piece (emphasis on the singular) to its predecessor.[3] The "true" sequel offers characters that have psychological depth, that seem to live and breathe beyond the screen, as opposed to the stock characters of series films who always behave in the manner that is conventional to them. The "true" sequel caresses a certain spectator's class sensibilities by appealing to his or her preference for works of quality. So, in opposition to the current trend that film critics have of labeling three or more films that draw on the same source texts (New Hollywood blockbusters and, retroactively, Classic Hollywood B-movies) as franchises, a term that clearly emphasizes the commercial over the artistic values of the films, I define the "true" sequel as a film that promotes itself as having distinctly more high-brow ambitions.

A group of films exists from the Classic period that on the surface offers examples from almost all of the recycling categories mentioned above: the Four Daughters films—*Four Daughters* (Michael Curtiz, 1938), which was remade as *Young at Heart* (Gordon Douglas, 1954); *Four Wives* (Michael Curtiz, 1939); *Four Mothers* (William Keighley, 1941); and a "reworking" of the first film, *Daughters Courageous* (Michael Curtiz, 1939), itself remade as *Always in My Heart* (Jo Graham, 1942).[4] While possessing this complex family relationship, the nuclear Four Daughters films seemingly function most as a short (in terms of Classic Hollywood), but successful, series. However, by the very nature of their conditions of production, distribution, and exhibition, the two films that follow *Four Daughters* are instead "true" sequels.

Four Daughters, Four Wives, and *Four Mothers,* the core films in the group, follow the love lives from courtship to marriage to motherhood of the four musical Lemp sisters, played by three real life sisters, Priscilla, Lola, and Rosemary Lane, with Gale Page as the fourth. Their widower father (played by Claude Rains), as a professor of music, holds the family together through good times and adversity, first, through the classical music and musical performance that bind all members, and second, through good sense, good humor, and unconditional love. The films were based on the popular Fannie Hurst story "Sister Act," which appeared in *Cosmopolitan* in 1937. Hurst properties had served Universal Studios and Warner Brothers well from the 1920s to the 1940s (and in the 1950s and early 1960s with several remakes and readaptations), leading to some of the definitive melodramas of the Classic Hollywood period: *Back Street* (John Stahl, 1932; Robert Stevenson, 1941), *Imitation of Life* (John Stahl, 1934; Douglas Sirk, 1959), and *Humoresque* (Jean Negulesco, 1946). A lesser known author's play was used for *Daughters Courageous,* which conveniently facilitated the refitting of its basic narrative structure and the dynamics of its characters' relationships toward a reorientation and an exploration of those elements cited and praised by film critics and audiences of *Four Daughters*: the palpable sensual magnetism between good-natured Priscilla Lane and surly bad boy John Garfield and the relationship between the girls and their father, here returning to the family after having abandoned them twenty years earlier.

James L. Limbacher's *Haven't I Seen You Somewhere Before? Remakes, Sequels, and Series in Motion Pictures and Television, 1896–1978,* and Bernard A. Drew's *Motion Picture Series and Sequels: A Reference Guide* both list *Four Daughters, Daughters Courageous, Four Wives,* and *Four Mothers* as a series. While Robert Nowlan and Gwendolyn Wright Nowlan's *Cinema Sequels and Remakes, 1903–1987,* does not officially include *Daughters Courageous* in its referencing of the Four Daughters "sequels," it does, nevertheless, cite it as a "pseudo-sequel," contrasting it with the two films featuring the daughters as wives and mothers, which were the "real sequels" (258). In his review of the film for the *New York Times,* Frank S. Nugent was at a loss for the correct classification: "Not exactly a sequel, yet not exactly a brand-new theme either, the Strand's 'Daughters Courageous' is the Warners' attempt to recapture the mood and the popularity of their brilliantly successful 'Four Daughters' of last season" ("Strand's 'Daughters Courageous' "). After mentioning the basic structural similarities between the two films as well as a shared mood, he nevertheless concludes that: "The resemblance ends there, in a way; for the story is new and quite disassociated from the earlier venture." And yet, he adds:

"Still the film cannot be considered completely apart."

The Nowlans' reference to "real sequels" does not offer, however, any theoretical role for the term beyond the concrete function of identifying a film that follows sequentially in production another film featuring the same characters, this whether the storyline is picked up again or whether an unrelated episode is offered. Indeed, *Cinema Sequels and Remakes* includes, for example, the Charlie Chan, Sherlock Holmes, and Thin Man films in its discussion of sequels according to the logic of the book's title, but acknowledges in the introduction that a distinction between the two practices does in fact exist: "The basic difference between a sequel and one film in a series is that in the former, the story of a previous movie is continued in some way, whereas in the case of the latter, there is no real connection between the films, save some central characters who reappear" (xi). In this less than rigorous vein, the reader has difficulty determining if the Nowlans consider the Four Daughters movies as operating in the same territory as the Charlie Chan, Sherlock Holmes, and Thin Man films (sequential films in unrelated episodes), or if they function as sequels with each successive film picking up the thread of the preceding one. Finally, Bosley Crowther, the film critic for the *New York Times* who reviewed only *Four Mothers*, referred to it as "the third and latest of this domestic series" ("The Lemps Again").

All indicators seem to point to a series: whether one speaks of an A-class series such as the Thin Man, or a B-class series such as Charlie Chan, the "four" in the Four Daughters films offers an apparently easy way to recognize that the movies are related, just as Warner Brothers had intended. While the "reworked" *Daughters Courageous* did not have "four" in its title, (1) it was released less than a year after *Four Daughters*, a film still fresh in the minds of audiences if not just for the five Academy Award nominations it received; (2) it directly advertised its filiation through the repetition of another title word "daughters"; and (3) it literally boasted the same ensemble cast. Not much has changed since the late 1930s. While series today more readily qualify as A-class pictures, if only from their budgets and big-name stars, studios continue to repeat an essential component of the title of the original film, usually, as noted earlier, by offering the same title and adding a number. While the numbers ostensibly indicate sequentiality, and some degree of continuity usually exists from one episode to another (much more so than in Classic Hollywood series), such films (the Lethal Weapon movies, the Superman movies, and so on), especially when studios release a third entry, are nine times out of ten series.

As noted earlier, the Four Daughters films present some of the basic characteristics of series. Like the Four Daughters films, many series from the Classic Hollywood era stemmed from only one source text or series of texts. The first of the eight Maisie movies (1939–47), for example, was officially based on a loose adaptation of Wilson Collison's novel, *Dark Dame* (1935); all of the subsequent nine entries retained only the title character. Like *Four Daughters*, whose popularity, it has been noted, inspired its "reworked" *Daughters Courageous* featuring the same cast as the earlier film, some series spawned "reworkings," but usually the studios conceptualized them as potential series. After the seventh entry in the Saint series, for example, author Leslie Charteris refused RKO any further rights to his novels. RKO responded by acquiring the rights to Michael Arlen's short story "The Gay Falcon," and put the *Saint's* George Sanders in the "carbon copy" lead role of the Falcon (Pitts 241): this time the name had changed but the basic narrative structure was the same. The Falcon movies were, in essence, a thinly disguised continuation of the Saint movies. And like *Four Daughters* and its remake *Young at Heart*, a series entry can lead to readaptations: the Falcon entry, *The Falcon Takes Over* (Irving Reis, 1942), was the first adaptation of Raymond Chandler's *Farewell My Lovely* (1940). It was remade (or readapted) as A-movies in 1944 as *Murder My Sweet* (Edward Dmytryk), and in 1975 as *Farewell, My Lovely* (Dick Richards).

All these similarities do not, however, necessarily make a series of the Four Daughters movies. On the contrary, recycling properties, casts, or pairings, and role types and narratives reflected the standard marketing strategies studios used in the hopes of minimizing the role of chance in any given film's reception, and this on all levels of production, low budget, and high budget. While winning formulas were typical, they functioned differently for the As and Bs. Regarding the recycling of properties, Warner Brothers, the studio that produced the Four Daughters films, "operated on a volume basis," producing all their films, big ones as well as small ones, "cheaply and efficiently," a practice that translated into the continual reuse of source materials (Balio, *Grand Design* 112–13). With respect to A-films, however, Tino Balio notes that, while it would seem logical that a studio, especially one like Warner Brothers, would seek to squeeze out of them a maximum number of similarly structured stories, the opposite was the case: they "seldom recycled expensive properties (for example, *Green Pastures*) because they were by definition easily recognizable by many people and therefore were likely to make audiences feel cheated if reused. The number and percentage of remakes Warner Brothers produced increased significantly after 1934, but the majority of these pictures were Bs" (100). One can infer that the studio felt that the audience for B-movies did not attach importance to works based on their literary or artistic pedigree.

Similarly, while studios subjected top-tier actors to a certain degree of the stereotyping with which lesser players were all too familiar, they strove for greater role diversification for the former than for the latter. After all, stars filled seats in a studio's first-run theaters, and stars determined the rental fees distributors paid for the better quality films (versus the flat fees paid for Bs). The key was to exploit stars just enough without overexposing and devaluing studio product. In terms of A-class stories and stars, then, finding that balance in which the studio got the most for its money while still promoting a quality product was essential.

As Balio notes regarding the development and exploitation of a studio's major stars: "A star's popularity and drawing power created a ready-made market for his or her pictures, which reduced the risks of production financing" (*Grand Design* 144). Such a strategy was at work in the recasting of the ensemble players of *Four Daughters* in *Daughters Courageous*. In fact, with respect to the relation between *Four Daughters* and *Daughters Courageous*, the two practices—star formulas and reuse of source materials—overlapped. Although the source materials for *Four Daughters* and *Daughters Courageous* were decidedly different, the screen adaptation of Dorothy Bennett's play *Fly Away Home* (1935) was tailored in such a way as to duplicate as much as possible the basic relations from *Four Daughters*. In this sense, like the Falcon films as a repackaged version of the Saint movies, *Daughters Courageous* is based just as much on Fannie Hurst's story as *Four Daughters* (that is, a remake). In another sense, however, the relationships between the characters of *Daughters Courageous* and the narrative built around them were determined by the stars' personas, which in turn determined the final shape the characters would take and the kind of trials they would encounter in the narrative. In the case of *Four Daughters*, Errol Flynn was originally slated to star in the film, a casting that would have radically changed the film in its focus on the male lead: the script would have been developed according to the dimensions of his star image. With his withdrawal from the production to do *The Adventures of Robin Hood* (Michael Curtiz, 1938), the script was rewritten to focus on the four daughters (Roberts).

While *Fly Away Home* contained many narrative points of intersection with *Four Daughters* (one parent raising four children), the plot had enough narrative dissimilarities (the parent is the mother, not the father, with the latter having left the family when the children were very young, and so on) that the film played against the expectations established by the first film (differentiation in Claude Rains's role, not as the glue that binds the family together, but as the disrupter of the family), which in turn allowed it to maintain the market value of its stars and to guarantee that the film was a quality, not an assembly-line (series), production.[5] Finally, regarding the transfer of the basic pattern of *Four Daughters* in *Daughters Courageous*, *Four Wives*, and *Four Mothers*, as well as the repetition of the core cast, although one can

perceive similar structural relationships in other cast reunions, most
notably in dynamic pairings—the Fred Astaire/Ginger Rogers, William
Powell/Myrna Loy (in the six non–Thin Man movies), and Spencer
Tracy/Katherine Hepburn groups of films, for example—one is disin-
clined to qualify them as "true" series in the same way one would do
so with the Charlie Chan, Sherlock Holmes, and Maisie movies. Once
again, the major indicators of distinction with respect to the Classic
Hollywood era are the class of movie involved and the degree of product
differentiation applied: the Charlie Chan films were B-unit productions
featuring minimal change in terms of narrative structure and personnel
as well as aggressive product exposure, the Tracy/Hepburn films were
A-unit productions possessing significantly more differentiation in order
to protect the studio's investments both in quality properties and in its
upper echelon personnel.

Apart from the Thin Man series, there are no other examples of
"true" A series. The Andy Hardy series, of which the second film is clearly a B-movie was technically upgraded to A-class when, in 1939, Mickey
Rooney became the number one star in Hollywood (a position he held
for three years) precisely because of his popularity in the role of Andy
Hardy. The Hardy family pictures "were grossing three to four times
their cost," and accordingly, the studios responded by elevating them
to A status, "at least outside the largest metropolitan areas" (Crowther,
Lion's Share 256; Balio, *Grand Design* 102), a notable distinction given
that the important first-run theaters were precisely in major cities. Balio
includes the Busby Berkeley Gold Diggers musicals from Warner Brothers as another example of an A series. Discussing them as a "true" series
rather than as a group of films is problematic. "The plots varied only
a little from picture to picture," notes Balio, a characteristic that can
technically qualify the films as series pictures, but it identifies them just
as readily as a subgenre (the backstage musical, a genre to which the
Broadway Melody "series" from MGM would also belong). The films
deviate in an important way from the series formula, however, in that
"the original leads were not repeated in the subsequent pictures. Rather,
the series was held together by Busby Berkeley's elaborately staged musical numbers" (*Grand Design* 102). In addition, the name that connects
the films, "Gold Diggers," does not encompass all the Warner Brothers
films from the period that featured the same theme and, contrary to what
Balio says, many of the same players in a variety of combinations: *42nd
Street* (Lloyd Bacon and Busby Berkeley, 1933), *Footlight Parade* (Lloyd
Bacon and Busby Berkeley, 1933), and *Dames* (Ray Enright and Busby
Berkeley, 1934). The minimal varying of personnel and the maximal
varying of characters points to the effort by Warner Brothers and MGM

respectively to associate the films carrying the words "Gold Diggers" and "Broadway Melody" with distinctive, non–series A productions.[6]

Like the other major studios, Warner Brothers attempted repeatedly to create dynamic couplings and partial encore casts both on and off the screen. This was, after all, unit production. *Four Daughters*, *Daughters Courageous*, and *Four Wives* had the same A-unit producers, Hal B. Wallis and Henry Blanke; the same A-unit director, Michael Curtiz; and the same A-unit screenwriter, Julius J. Epstein (all nominated for Oscars in their categories for the first film). As for the actors, if one takes Priscilla Lane's motion pictures as an example, the actress appeared in two other Warner Brothers films with May Robson, who played her aunt in the Four Daughters films. The studio paired several promising male A-list stars with her as well: she appeared on the same bill with her Four Daughters films costar Jeffrey Lynn in eight films from 1938 to 1941, with Wayne Morris in four films from 1938 to 1940, and, in an effort to repeat the magnetism between her and John Garfield in *Four Daughters*, *Daughters Courageous*, and *Four Wives* (despite the death of his character in the first film), she was paired with the latter in *Dust Be My Destiny* (Lewis Seiler, 1939). While in this respect, A-unit and B-unit production by core teams are mirror images of one another, the important difference is that in whatever the pairing, and consequently, whatever film in which she figured, the "film star" Priscilla Lane was never eclipsed by the characters she played. The poster for *Dust Be My Destiny* advertised in its boldest letters the names of its stars, Priscilla Lane and John Garfield, and not those of Ann Lemp and Mickey Borden (the characters that they portrayed in the Four Daughters films): in proclaiming that they are "Together Again!" the poster deliberately incorporates Ann Lemp's and Mickey Borden's character traits into the overall persona of movie stars Priscilla Lane and John Garfield. Even *Four Wives*, the second of the Four Daughters movies, emphasized the stars over the characters by inviting the spectator to "Join the Honeymoon Lanes [not the Honeymoon Lemps] as they start out on their happiest adventure."[7]

In contrast, as an example of the different mindset involved in the forming of a studio's minor series actors, MGM treated Ann Sothern overall as a B talent, even after her successful supporting role as Jean Livingstone in Tay Garnett's *Trade Winds* (1938). Precisely because of her popularity as Jean, B-unit producer J. Walter Ruben looked for a suitable B series fit for her, especially one between her and a male costar. In the same year that she starred in *Maisie* (Edwin L. Marin, 1939), Ruben also had her play Garda Sloane against Franchot Tone in what was to be the third and final entry of the Joel and Garda Sloane mysteries—*Fast and Furious* (Busby Berkeley, 1939)—and Ethel Turp against William Gargan in *Joel*

and Ethel Turp Call on the President (Robert B. Sinclair, 1939), the first film
in a planned series that never materialized. Maisie was the character that
really clicked with audiences. Unlike Priscilla Lane, whose star personality
shaped the characters that she played, Ann Sothern became synonymous
with Maisie, so much so that, as the series wore on, she struggled to shake
the character's hold on her. Although actors no longer technically need
fear such fates in the poststudio era—Harrison Ford has played in several
series without suffering any repercussions to his status as a major star (the
Star Wars and Indiana Jones series, and two Jack Ryan entries)—the superstition still runs strong. One reads on the Internet Movie Database, for
example, that Kevin Costner has become more the exception than the rule:
he has "purposely avoided doing sequels to his films. So far, he is one of
the few blockbuster stars to never come back for a sequel" ("Biography").
Regarding Ann Sothern, MGM's publicity department deliberately encouraged the confusion between actress and role, designing posters in which
the boldest letters announced the newest Maisie movie, for example, with
the actress's name in demonstrably smaller print in the bottom corner.[8]
In this instance, the character clearly dominated her star persona. For this
reason, ostensibly any given Classic Hollywood studio's prominent actors
were with rare exception associated with series' roles.

The calculated weighting of publicity toward the star in the Four
Daughters movies and toward the lead character in series movies works
to identify the former as A-movies and the latter as B-movies. This does
not, however, lead us to reject classifying the Four Daughters movies as
a series, because after all, the Thin Man movies were an A-class series.
However, according to the class of the Thin Man films, instead of high-
lighting the characters Nick and Nora Charles, posters advertised its stars
just as studios did nonseries star vehicles: at the top of the poster for
The Thin Man Goes Home (Richard Thorpe, 1944), the fifth entry in the
six-film series, one reads: "Together again in MGM's riotous comedy!"
Directly underneath in the boldest letters, one finds the names of its
stars, William Powell and Myrna Loy. In addition, MGM staggered the
release of Thin Man episodes so that (1) a new entry appeared only every
two to three years; and (2) there was enough product differentiation in
the film roles between the Thin Man movies to maintain William Powell
and Myrna Loy's star ranking. Similarly, the Four Daughters films were
issued roughly every two years. In contrast, in 1940 alone, Twentieth
Century-Fox issued four installments in the B-class Charlie Chan series.[9]
Clearly, the studio philosophy was to milk a B series for as long as possible. This does not resolve, however, the issue of identifying the category
to which the Four Daughters films belong because, according to the logic
of the Thin Man series, they technically qualify as an A series.

Continuity distinguishes the Thin Man series from the Four Daughters films. Continuity refers here to (1) the thread of one story being picked up in the film that follows (indicative of the sequel), as well as to (2) the virtual ability to invent indefinitely new adventures for a character or characters (indicative of the series). As stated earlier, in contrast to the period's serial productions (sequential episodes of a single story with each episode usually ending in a cliffhanger, as in the *Flash Gordon Conquers the Universe* serial that was divided into twelve episodes [Ford Beebe and Ray Taylor, 1940]), which targeted the underage patrons of Saturday matinees, Classic Hollywood series films generally had little to no narrative continuity between episodes. Aimed at adult audiences, the Four Daughters films were not serials, yet possessed the serial's continuing storyline (without, of course, the cliffhanger). Nugent clearly treated these films as an A-series, commenting that *Four Wives*, "is a singularly happy film, well-written, well-directed and well-played, and it reconciles us tranquilly to the vista it has opened of a 'Four Mothers' (although part of that already has been realized), a 'Four Grandmothers' and possibly a 'Four Granddaughters' " (" 'Four Wives' "). Nugent's list of potential future entries in the "series," while positing multiple installments, at the same time reveals the impossibility of the realization of such a series: series, whether in film, popular literature, comic books, or radio plays, deny the passage of time, focusing on an eternal present; sequels, however, are anchored in the beginnings and endings of life cycles. The Four Daughters films exhausted the premise that grounded them with *Four Mothers* and could go no further, regardless of Hollywood's ability to age actors beyond their years. Indeed, *Four Mothers* was perhaps the result of singular studio misjudgment, if not outright error: while the qualities that assured the success of the first sequel (first-rate production, direction, writing, and acting) had dropped a notch in the final film (although director William Keighley and screenwriter Stephen Morehouse Avery were hardly B-unit personnel), the latter could not logically spawn new adventures for the Lemp sisters. Similar temporal restrictions on the narrative are evident in Vincente Minnelli's *Father of the Bride* (1950) and its sequel *Father's Little Dividend* (Vincente Minnelli, 1951) and, more recently, in *Before Sunrise* (Richard Linklater, 1995) and its sequel *Before Sunset* (Richard Linklater, 2004). In particular, the latter film's reunion of Jesse and Céline nine years later plays itself out not only in the real time of the characters but also in that of the spectators as well.

To determine whether *Four Wives* is a "true" sequel, given its place in between the first and the third film, it is perhaps useful to work backward by identifying what is not a sequel. George Seitz's *A Family Affair* (1937) featuring the Hardy family was followed by *You're Only*

Young Once (George Seitz, 1937), which is often referred to as its sequel. Any further additions would constitute a series, henceforth marked by minimal sequential and maximal episodic development. Accordingly, the fourteen pictures that followed *You're Only Young Once* would ostensibly have established the Hardy family series, had not the "sequel" declared itself a series from the outset: the film opened with Lewis Stone "directly addressing and informing the public of the new Hardy family series" (DeCroix 154). *You're Only Young Once*, therefore, is not a "true" sequel. In another example, audiences enjoyed the supporting characters of the *The Egg and I* (Chester Erskine, 1947) so much that Universal issued *Ma and Pa Kettle* (Charles Lamont, 1949), "The hilarious sequel to 'The Egg and I,'" two years later. Both *You're Only Young Once* and *Ma and Pa Kettle* were series entries and could be read as such by the drop in production values and headliners. Because neither cast nor production values changed, *Four Wives* (and to a limited degree, *Four Mothers*) can provisionally qualify as "true" sequels.

The second film grouped among the Four Daughters films, *Daughters Courageous*, too, is neither a sequel nor a pseudosequel, but, for different reasons: as noted earlier, it was based on an entirely different source text and was advertised as such. Its poster boasted both a modicum of sequel status to capitalize on the critical and popular success of *Four Daughters*—"It's another 'Four Daughter's' hit!"—as well as emphasizing difference—"Only the stars are the same. The story, characters, romances are all different." The poster continued to alternate between invoking fond memories of the previous film—"If you liked 'Four Daughters' (and who didn't), we wholeheartedly recommend for you and all your family 'Daughters Courageous'"—and bringing both reel and real lives into play: the movie starred the "Four Daughters," listed, not as the Lemps, but as Priscilla Lane, Rosemary Lane, Lola Lane, and Gale Page. The melding of reel and real personas accounted for the greater illusion of reality in the performances of this A production. With *Daughters Courageous*, Nugent emphasized the fullness of the characters as one of the qualities endowing it with as legitimate a claim to distinction as *Four Daughters*: "They [the characters] are not simply creations of the camera, but men and women whose lives began, and will continue, beyond the camera's range of vision." The message to the new film's potential audience was clear, even if Nugent hesitated to classify it: "Not exactly a sequel, yet not exactly a brand-new theme either." Notable in his discussion of the film, Nugent did not use terminology generally associated with series entries ("routine," "formulaic," and so on), an important consideration no doubt being the high production values associated with the film and, most important, the stature of the production team and the actors involved. The latter were important players in the Warner

Brothers stable, and the studio was careful to treat them like luxury commodities and not squander them indiscriminately in lower quality productions. Studios carefully handled their top talents and the productions
in which they appeared because, as Cathy Klaprat has shown, neither a
particular studio nor its film narratives ultimately attracted spectators;
stars did (353–54). The presence of a star in a film minimized the risks
involved in production, maximized the rental fees that could be charged
to distributors and exhibitors, and drew audiences to first-run theaters,
which were owned by the studios and whose tickets were top dollar. The
importance of selling high-price tickets in first-run theaters is revealed
in that, although "they comprised only 25 percent of the total exhibition
seats, they returned over 50 percent of the box office receipts" (355).
These studios' theaters possessed greater luxury and aesthetic appeal than
second-run theaters, and catered to the class-consciousness and sense of
distinction of those patrons capable of buying more expensive tickets.
In contrast, a *New York Times* reviewer of the Maisie series entry found
questionable the decision to show *Ringside Maisie* (Edwin L. Marin, 1941)
in a first-run theater such as the Capitol because the Capitol was "strictly
a class joint. It was a little too classy, in fact, because Maisie is a sweet
girl with a heart as big as a pumpkin, but her refinements are limited"
(T. S. " 'Ringside Maisie' "). Studios generally knew that the patron of
the Capitol possessed those refinements that Maisie lacked and that he
or she expected the theater experience to reflect his or her sensibilities: comfortable and attractive surroundings, patrons possessing similar
cultural capital, a star vehicle, a quality production, and a film that in
varying degrees was one (or in the case of sequels, two) of a kind. One
did not generally show series films at the Capitol: a notable exception,
of course, was the Thin Man series, which could and did play at the
Capitol. One would, however, show "true" sequels. Both follow-up Four
Daughters movies played at a first-run house, the Strand.

Among the definitions offered for series and serials in Ephraim
Katz's *The Film Encyclopedia*, one finds no category for the sequel. This
absence perpetuates the indiscriminate use of the term by film scholars,
critics, and the industry to refer to any revisited material rather than
to a particular industry practice that continues to this day. Isolating the
"true" sequel in the confusing trail of the Four Daughters movies—the
sequels that were not a series—is useful for an understanding of the
rationalization behind the Classic Hollywood industry practice among
the major five film studios of grouping film production into A- and
B-pictures, with the former aiming for a spectator of a certain cultural
capital, and the latter for popular audiences. Budgets determined not
only the core production values that went into a film, but also affected
every facet of production, important considerations of which, we have

seen, were how, and how often, and which actors were assigned roles, and how, and how often a property was reused. Isolating and defining these practices may seem trivial (that is, the basic motivation behind all groupings of films, A- and B-class, is the minimizing of production costs with the maximizing of returns), especially because the industry itself often seems little interested in such taxonomies. Although studios' attempt to appeal to the widest spectrum of tastes, the core audience of "true" sequels clearly was and still is the more sophisticated spectator trained to consume only originals.

Notes

1. One generally refers to a group of nonseries films possessing two sequels as a trilogy, as in the Lord of the Rings trilogy. Like most trilogies, these films resemble somewhat the serials of the silent and Classic Hollywood period in that, while not ending in the characteristic cliffhanger, each installment leaves the tale nevertheless incomplete, awaiting the final film for narrative resolution.

2. When a proposed series never gets beyond two films, one generally speaks of a failed series, not of an original and its sequel. An example of this was the unrealized series that was based on P. J. Wodehouse's Jeeves stories, starring David Niven as the clueless Bertie Wooster and Arthur Treacher as his all too competent butler Jeeves.

3. As an indication of the tendency of the "false" sequel to become part of a more complex family of films, the Internet Movie Database lists among its results in a keyword search all those sequels that led to something else: "sequel-to-remake," "prequel-to-sequel," "prequel-to-sequel-of-remake," and so on.

4. Regarding *Daughters Courageous*, "reworking" is a more appropriate term than "spin-off," because the latter is technically a film that takes popular supporting characters from an earlier film and gives them adventures usually unrelated to those of the earlier film's main characters. A good example is the Ma and Pa Kettle series, which was a spin-off of *The Egg and I* (Chester Erskine, 1947). The principal actors of the first film, Fred MacMurray and Claudette Colbert, and the characters that they played never appeared in the series. *Daughters Courageous* does not technically apply to this category because no recurring lead or supporting characters appear from the earlier film.

5. My argument is based on Cathy Klaprat's discussion of the economics of the star system in "The Star as Market Strategy: Bette Davis in Another Light."

6. Interestingly, the Nowlan's *Cinema Sequels and Remakes* lists the Gold Diggers movies as remakes.

7. The irony, of course, is that one of the four actresses, Gale Page, was not even a Lane.

8. A glance at posters for any B series replicates the same practice.

9. The series usually averaged two to three releases per year. This average holds for most Classic Hollywood era series.

3

THOMAS LEITCH

Sequel-Ready Fiction

After Austen's Happily Ever After

THESE ARE HEADY TIMES FOR connoisseurs of intertextuality. Beeban Kidron's film adaptation of *Bridget Jones: The Edge of Reason*, not exactly the most complicated release of 2004, is a sequel to an adaptation that is also an adaptation of a sequel. The 1999 Helen Fielding novel that provided its avowed source had already contributed materially to Sharon Anderson's 2001 film adaptation *Bridget Jones's Diary*, which was based more directly on Fielding's 1996 novel of the same title, which was in turn rooted in a weekly column Fielding had been writing for *The Independent* (and later for the *Daily Telegraph* before returning to *The Independent*). Encouraged by the Jane Austen frenzy sweeping the nation in the wake of the 1995 BBC miniseries *Pride and Prejudice*, Fielding based the character of Bridget's stiff beau Mark Darcy in the *Independent* column on Colin Firth's portrayal of Elizabeth Bennet's stiff beau Mr. Darcy in the miniseries. Invited to turn her column into a novel, Fielding lifted the plot of *Pride and Prejudice*, and later claimed to have used the plot of *Persuasion* as a basis for *Bridget Jones: The Edge of Reason*. When *Bridget Jones's Diary* was filmed, Fielding insisted that the adaptation be directed by her friend Sharon Maguire, a television director who had been the model for Bridget's friend Shazzer, and that

Figure 3.1. *Bridget Jones's Diary* (Sharon Maquire, 2001). Courtesy Miramax/ Universal/The Kobal Collection/Bailey, Alex.

Darcy be played by none other than Colin Firth, whom Fielding wrote into her sequel in propria persona in an episode in which Bridget flies to Rome to interview him about his new film, *Fever Pitch*, but ends up fixating on his emergence from the lake at Pemberley with a wet shirt as Mr. Darcy. On top of the vast web of intertextual references movie audiences expect as their due in even the most artless films, Fielding's novels and their film adaptations provide still more, more, more.

The resulting heteroglossic stew has already been subjected to closer intertextual analysis than most romantic comedies can ever hope or fear to attract. This chapter does not retrace the steps of Bridget Jones's legion of analysts, beginning of course with Bridget herself, but rather considers Bridget's success in a broader context, broader even than the chick-lit phenomenon with which Fielding is so often identified. Numerous contemporary authors have undertaken sequels to Austen's novels, but the novels do nothing to encourage any speculation about what happened next, and many of Austen's readers have treated the modern sequels as excrescences or travesties.[1] Although *Bridget Jones's Diary* had concluded with the same sort of romantic rapprochement as *Pride and Prejudice*, however, nothing seemed more natural and inevitable than the swift arrival of a sequel that would be eagerly embraced by both hundreds of thousands of eager readers and millions of filmgoers. What features of *Bridget Jones's Diary* make it so hospitable to a sequel that even audiences who professed their disappointment in *Bridget Jones: The Edge of Reason* acknowledged that its appearance as book and film was perfectly consonant with Fielding's original? Or is the widespread appetite for such a sequel less a function of any particular features of Fielding's novel than of more general changes in audiences' dispositions since Austen's time? This chapter considers both the specific qualities of Fielding's heroine that made her so ripe for a sequel and the ways in which the two films to feature her exaggerate her sequel-ready status still further by undermining the teleological import of her adventures. But it begins by placing the films, the novels, and the weekly newspaper column that gave birth to them all as the latest arrivals in a long tradition of sequels Fielding's work both continues and transforms.

Present-day Hollywood is so dominated by the rush to franchising that even apparent stand-alones such as *Gone with the Wind*, *Psycho*, and *The Silence of the Lambs* have delivered sequels (the second and third spawning prequels as well) whose success, according to the market research that drives commercial filmmaking, will be assured by presold brand names. But simply arguing that *Bridget Jones: The Edge of Reason* represents a reflexive Hollywoodization of its heroine is not enough. For one thing, the film sequel, although it did not duplicate the record of *Bridget Jones's Diary* in becoming the highest grossing film yet released in Great Britain, was eagerly awaited and economically successful.[2] Clearly it fed a mass-audience hunger as palpable, if perhaps as adventitious, as Bridget's own investment in *Pride and Prejudice* and Princess Diana. For another, the sales figures for Fielding's second novel were just as impressive in the world of publishing as those of its film adaptation in the more stratospheric heights of commercial filmmaking. Bridget, unlike Austen's heroine Elizabeth Bennet, evidently left a vast audience clamoring for more. The power of Fielding's heroine to arouse and fulfill such an appetite raises questions about why it seemed so logical for any contemporary fictional success, this one in particular, to generate the kind of transmedia franchise that had eluded Austen for 200 years.

Part of the answer clearly has to do with the explosive growth of new media unavailable to Austen. Yet sequels of several kinds were already well-established when Austen wrote. Indeed the rise of the novel marked in some ways not only what Ian Watt has identified as a new emphasis on "truth to individual experience" (13) rather than adherence to some traditional literary formula but a new movement toward self-contained stories with a beginning, a middle, and an end, which, as Aristotle ruled, "naturally follows some other thing, either by necessity, or as a rule, but has nothing following it" (31).

My claim that the novel represented a relatively new emphasis on self-contained stories may seem perverse in view of Aristotelian tragedy's emphasis on a decisive end that is "the chief thing of all" (Watt 27). Even Athenian tragedy, however, offers two obvious models for sequels. Aeschylus's *Oresteia* (458 BC) provides the only surviving example of the planned dramatic trilogy, the sequence of three plays designed expressly to be staged on the same day, each presenting a cohesive episode in the ongoing story of the house of Atreus, each connected to the others by the continuing search for vengeance that made the trilogy more coherent and penetrating than the sum of its three individual parts. And Sophocles's Theban plays provide an example of an unplanned trilogy, its three plays written out of sequence (*Antigone* around 441 BC, *Oedipus the King* at an unknown date some years later, and *Oedipus at Colonus*, which makes only sporadic attempts to reconcile apparent contradictions between the other two, shortly before Sophocles's death in 406 BC), yet still frequently read, although never staged, as chapters in a single story. Both these models resurface in Shakespeare, the first in the two historical tetralogies (especially the second, from *Richard II* to *Henry V*, which Alvin B. Kernan has dubbed the Henriad because of its Aristotelian emphasis on "a large-scale, heroic action" [245]), the second in the unplanned *Merry Wives of Windsor*, which brings Falstaff back from the grave in response to Queen Elizabeth's wish to see Sir John in love. The most important unplanned sequel by a Shakespearean contemporary is Marlowe's *Tamburlaine the Great, Part II* (1590). This model has endured in the second part of John Bunyan's *Pilgrim's Progress* (1684), Lewis Carroll's *Through the Looking-Glass* (1872), and the unplanned sequels to films such as *The Godfather* (1972, 1974, 1990) and *The Matrix* (1999, 2003, 2003)—and perhaps in Austen's own *Persuasion* (1818), whose second-chance-at-love story makes it read like an informal sequel to an unwritten Austen novel.

In addition, the publication of a novel in multiple volumes rather than its staging on a single day meant that novels such as Laurence Sterne's *Tristram Shandy* (1760-1767), unencumbered by a strong sense of Aristotelian teleology or even a consecutive storyline, could in principle go on forever. The tropism toward endless narrative persists in eighteenth-century contemporaries such as Denis Diderot's *Jacques le fataliste et son maître* (c. 1778), nineteenth-century sagas such as Honoré de Balzac's *La Comédie humaine* (1830-1848), Eugene Sue's *Les Mystéres de Paris* (1842-1843), Anthony Trollope's cycles of six Barsetshire novels (1855-1867) and six Palliser novels (1864-1880)—the second set incidentally incorporating the more closely related albeit unplanned pair of *Phineas Finn* (1869) and *Phineas Redux* (1873)—and the multiple-authored twenty-first century narrative blogs made possible by the Web and prefigured by Fielding's *Independent* columns. Such endless narratives have their basis in the prenovelistic tradition of picaros such as Lazarillo de Tormes, who go from place to place enjoying a string of self-contained adventures with no apparent end, and Robin Hood, whose merry men are capable of having essentially the same adventure over and over indefinitely. The rich oral gestes of Troy, Araby, and Camelot—each a stockpile of adventure-worthy characters and typological conflicts—represent still an older tradition of stories without end. The most distinguished sequel in this mode is the *Odyssey*.

Finally, there is the metasequel: the sequel that not only continues but also comments explicitly on a specific predecessor. The obvious example is the second part of *Don Quixote* (1615), in which the Knight of the Dolorous Countenance and his squire, although no more self-conscious themselves than they were in Part One, have become public paragons of delusion, frequently recognized as such and occasionally feted as celebrities or confronted with doubles striving to live up to the chivalric models they presented ten years earlier. The most ambitious of all metasequels is the New Testament, which, by offering itself as a completion of the Hebrew Bible, recasts all earlier scripture, not just prophetic books such as Isaiah and Ecclesiastes, as a series of prophecies fulfilled in the life and ministry of Jesus. *Paradise Regained* (1671) retraces this narrative trajectory while reversing its scope because Milton's brief epic stands more as a postlude to than as a completion of the more ambitious *Paradise Lost* (1667). But the tradition survives in a form much closer to Bridget Jones in a series of novels by Stephanie Barron beginning with *Jane and the Unpleasantness at Scargrave Manor* (1996) that recast Jane Austen as a fictionalized sleuth undergoing a series of adventures complete with faux-scholarly footnotes that place it both inside and outside Austen's universe, and a subgenre of quasi-biographical films from *Shakespeare in Love* (1998) to *Becoming Jane* (2007) that invent fictional romantic intrigues on which their authors are alleged to have drawn in creating their most memorable works. Apart from the doubtful example of *Persuasion*, Austen apparently never indulged in writing sequels. But there were many models for such continuations available to her, beginning with Daniel Defoe's two sequels to *Robinson Crusoe* (1719, 1719, 1720) and the two-volume sequel Samuel Richardson wrote to *Pamela* (1740, 1741) to preserve his legal rights in the story in the face of John Kelly's unauthorized sequel *Pamela's Conduct in High Life* (1741). When Austen was producing her novels, single, highly wrought, self-contained narratives such as *Tom Jones* (1749) whose end defined not only the limit of the characters' adventures but also the capstone of the tale's formal structure were the exception rather than the rule.

What changes between Austen and Helen Fielding is not the possibility or acceptability of sequels, which were already in wide currency when Austen wrote, but the emergence of different kinds of sequels that reflected both new technologies and a fundamentally new attitude toward the originality of original stories and the value of Aristotelian ends and endings. The most distinctive, although the least numerous, of these is the nonce sequel arising when a film originally designed as a single story is split into multiple parts because it runs inconveniently long. Leading examples include Richard Lester's *The Three Musketeers* (1973) and *The Four Musketeers* (1974) and Quentin Tarantino's *Kill Bill, Volumes 1 and 2* (2003, 2004). Peter Jackson first envisioned Lord of the Rings as a two-part film, then considered squeezing J. R. R. Tolkien's epic of Middle-earth into a single feature before following Tolkien's lead and casting the story in three parts (2001, 2002, 2003), although insisting, as Tolkien had done before him, that it was a single work in multiple installments, not a trilogy.

A second new kind of sequel, almost equally uncommon, takes its cue from the title of Alexandre Dumas's *Twenty Years After* (*Vingt ans après*, 1845). The impetus behind these sequels is to develop a character or group of characters originally conceived to carry the burden of a single story and revisit them grown older in an adventure that will display them in a new light. Examples include Henry James's *The Princess Casamassima* (1886), designed in part as a platform for Christina Light, the equivocal heroine of *Roderick Hudson* (1876); Lester's *Robin and Marian* (1976), based on a rarely filmed strain of legends recounting the outlaw's death; and stories by divers hands of Sherlock Holmes's retirement, from H. F. Heard's *A Taste for Honey* (1941) to Laurie R. King's *The Beekeeper's Apprentice* (1994) and its own sequels. Interestingly, none of the Hollywood films based on Dumas's *The Man in the Iron Mask* (1939, 1989, 1998), an 1847 sequel to *The Three Musketeers*, emphasizes its status as sequel, presumably because only the first of them, Allen Dwan's 1929 *The Iron Mask* starring Douglas Fairbanks, is produced by a company that had released a recent adaptation of *The Three Musketeers* or cast with the same performers as those earlier adaptations.

The death and resurrection of Sherlock Holmes marks a crucial turn in both Holmes's own career and the history of sequels generally. For seven years after Arthur Conan Doyle's impatience with the detective hero who had brought him fame led him to send Holmes and his nemesis Professor Moriarty over a cliff and into the Reichenbach Falls in "The Final Problem" (1894), Doyle resisted all entreaties to bring Holmes back for further sequels. He returned to him in 1901 to write Holmes into *The Hound of the Baskervilles*, a tale originally conceived without him by setting the story before Holmes's ostensible death.[3] Unlike Elizabeth I, who had apparently accepted Falstaff's unexplained return from his death between *Henry IV, Part 2*, and *Henry V* to assume the leading role in a very different kind of play, Holmes's fans, although eagerly devouring *The Hound*, demanded not simply more retrospective installments of his adventures but the assurance that he had not died in the first place. Two years later, Doyle capitulated in "The Adventure of the Empty House," a sequel to "The Final Problem" that naturalized Holmes's resurrection by providing a rational, if not especially convincing, explanation of how Dr. Watson had mistakenly come to believe him dead and anchoring his return in a specific historic time (the spring of 1894) after his apparent death.

Several differences are found between the specific demands Doyle had to accommodate to secure Holmes's resurrection and Shakespeare's more casual resurrection of Falstaff. One is the difference in the hero's relation to his world. Although both Falstaff and Holmes were already veterans of sequels when they died, both Holmes's relative durability (two brief novels and twenty-three short stories before his alleged death) and his relative abstraction from his world (through his status as a consulting detective whom readers might reasonably have expected to be professionally available indefinitely until they were brought up short by the title and the opening sentence of "The Final Problem") must have made his death seem more shocking and less acceptable. In addition, the narrative mode of the magazine story that had made Holmes famous was more naturalistic and continuous than that of a Shakespeare play, which, presented as a discrete entertainment experience, most likely would have explained the peculiarity of Falstaff's resurrection only in a framing prologue or ignored it entirely. No wonder Doyle, as quoted by his biographer Andrew Lycett, claimed to have invented something radically new in devising the fictional form of linked but independent adventures starring a single durable hero: "I was a revolutionist, and I think I may fairly claim . . . the credit of being the inaugurator of a system which has since been worked by others with no little success" (164). Finally, Doyle's relation to his public was different from Shakespeare's because he no doubt learned when his initial attempt at a retrospective sequel failed to still the demand for a resurrected Holmes. Shakespeare needed to suit only the whim of a single fan, however powerful; Doyle had the pressure of thousands.

The case of Sherlock Holmes opens the doors to a far more vast category: the hero, almost always male, who can be endlessly recycled because he remains sufficiently unchanged by, or remote from, the action of any given story to be available in unaltered form for further nondevelopment. Such characters trace their ancestry to Robin Hood, King

Arthur's knights of the Round Table, and picaros such as Lazarillo de Tormes. But their relation to their adventures is more complex because they are not really adventurers. The pivotal example is the nameless monster Victor Frankenstein created who is conceived in terms of a tragic teleology that can be overridden by the simple expedient of bringing him back to life. His progeny include heroes who cannot die because they are superheroes (Superman and his DC and Marvel counterparts, and the evergreen, if not literally immortal, James Bond), villains who cannot be killed because they are immortal or undead (Dracula and the legion of vampires that followed him, along with such franchise movie monsters as the Mummy, the Invisible Man, the Wolf Man, Michael Myers, Freddy Krueger, and Jason Voorhees), and heroes such as Tarzan whom audiences can imagine enduring forever because their world seems so remote. Despite the early-blooming example of Frankenstein's monster, the vogue of these franchise heroes corresponds roughly to the rise of twentieth-century technologies such as comic strips, movie serials, radio, and television that favor indefinitely continuing episodic stories over self-contained Aristotelian actions. Even when these stories move each toward a preordained ending, that ending is a reluctant contrivance such as the coming of dawn that interrupts each of Scheherazade's stories. Each ending provides an excuse for the storyteller to break off a tale both the teller and the audience wish could continue forever.

Although Scheherazade specializes in stories of action heroes such as Ali Baba, Aladdin, and Sinbad the Sailor, the female counterpart to this mainly male-oriented series of endless adventures can be found alongside Superman's comic-strip adventures in the increasingly female-dominated franchises of *Little Orphan Annie, Mary Worth*, and *Apartment 3-G*. If the eternal returns of Sherlock Holmes, Tarzan, and Frankenstein's monster depend largely on the cinema, these female franchises have their parallels in genres fueled by other post–Austen technologies: television and radio soap operas and magazine serials. These stories owe less to the repeated death and resurrection of Hollywood heroes and monsters than to what Henry James called the "adventure" of Bessie Alden's rejection of Lord Lambeth in "An International Episode" (1878) for the kind of "psychological reason" James found "adorably pictorial" ("The Art of Fiction" 61). Instead of staging physical conflict in public exterior spaces, these stories of psychological conflict and self-conflict threaten to break with Aristotelian teleology by their refusal to end at all. The quintessential example is *The Guiding Light*, which first aired on radio in 1937 and went on to survive hundreds of plot twists, the departures or deaths of dozens of performers, a change of medium from radio to television in 1952, and numerous format changes thereafter (the move from black and white to color in 1967, the lengthening of individual episodes from half an hour to a full hour in 1977) to continue until 2009. *Guiding Light*, as it had been called since 1976, seemed likely to continue indefinitely because its format had demonstrated the ability to adapt to new media—it would be a natural for webcasting—and because its employees, producers, sponsors, and viewers were united in their desire to keep it afloat. Because the format of the series implied a promise that it would tie up individual subplots but never come to an end, it could be ended only by an unforeseen production catastrophe, a deliberate change of plans occasioned presumably by competition from a stronger story, or by declining ratings, not by its own natural tropism toward ending.

A final model of the sequel generated by radio and popularized by television shows how differently contemporary sequels treat the notion of teleology from the kinds of sequels Austen knew. Since the mid-1950s, the principal alternative television has offered to continued stories indefinitely is not self-contained dramas of the sort that once flourished on *Kraft Television Theatre* (1947–58) or *Playhouse 90* (1956–61), but the series that immerses a continuing cast of characters in a new but generically similar adventure every week. In sitcoms such as *I Love Lucy* (1951–57), *Gilligan's Island* (1964–67), and *Seinfeld* (1990–98) or dramatic series such as *Law and Order* (1990–) and *ER* (1994–2009), every episode is self-contained, readily intelligible to viewers who have not seen the preceding episode. Yet the continuity provided by the strongly established characters who anchor the series means that each episode covers such similar ground, even in *Seinfeld*, that it is a remake in the guise of a sequel to the earlier episodes. This tendency has been complicated in recent years by programs as diverse as *The Mary Tyler Moore Show* (1970–77), which introduced longer narrative arcs that changed several of the characters irreversibly over the life of the series; *24* (2001–), in which each hour-long episode, filmed to simulate a congruence of dramatic and real time, builds inexorably on the preceding episode while introducing new complications of its own; and *The Simpsons* (1989–), whose every episode is a feast of heteroglossia that refers both to the program's own world and to the broader world of cultural references outside. Yet the impetus toward sequels that provide the pleasures of remakes continues not only in the ensemble casts and predictably conflicting agendas of such programs but also in the recent rise of reality-based programming, quiz shows, and even news broadcasts that have emphasized indefinitely continuing stories ever since the 1979–81 Iran hostage crisis, whose 444-day duration, faithfully memorialized day by numbered day on the nightly news, went far to establish a pattern of subordinating incidental developments to the presentation of a distinctive narrative universe guaranteed to remain identical week after week.

This overview of sequels before Bridget Jones emphasizes two distinctive features of Fielding's heroine. The first is simple. Influential as cinema may have been in fostering a mass culture receptive to sequels, Bridget's roots are not in the movies but the popular press. Once a thriving periodical industry had created "a huge, open mouth which has to be fed" by new book reviews, for example, it was only a matter of time before Henry James would compare the reviews to "dummies" designed to make it look as if a long train is fully occupied, each dummy readily recycled: "The guard attends to it when the train is shunted, blows the cinders from its wooden face and gives a different crook to its elbow, so that it may serve for another run" ("The Science of Criticism" 95). The tendency James notes of even nonnarrative forms such as book reviews to generate their own well-nigh indistinguishable sequels produces not only continuing magazine serials but also publishing heroes such as Buffalo Bill, Nick Carter, and Nancy Drew, as well as endless streams of paperback fantasies, romances and Choose-Your-Own Adventures. This model of the sequel as a virtual remake has given the world the Police Academy franchise (seven feature films from 1984 through 1994, followed in 1997 by a short-lived television series), the three Matrix films, and Bridget Jones.

The second, altogether less simple, feature that makes Bridget so distinctive is her alliance of several thematic elements drawn from twentieth-century technologies whose stories are typically directed to female audiences—magazine serials, continuing comic strips, and soap operas—with an approach to teleology best illustrated by the resurrections of Frankenstein's monster and Sherlock Holmes. Because each of Holmes's stories comes to a definitive end for his clients while leaving him available for further adventures, their teleology might be described as both open and closed. "The Final Problem," however, promises an ending that is apparently irreversible. However rapturously fans may have greeted "The Adventure of the Empty House," Holmes's resurrection is a fictional scandal on a par with a fictionalized Mary Shelley's revelation, at the beginning of *The Bride of Frankenstein* (1935), that her monster had not died in the blaze that apparently consumed him at the end of *Frankenstein* (1931). It is as if Austen had written a sequel in which Mr. Darcy had decided that despite his unstinting and apparently incontrovertible pledge of love at the end of *Pride and Prejudice*, he did not wish to marry Elizabeth Bennet after all. When Fielding brings Bridget back in *The Edge of Reason*, she is not so much continuing her heroine's story as shattering the teleology of her earlier novel, indicating that the true love

Bridget had found at the end of that novel did not carry the teleological power that it once had in Austen, and that many of Fielding's readers had presumably assumed it would this time as well.

As it turns out, Bridget, a child of *The Independent*, is only a distant relation of Elizabeth Bennet. She was designed from the first not as a character that implied an Aristotelian action but as a voice that could amusingly dramatize contradictions facing educated, romantically minded career women of the 1990s. Although Fielding acknowledged pressing the plot of *Pride and Prejudice* into service for *Bridget Jones's Diary*, practically everything that made Bridget appealing came from other sources, as a look at the opening page of Bridget's New Year's resolutions, based on Fielding's *Independent* column for 3 January 1996, makes clear:

I WILL NOT

Drink more than fourteen alcohol units a week.

Smoke.

Waste money on: pasta makers, ice-cream machines or other culinary devices which will never use; books by unreadable literary authors to put impressively on shelves; exotic underwear, since pointless as have no boyfriend.

Behave sluttishly around the house, but instead imagine others are watching.

Spend more than earn.

Allow in-tray to rage out of control.

Fall for any of the following: alcoholics, workaholics, commitment phobics, people with girlfriends or wives, misogynists, megalomaniacs, chauvinists, emotional fuckwits or freeloaders, perverts. (2)

The voice is inflected by journalistic canons of telegraphic brevity ("pointless as have no boyfriend"), the rhetoric of diet and self-help books ("alcohol units"), and the dialogized voices of Bridget's mother ("but instead imagine others are watching") and her friend Sharon ("emotional fuckwits"). What makes it both funnier and more desperate than any of its sources is its indiscriminately mechanical internalizing of their norms (the word Bridget most frequently omits from her diary entries in the interests of brevity is "I"), its hopeless attempt to incorporate the contrary ideals behind them all, and its transparently misguided faith in both the need for and the efficacy of self-improvement regimens. Every day is New Year's for Bridget, who emerges from even her most disastrous misadventures resolved that although she can never forgive herself or anyone else for the debacle du jour, she will do better next time. The contradictions in Bridget's voice thus guarantee endless tribulations but no teleology.

In rooting her heroine in a voice whose naïve faith in individual agency mocks her potential for agency, Fielding was following in the venerable tradition of the *skaz*, or sketch, a form Boris Tomashevsky had identified as an alternative to the well-plotted short story as early as 1925 (67). The sketch, typically designed to display the attractions of a distinctive place or the dynamics of a self-conscious voice, was peculiarly suited to journalism because it flourished on the frontier between fiction and nonfiction, as Fielding realized when she adopted the persona of Bridget instead of writing the column, as she had originally been asked to do, as herself. Half a century earlier, many writers from *The New Yorker*—Dorothy Parker, Richard Lockridge, Eric Partridge, and most notably John O'Hara—had graduated from the humorous sketch about a particular group, situation, or subculture to short stories or novels on the same subjects. For Fielding to make a similar transition with a novel that incorporated many people and situations she had already invented for her column was only natural: Bridget's neurotic fretting about her weight; her smoking and drinking; her anxiety about whether she should sleep with her boss Daniel Cleaver; the dangers of carrying on an office romance; her distaste with her philandering mother; her dread of her inquisitive relatives and the Smug Marrieds; her humiliation when she is the only guest to arrive in costume at the Vicars and Sluts party; her discomfort with the relentless coarseness of Richard Finch, her new boss at *Wake Up Britain* (which became *Sit Up Britain* in the films); and her obvious unsuitability as a television correspondent. The humor Fielding spins out of her earliest columns for *The Independent* depends on Bridget's self-perceived inadequacies, her inability to enjoy everything, or anything, that her friends, her relatives, and her library of self-help books assure her is rightfully hers. The implicit promise of these columns is precisely the opposite to the promise of the genre romances that take their cue from Austen: that Bridget will never grow, never change, never fulfill a single one of her self-therapeutic promises, so that like her friends, we will always love her just as she is.

Even Bridget's yearning for romance originates as a contradictory series of negative impulses that engender sketch comedy rather than the sort of teleology associated with consummation. When the BBC *Pride and Prejudice* captivates her along with the rest of the nation—a fact she first mentions in Fielding's 18 October 1995 column as a counterweight to her apprehensive preparation for her interview with Richard Finch—her ruminations are couched in terms not only of a neurotic addiction to Elizabeth and Darcy's idealized romance but also of a neurotic resistance to the teleology of romance generally:

> 8.55. Just nipped out for fags ready for *Pride and Prejudice*. Hard to believe there are so many cars out on the roads. Shouldn't they be at home getting ready? Love the nation being so addicted. The basis of my own addiction, I know, is my simple human need for Darcy to get off with Elizabeth. The football guru Nick Hornby states in his book *Fever Pitch* that men not wish themselves on the pitch, claims Hornby. Instead they see their team as their chosen representatives, rather like Parliament. That is precisely my feeling about Darcy and Elizabeth. They are my chosen representatives in the field of shagging, or rather courtship. I do not, however, wish to see any actual goals. I would hate to see Darcy and Elizabeth in bed smoking a cigarette afterwards. That would be unnatural and wrong and I would quickly lose interest. . . . That is not to say, however, I would not delight in sleeping with the actor Colin Firth.

When she goes to the interview with Richard Finch, "who has merged bewilderingly with Mr. Darcy in my mind," Bridget answers his story-baiting question, "What do lesbians actually do in bed?" by replying, "I think we should be doing the off-screen romance between Darcy and Elizabeth"—a non sequitur that instantly wins her the job.

Two weeks later, as Bridget is preparing for her first day in her new position, she records her profound disappointment with "the Elizabeth and Darcy wedding episode." Her criticism prompts her mother's response: "Oh, don't be silly, darling, no one's the slightest bit interested in love once the pursuit is over. As my father used to say, 'You don't run after the bus when you've caught it, do you?'" But just as Pamela Jones is still interested in love once the pursuit is over—just not that of the boring, affectionate husband who no longer pursues her—so is Bridget. In fact, Bridget, who continues to confuse Austen's Darcy with Colin Firth ("there are no such men as Mr. Darcy any more. Even Mr. Darcy himself—who would never do anything so flighty as to be an actor—is, in fact, an actor"), not only persists in running after the bus once the pursuit is over; she is incapable of seeing that she has caught it. Although she is slotted into the role of the romantic-comedy heroine with the arrival of Mark Darcy at her parents' New Year's party in the *Independent* entry for 3 January 1996—a scene Fielding created some ten months after beginning her column, but one that became the opening scene in both the novel and film *Bridget Jones's Diary*—she is endlessly available for sequels even after Darcy vanquishes the unsuitable Daniel Cleaver and declares his love because she is too invested in her neuroses ever to be cured. Bridget's first entry in *Bridget Jones: The Edge of Reason* begins with an obvious set-up line ("Hurrah! The wilderness years are over") whose punch line arrives promptly at the end of the paragraph ("Ooh. Mark Darcy just moved. Maybe he will wake up and talk to me about my opinions" [3]). The moony voiceover that introduces Kidron's film ("I've found my happy ending at last, and nothing in the world can spoil it"), which would seem to carry decisive teleological force if only it were deferred until the end of the film, is instantly followed by a deflating segue ("Well, almost nothing") to Bridget's farcically terrified skydive into a pigpen for *Sit Up Britain*.

For all the parallels Fielding draws between Bridget and Elizabeth Bennet, whose romance strongly implies a resolution from its beginning, the foundation of Bridget's humorous appeal is a neurotically self-critical voice that would be silenced forever by such a resolution. Unlike Emma Woodhouse's discovery of the capacity for corrective self-criticism, which promises to end her story by making her a suitable mate for Mr. Knightley, Bridget's neurotic and hopelessly unconstructive self-criticism can have no such teleological force because she is stuck with it from the beginning. As the cure of Don Quixote at the end of Cervantes's second volume means the end of his life, the promise of enduring happiness in love would be the death of everything that makes Bridget Bridget. Elizabeth Bennet, her ostensible model, is a heroine divided by her desire for love and acceptance by her equals and her forthright sense of independence. In the case of Bridget, both these warring impulses are put on one side of the scale as Bridget's yearning for professional success, romantic validation, respectable parents, and a steady diet of shagging. The other side is occupied by an insatiable impulse toward self-criticism that makes her altogether more unstable than any Austen heroine. To be more precise, Elizabeth is unstable—torn between Darcy and Wickham, between her loyalty to her parents and her recognition of their failings, between her attraction to Darcy and her repulsion from his contempt for her family and his own love—only until her instability is resolved by Darcy's unconditional second confession of love, which makes her whole by uniting her in a couple that spells the end of both her instability and her story. Bridget, by contrast, is stable in her instability. Nothing can complete her or dull her self-lacerating edge: not romantic pursuit, professional achievement, satisfying sex, even marriage and children.

Throughout the novel Fielding drew from her newspaper columns and the sequel inspired by them, Bridget is much more resistant to teleology than Elizabeth because Fielding's world, even when it is enshrined between the covers of a single volume, offers men and especially women so many fewer teleological options. In *Pride and Prejudice*, matrimony may or may not provide the opportunity to consummate a grand passion or a marriage of true minds, but even at its worst it is an honorable estate with due rewards for Charlotte Lucas, who clear-sightedly accepts the odious Mr. Collins for the advantages it will give her over being a dependent spinster, and Lydia Bennet, who purrs with contentment after Darcy succeeds in getting the unscrupulous seducer Wickham to marry her. As early as Guy de Maupassant's *Bel-Ami* (1885), the possibility of divorce loosens the teleological force of marriage, opening the way for the question Bridget asks in voiceover as she is skydiving into the pigpen at the beginning of *The Edge of Reason*: "What happens *after* you walk off into the sunset?"—prompting Richard's unwitting but gorgeously deflating response, "Close-up of the porker," and a tight close-up of Bridget's rump.

This opening sequence, whose most direct source in Fielding is the episode in *Bridget Jones's Diary* (194–95) in which her plan to slide down a firehouse pole and interview a firefighter is scotched when she begins to slide too soon and the camera catches her scrabbling to climb back up, shows how Bridget's resistance to teleology becomes still greater when she is transferred from novel to screen. Once Richard hires Bridget as a correspondent for *Sit Up Britain*, she is obviously available for any number of on-air pratfalls. The logic of the film sequel demands that she at least endure a pratfall more elaborate and humiliating than the episode of the firehouse pole. The result is an inflated remake in the guise of a sequel, something that covers the same ground as the first film but at greater length, with a bigger budget, and with apparently higher stakes. If Bridget fails to pull her ripcord, she will be killed rather than simply humiliated. But of course she eventually pulls the cord, and of course her humiliation, though intense, has no lasting impact on her. In fact, her "crap skydiving report," which logically ought to get her fired, has no effect on her future because, as Richard tells her, "they loved it upstairs." No matter what happens to Bridget, good or bad, she will always be available for further dreams, adventures, and ridicule.

Because Fielding had already published her second novel when *Bridget Jones's Diary* went into production, the film felt free to lay much more methodical groundwork for a sequel. Its main technique for doing so is to soften the teleological impact of every plot development in its final scenes that would normally herald a definitive ending. Refusing Daniel's tepid blandishments, she tells him, "I'm still looking for something more extraordinary than that," intimating that she is an eternal seeker who can never be satisfied. When her philandering mother returns in remorse to her father pleading to be taken back, he replies: "I just don't know," before adding, "I'm joking, you daft cow." The film echoes Austen's Darcy-Wickham rivalry in revealing that Daniel has seduced Mark's wife rather than learning that Mark has slept with his girlfriend. But instead of allowing Bridget to fly into Mark's arms, it introduces the threat of his engagement to his legal colleague Natasha and packs them off to New York, from which Mark must abruptly return for the film's final sequence. Even after he tells Bridget that he loves her, the film has one last-minute complication—his discovery of the diary in which she has described him so recently and unflatteringly—that could torpedo the ending. The implication of all these sudden obstacles and changes of course is that nothing is ever certain because things can always change, and "The End" of the film's credits can be crossed off and replaced with "The Beginning."

If the leading strategy Maguire's film adopts is to weaken the teleological force of the romance plot it borrows from Austen, the leading strategy of Kidron's film is to transform every incident from a potentially developmental stage in a teleologically oriented plot into an endlessly repeatable spectacle. Bridget's prophetic quarrel with Mark over the upbringing of their nonexistent son culminates in a moment when Mark, returning from the loo, says even more prophetically: "Oh, Christ, now what?" The quarrel, as Mark subliminally recognizes, will lead nowhere except to a reconciliation, followed by more quarrels. Pam Jones, emerging from a dressing room swathed in violet, announces, "Daddy and I are going to get married!" When her daughter protests, "But you're already married!" Pam crows, "We're going to do it again!"

Marriage vows are far from the only apparently definitive ritual the sequel needs to renew. Bridget, about to fall into bed with Daniel, tells him, "If I stay with you tonight, it's definitely the end of something important." He asks her, "Doesn't everyone deserve a second chance?" Her reply—"Except Hitler"—both indicates her susceptibility to him and puts an anticlimactic spin on the question of whether Daniel can ever change. Moments later, when she is confronted by the full-body masseuse he has hired for the evening, she rages: "I can't believe I fell for it again!" But of course the audience can believe it. They have been prepared for this moment by the inflation of Daniel's role in the film so that he is not an incidental temptation but a symmetrical alternative to Mark and by the endless soundtrack of pop tunes, from "The Sound of Music" and "Nobody Does It Better" to "Material Girl" and "I Believe in a Thing Called Love," that turn every action, from skydiving to kissing, into a timeless, self-contained spectacle that floats free of the context that moors it to the film's story into a more broadly romantic and satirical context in which it can be endlessly repeated.

Hence Lizzie Skurnick's observation that chick-lit has "grown up" to "mom lit" (1) with the arrival of babies in the neighborhoods of Sophie Kinsella, Jill Kargman, Carrie Karasyov, and Fielding herself, adroitly traces the latest development in a genre that "is now seen to have run its course" (2) while overlooking a more fundamental point: that even as a mother and grandmother, Bridget will never grow up because she can never settle down. Snagging the rich boyfriend her mother had been urging on her for a year, Bridget realizes, does not resolve Pamela Jones's tendency to nag but simply makes her switch gears and preach chastity, and Bridget's friends, having urged her for years to get a steady boyfriend, now urge her to dump him. When the final page of *The Edge of Reason* promised that Bridget would follow Mark to Los Angeles, seasoned fans knew that the move would merely provide a new arena for neuroses that had already been staged in Bridget's parents' home, a publishing office, a television program, and a Thai prison. When Fielding celebrated Darcy's return from Los Angeles, Bridget evidently not having accompanied him after all, in a 2001 story, "Bridget Jones: This Time I Really Have Changed," the story's leading joke was telegraphed not only by the opening entry from Bridget's diary ("This is my chance to prove to him that life with me can be tranquil and orderly") but also by its title. And when Fielding resumed her weekly Bridget Jones column for *The Independent* on 4 August 2005, seven years after ending her final column for the *Daily Telegraph*, like her novel *The Edge of Reason*, with Bridget's impending departure for Los Angeles, the very first thing she did was to have Bridget get pregnant.

The promise of motherhood did not mark the end of Bridget's adventures in the way Skurnick's remarks suggest. Instead, in the time-honored tradition of *The Guiding Light*, she found that the father of her baby was not Mark Darcy but Daniel Cleaver, whom she had "accidentally" shagged after fortifying herself with Chardonnay during an unsought meeting with him. Fielding suspended Bridget's weekly diary entries on 15 June 2006 with Daniel bringing Bridget and her newborn baby home to his flat. But the final lines of that entry make it clear that motherhood has not provided any closure for her heroine:

> Whole world seems too dangerous for baby—even Daniel's flat. What if I accidentally drop him in the toilet and flush it? Or put him in the tumble-dryer? What if Daniel and I split up, then I

die and there's no one to care for him? What if am alone with
baby when die and no one realises and he's left just crying for his
mummy?

Oh, God, thought all neurosis and anxiety would end when
had baby, but realise has opened up a lifetime of fears for him.
Have to stop worrying. Anyway, given way he lunges at me like a
little snuffle-pig, he would probably survive by eating me.

And truth is, although scary, I like this worrying re being
eaten by own child so much better than years of worrying that
would die alone, as tragic barren spinster, and be found weeks later
half-eaten by an Alsatian.

This last observation is as close as Bridget ever comes to admit-
ting how invested she is in her sempiternal neuroses and how resistant
she is to the therapies of love, marriage, and motherhood traditionally
prescribed for the weaker sex. Nor do her readers want her to respond
to therapy. It is a truth universally acknowledged that neurosis is funny
only until it is cured, and a vast audience agrees with Bridget that it
would be better for her to be neurotic than content. One might argue,
as Fielding does in the 15 November 1997 column introducing Bridget's
move to the *Daily Telegraph*, that Bridget's neuroses are simply reflections of her audience's: "If Bridget is popular . . . it's because she lives
in a state of nameless dread, thinking everyone knows how to live their
life except her. What she doesn't realise is that lots of other people feel
the same way." Bridget's distinctively neurotic voice is representative of
a large audience not only because they feel as insecure and alienated as
she does but because, despite the well-publicized clamoring for "closure"
reported by every crime victim ever to address a television camera, they
recognize subliminally that closure would be death.

Yet this resistance to closure, this preference for more adventures
rather than any definitive resolution, seems neurotic only when it is measured against an Aristotelian norm. E. M. Forster makes his resistance
to Aristotle explicit in his defense of character as a constitutive trope of
the modern novel, which Forster sets against Athenian tragedy: " 'All
human happiness and misery,' says Aristotle, 'take the form of action.'
We know better. We believe that happiness and misery exist in the secret
life, which each of us leads privately and to which (in his characters) the
novelist has access" (83). In a world peopled entirely by Prince Hamlets
whose pride or shame is that they have that within which passes show,
the resistance to teleology Bridget and her audience share may be a
sign that even if chick-lit's day has passed, the problems it raises so poi-

gnantly have not. It may well be the nature of contemporary heroines and their audiences to remain increasingly unfulfilled not because they are neurotically alienated from a functional society that calls forth their most authentic selves in public action but because contemporary social norms both alienate and colonize the individual consciousness so irresistibly that its most representative heroes and heroines are those least inclined toward closure. An important implication of Hillel Schwartz's argument that we live in "a culture of the copy in which repetition is psychologically, physiologically, cinematically, and commercially compelling" (300) is that every adventure invites a sequel that is tantamount to a remake. In such a world, it makes perfect sense, as Paul Budra points out, that "the perfect postmodern monster" has "no personality" but is "possessed of the charisma that comes with stability through sequelization" (198). Bridget's overpowering personality, directed in part toward the indefinite deferral of teleology and in part toward the systematic undermining of the teleological cues in whatever narrative model her creators adapt, suggests that the definitive accord Aristotle saw between psychology and action, between private self and public world, may have been nothing more than a bump in the road, a temporary blockage of the desire to desire.

In the end, Bridget is not a reducto ad absurdum, but more fittingly a step on the road to something else. After all, a female-oriented franchise spanning two newspaper columns, two novels, and two movies pales beyond the media conglomerates of action heroes such as Superman and James Bond. Although Kidron's film puts a new spin on Bridget's romantic rivalries by making her apparent rival Rebecca Gillies a lesbian who actually fancies Bridget rather than Mark, that twist has an air of finality (what sort of rival could Bridget possibly be more mistaken about?) rather than a promise of endless iterations in sequels still to come. Even the extras included in the DVD of *Bridget Jones: The Edge of Reason*—an alternate opening sequence, a filming of Bridget's interview with Colin Firth adapted from a chapter in Fielding's novel (136–42) that was not used in the feature, and a featurette entitled "Mark and Bridget Forever?"—have a disconcerting air of definitiveness. Sequel-ready heroines such as Bridget may be no more than transitional figures pointing toward female leads who can play as endlessly at romantic consummation as male leads such as Bond can play at definitive world destruction and redemption. The closest approach so far to this ideal of endless romance is not Bridget's adventures but *Apartment 3–G* and *Sex and the City*. Bridget's perch on the very edge of reason suggests that there is a still further path for other heroines to follow.

Notes

1. Even the Republic of Pemberley, a Web site at www.pemberley.com that includes in a section called "Bits of Ivory," brief Austen pastiches and sequels by Pemberleians, reflects this distaste in its description of Austen sequels as "Austenuations."

2. It would have been even more successful had it not been budgeted at an estimated $70 million, nearly three times the $26 million budget of *Bridget Jones's Diary*.

3. Although Dr. Watson sets *The Hound of the Baskervilles* in 1889, Sherlockians do not agree when the events of the novel take place. Only three of the fourteen scholars whose opinions Leslie S. Klinger summarizes in his edition of the four Holmes novels (3: 626–27) agree with Watson on the date, and more than one-third of them date it after Holmes's resurrection in 1894.

4

R. Barton Palmer

Before and After,
Before Before and After

Godfather I, II, and III

"THE *GODFATHER* FILMS," cinema historian Nick Browne declares, "are monuments on the landscape of American cinema" (1). Browne concedes that this judgment of excellence does not indicate that, aesthetically speaking, the three films are the same: "there are, of course, differences of intention and achievement among the three" (1). The parenthetical qualifier "of course" means, I suppose, that we should suspect these marks of individuality to be present, and indeed it does seem an unarguable point. All monuments, we might agree, are not created equal, and the plurality of these particular films in terms of "intention and achievement" is a well-supported critical commonplace too evident to deny. The Godfather films (1972, 1974, 1990) are three productions released at different times as the result of divergent "makings," as well as three texts that can be evaluated separately with regard to the contrasting intentions that can be read from them. Such a critical operation, naturally enough, depends on the fact that these texts continue to present themselves in some sense as individual objects whose meaning is self-contained. But (pun intended) is this the whole story?

Figure 4.1. *The Godfather Part II* (Francis Ford Coppola, 1974). Courtesy
Paramount/The Kobal Collection.

    Despite the evident plurality of the series at the most basic levels
of production and what we might term "textual ontology" (their mode
of being in film culture), the three films also constitute a larger unity
in Browne's view, or at least they can be seen that way: "it is natural to
regard these films as a trilogy to deal with the continuity of a directorial vision of the century-long working through of economic crime and
punishment in the inner sanctum of an American dynasty" (1). Several
points here of interest reflect familiar critical protocols about textual
"unity" and its importance within established traditions of evaluation.
The Godfather films constitute a trilogy because (an invocation here of
classic auteurist thinking) they are unified by "a directorial vision." The
reflex of that vision is that they share the same theme ("economic crime
and punishment") and the same subject matter ("the inner sanctum of an
American dynasty"). Finally, for practical reasons they became a trilogy
because their narrative "reach" is of an extent hardly containable within
the boundaries of a single film (a "century-long working through"). Identifying these films as a "trilogy" does seem a critical move to contain
and reorient their previously acknowledged singularity, easing the sense
in which they can be understood as belonging to their presumed author.
And yet more than auteurist protocols can be seen at work here. Most

critics would agree that in some sense the three films do "naturally" constitute a collectivity.

At the same time, the conception of a collectivity seems problematic and hardly self-evident. The title of Browne's very useful collection of essays is *Francis Ford Coppola's* The Godfather Trilogy, even though no text bears this name. If this designation is perhaps unconvincingly tendentious, it reflects two widespread notions: first, that while they remain singular in some important senses, a relation exists among the Godfather films that makes considering any one in absolute isolation from the others impossible; second, that this relation (somehow, if incompletely) elides the fact of singularity because the two films that follow the original not only continue its diegetic world but also the chronological unfolding of a web of events first recounted in *The Godfather*. Yet thinking of the series as a trilogy is not the only way, or even the most useful or accurate way, to account for what connects them to one another.

Significantly the term "sequel" does not occur in Browne's auteurist account of the series, although certainly those who produced the second and third films, as well as the audiences around the world, thought of them in this way. Indeed the titling scheme chosen for the two later productions, which was retrospectively imposed on the first, reflects industry wisdom that sequels should be marketed, often if not always, by alerting viewers to their connection to a well-loved and "presold" original (or, also in this case, originals). Recycling the exact title of the original (with Roman numerals somewhat grandly indicating production/release order) is perhaps the most obvious, but certainly not the only, way to do this. The marketing ingenuity of the industry is admirable, perhaps unlimited in this regard: compare, among many other less artful examples, the case of *Alien* (Ridley Scott, 1979) and *Aliens* (James Cameron, 1986), and *Grumpy Old Men* (Donald Petrie, 1993) and *Grumpier Old Men* (Howard Deutch, 1995). Because of its associations with the artless extension of commercially successful originals, most familiar these days in those groups of continuations designated by the damning term "franchise," such as the Rocky or Jurassic Park series, the concept of the sequel, which it is the avowed object of this volume to elucidate, is perhaps perceived to be incompatible with, or at least inconvenient to, conceptions of, authorship.

But good reasons exist to respect the actual history of the making and distribution of these three films, seeing, like filmgoers at the time, the second film as a sequel to the first, and the third a sequel to the first two. At least this is what this chapter demonstrates. Seeing the suite as connected by the concept of the sequel is fundamental to the understanding of the Godfather films, but it is ignored completely in the otherwise

fine essays in the Browne collection. To be fair, of course, textual singularity as such means little to an auteurist account of a directorial oeuvre,
even if the acknowledged focus is limited to three texts. However, as
literary critic J. A. Burrow rightly points out, considering the role that
context plays in determining the nature of the critical act: "One cannot
interpret or evaluate a text without identifying what *kind* of text it is"
(17). We know perfectly well what kinds of texts *Godfather I, II,* and *III*
are, considered separately. But what are they exactly when considered
together? How can we define their relation and its components?

The films certainly do not constitute a trilogy in the way Browne
suggests, that is, a coherent, step-by-step unfolding of a foundational
artistic vision. No one involved in the production of what was at the
time simply called *The Godfather* (including Mario Puzo, author of the
source novel) contemplated a "century-long working through" of themes
and subject matter conceived broadly enough to merit such a treatment.
Once again, as is well known, only the phenomenal box-office success of
the film once identified only as *The Godfather* led to the decision on the
part of those involved in the production (particularly the executives at
Paramount Studios, including the dynamic Frank Yablans) to begin work
almost immediately on a sequel. If a "directorial vision" can be seen legitimately as the major shaping force of the Godfather "trilogy," it can be seen
first to operate in a superordinate fashion only in the planning and execution of the second film. *The Godfather* was marked by substantial disagree-
ments between its director and the producer (Robert Evans), who strongly
insisted, for example, that Coppola's final cut be drastically revised (it was);
as a result, the film in many ways belongs not only to the director, but
also to the author of the original property and its producer. For the second
film, in contrast, the director was given much more control, as Jon Lewis
reports: "The production of *The Godfather: Part II* was significantly less
contentious than the production of the first film, largely because Coppola
was contracted not only to co-write but to produce the film himself. . . .
Coppola seemed to have had a free hand" ("If History" 40).

Because of circumstances too complicated to review here, when
Coppola was finally persuaded by the studio to direct yet another sequel
(a sequel, in effect, to the first two films) at the end of the 1980s, he
was allowed to make many important creative decisions (including hir-
ing his daughter Sofia to play the part of Mary Corleone, Michael's
daughter, when Winona Ryder suddenly dropped out of the project), but
proved unable to influence others. Producer Frank Mancuso refused to
pay Robert Duvall's asking price to reprise his role as Tom Hagen from
the two previous films, even though Mancuso had previously agreed to
a significantly higher figure to re-sign Diane Keaton as Michael's ex-wife

Kay. This casting decision not only forced Coppola to do significant rewriting of the script, eventually introducing a new lawyer character, B. J. Harrison, played by George Hamilton, who came much cheaper; it also decisively, and unfortunately, altered the carefully established continuity of the principal "family" characters that had tied the first film to the second and was to have provided the same linking function from them to the third (see Lewis, "If History" 43–52, and Biskind, *Godfather Companion* 131–81).

Authorship in Installments

It is beyond argument, in any event, that the three films were conceived and produced separately, not as three parts of a whole predetermined by some creative urge we can, with neoromantic elegance, term "directorial vision." Auteurism demands commonality and connection. And there is no reason to deny that such qualities could be found in the three films, an obvious point explored later in this chapter. As a critical protocol, however, authorship cannot be allowed to blind us to inalterable facts of structure, including and especially textual boundaries. These boundaries make a difference. And I do not mean something along the lines of the distinction (theoretically and hermeneutically interesting, but formally irrelevant) that narratologists make between "story" and "discourse." For if the story can, with the textual unfolding at an end, be conceived as a whole, it is only because it is a construct (not a textual element as such), based on information and inference, from the way in which the events of the plot have been presented in linear fashion by the discourse. Put simply, a narrative is always already both story and discourse. In contrast, the Godfather films must be either a trilogy (three parts of a whole) or a succession consisting of a foundational text plus two sequels (a three-part series rather than a whole).

Consider the evidence. Who would be bold enough to defend the proposition that the merging of what were then the only two parts of *The Godfather* into a single text for exhibition on network television called, variously, *The Godfather Saga* or *The Godfather 1902–1959: The Complete Epic* (1977), did not create an artifact qualitatively different from its two constituent films, even if these are considered two parts of a superordinate structure then thought complete? And that difference resides only partly in the fact that the narrative line of what could then be identified as the history of the Corleone crime family from 1902 to 1959 has been, as it were, straightened out, with *The Godfather: Part I* becoming the "medias res" of the story whose beginning and ending sections were derived from the 1902 and 1959 sections of *The Godfather: Part II*.

Most important for our purpose here, the process of amalgamation involved in remanufacturing the first two Godfather films into something like a television miniseries also eliminated those relations that we customarily consider as resulting from the process of "sequelization." Put another way, the amalgamation completed a process of incorporation that had been left intriguingly unfinished with the release of the second film. For the television version, two texts that had been connected to one another, yet hitherto had remained separate, became one. The connections between what, after amalgamation, were parts of a singular whole lost the decisive element of textual boundaries. No transforming amalgamation, however, has produced a new, and unitary, critical object from the three *Godfather* films. From the point of view of production, distribution, and exhibition, there is no "whole" as such containing three parts. Thus there is no Godfather trilogy. Any sense we might have of an overarching structure emerged only after its "parts" came into existence and when, because of the death of Michael Corleone, the main character, in the concluding scene of *The Godfather: Part III*, it became likely, if not inevitable, that no more such parts would be forthcoming.[1] The films are singular, though subordinate to one another; they are complete, yet unfinished in themselves. Parts *II* and *III* begin with an ending, *I* and *II* end with a beginning. The trajectory of the series hardly runs smoothly: a diegetic world begins and ends, begins and ends again, only a third time to begin and then end (if perhaps only provisionally). The films were produced singularly, and this is how they were exhibited.

I am not concerned here with the fact of the three films' singularity as such. Belaboring the obvious serves no purpose because it is a point even conceded in advance by those such as Browne who would prefer seeing the series of films as a trilogy. Even Browne does not insist that what he calls the three parts of *The Godfather* are (to invoke a theological metaphor) separate only in the sense of being identifiable persons that share a single substance. Instead, the ineradicable singularity of the three films serve here as the starting point for an examination of the particular fashion in which "sequeling" plays itself out in the constitution of the series.

But first, some further light must be shed on the notion of the sequel. An important concept in film studies that has, from a theoretical standpoint at least, received far too little attention, the sequel has been mistakenly seen for the most part only as the material result of a certain practice within commercial filmmaking (exploiting the evident popularity of a previous release). But it is also a crucial aspect of textual ontology, which can be easily summarized. Sequelization reorients (while reinforcing rather than eliminating) the singularity of the texts thus connected, precluding the possibility of a boundary-eliminating collective. Consider the following: After the release of *The Godfather: Part II*, *The Godfather* became *The Godfather: Part I*. From a "text in itself" it became the "text that will be followed." For ease of reference here, I will use the Latin term *sequendum* ("that which must or will be followed") to designate a text that finds itself succeeded by a sequel. The resulting reorientation, of course, is not a textual feature as such, but a contextually imposed strategy of nomenclature and reading.

The renaming of *The Godfather* recognizes that the film must now be understood differently (that is, as suffused by the qualities of "before" and "incompleteness"), but it points to no formal change per se. The extratextual knowledge that a text is followed by another becomes a protocol of reading that conditions how we understand both the text (now connected to another just as individual) and also its various features, for these can, perhaps even ask to, be read in a context wider than the boundaries of their generating text, which continues to strive, but must fail in the final instance, to contain them absolutely. Sequels are often designed to minimize, even eliminate, this backward/forward-looking mode of appreciation. *U.S. Marshals* (Stuart Baird, 1998), for example, carefully recycles the most commercially successful elements of *The Fugitive* (Andrew Davis, 1993), including a major character and star (played by Tommy Lee Jones) and a narrative pattern (the exciting pursuit of a fugitive who turns out to be innocent), but no attempt is otherwise made to link the narratives, which remain resolutely singular, making the productions self-contained and hence more easily marketable, or so industry wisdom suggests. Titling did not encourage viewers to consider *U.S. Marshals* as a sequel (apparently something along the lines of *Another Fugitive* was rejected), suggesting that what comes after *The Fugitive* is simply the close repetition of a formula proved successful by that film's excellent box office; the sequel in this instance then does not reorient or redefine the nature of its sequendum, which functions instead as a more or less disposable pretext.

In contrast, the Godfather films offer an instructive example of the opposite tendency. In fact, one of the most interesting aspects of this series is what Browne terms a "directorial vision," which can be seen at work in its overall architectonics as these were worked out during almost two decades of intermittent production activity.[2] Far from merely a canny recycling of elements that had proved popular, this authorial design encourages viewers to read the elements of *The Godfather* in relation to similar elements in the two sequels. Interestingly, the one study devoted to the first two Godfather films as a series of an original film and its sequel (Tom Berliner's "The Pleasures of Disappointment") approaches them only from the point of view of how such remakings always fail to be as appealing as the original. Berliner remarks: "The almost inescapable failure of sequels results from the fact that, at the same time a sequel calls to mind the charismatic original, it also recalls its absence, fostering a futile, nostalgic desire to reexperience the original aesthetic moment as though it had never happened" (109). True enough, perhaps, but this sense of looking backward (for what else is nostalgia?) can be used effectively as theme. A source of aesthetic pleasure, if we must use this kind of language, in the Godfather series is the pervasive sense of loss over time, as Michael fails to be his father, and as his father's world disappears forever. That the sequels fail somehow by virtue of the fact that they are sequels provides the viewer with an emotion that reflects that of Michael himself. In fact, this chapter argues, the ending of *Godfather III* spectacularly fails to be the ending of *The Godfather*, and that seems to be Coppola's point.

Coppola seems clearly to have recognized the authorial aspect of sequeling and, interested in establishing a particularly rich menu of parallels that reached across the series, designed the endings and beginnings of the second and third films as variations on themes announced in the first: curtain-raising ceremonies that express family solidarity while hinting at its potential weaknesses and vulnerabilities; the concluding elimination of these threats through skillfully managed assassinations of enemies both outside and inside the family. The techniques that express these themes play with notions of unity and singularity, much as the sequelized series of films does the same more globally. For the openings, Coppola fragments a collective event taking place in a single setting into a series of mininarratives, in the style of Robert Altman; for the all-resolving vendetta, he deploys elaborate patterns of crosscutting to confer representational unity on events occurring simultaneously, or nearly simultaneously, in a series of disconnected spaces.

These moments in each film are privileged set pieces, calling attention to the ways in which the narrative beginning, spectacularly initiated, is given a spectacularly fashioned conclusion. In designing the suite of films in this fashion, Coppola devises an aesthetic that perfectly suits the nature of the sequel, which is defined by a perhaps unexpectedly complex treatment of beginnings and endings, which come to bear the burden of expressing the ideas of before and after. That there is only an apparent difference between before and after becomes a central theme in this narrative of a family's rise to prominence and wealth. This success is thoroughly unstable, the result of an only partial assimilation that makes either escaping the past (in order to embrace thoroughly a promising future) or reliving its fullness (and so forestall the fading or loss of what renders it so worthy of preservation) impossible for the Corleones.

The aesthetic experience of the series is not flow, but rather intermittency and reorientation. From the point of view of succession, *Godfather I* has become a sequendum, followed by the sequel, *Godfather II*, which in turn also becomes a sequendum, along with *Godfather I*, with the appearance of *Godfather III*, a text that is, at least currently, only a sequel. The three texts do not form a whole, but a series of singularities connected by notions of before and after. What had ended has been prolonged and that prolonging has produced a second ending, which, itself prolonged, has eventually resulted in a third and, at the moment, final ending. Not parts filling their appointed slots, one after another, in a foreseen whole, the Godfather films deploy a series of endings that begin again, prolonging (and in consequence providing the opportunity for a profound meditation on) the notion and form of closure, the ending that problematically marks the boundary and thereby establishes the distinct and singular identity of the text.

Distinct singularity is a definitive feature of the sequel. Superficially resembling two other, related processes of textual succession, adaptation, and remaking, sequelization differs fundamentally from both in its rejection of a shared identity for the texts in question. The adaptation is another version of what it adapts, defined by what it stands in for, by what it replaces; adaptations can, and often are, given the same title as the works they adapt. Similarly, the remake is another version of an existing text, with which (however problematically) it shares an identity. Once again, the two texts often share exactly the same name. The remake is defined by what it offers an alternative to (but does not stand for). The sequel, in contrast, repeats in some sense, but does not stand in for its sequendum, not being identical with it. The sequel does not replace but redefines what it follows, revealing its unfinished nature. In the process, the sequel demonstrates that its own singularity is not a self-sufficiency because the later text owes its form and content in some fashion to the one that preceded it. The title *Godfather II* refers backward to its sequendum (expressing the notion that here is more of the same) even as it somewhat paradoxically indicates that this text is not the same as what it follows.

The nature of the redefinition effected by the sequel is, as one might expect, different in every case. Any literary text may generate an unlimited number of cinematic adaptations, uniquely shaped by what features of the source are selected for transformation.[3] Similarly, any text, literary or cinematic, may generate an unlimited number of sequels.

The zero degree of connection between the two texts may simply be an indication that "there is more" in the sense of yet another narrative movement to be completed. In taking a close look at the *Godfather* series, we will see what "there is more" means in a particular example. But the fact of more, as well as the sense of after, always imply the sense of what came before and of what has been left behind. Like adaptation and remaking, sequelization identifies relations (or, perhaps better, ties) that connect texts with one another. It is to such considerations of what, following the lead of theorist Gérard Genette, I will term transtextual connections that we must now turn, framing sequeling within a wider field of similar, yet distinct, processes.

Transtextuality, Hypertextuality, and the Sequel

Like others of his critical generation, Gérard Genette would have us believe that texts do not exist in splendid isolation, their borders impermeable to connections with other texts, their meaning deriving strictly in se and per se. This perspective on what has most often (and somewhat confusingly) been termed "intertextuality" is usefully summed up by Graham Allen:

> Texts, whether they be literary or non-literary, are viewed by modern theorists as lacking in any kind of independent meaning. . . . The act of reading, theorists claim, plunges us into a network of textual relations. To interpret a text, to discover its meaning, is to trace those relations. . . . Meaning becomes something which exists between a text and all the other texts to which it refers and relates, moving out from the independent text into a network of textual relations. (1)

For poststructuralists such as Roland Barthes and Julia Kristeva, "intertextuality," a concept that finds its origins in the work of Russian theorist Mikhail Bakhtin, refers to a general condition of language, already "pre-owned," as in Barthes's oft-quoted formulation: "The text is a tissue of quotations drawn from the innumerable centers of culture. . . . The writer can only imitate a gesture that is always anterior, never original" ("Death" 13).

Barthes, Kristeva, and their followers offer what Allen terms a more foundational and global account of "the semiotic processes of cultural and textual signification" (1). In contrast, Genette concerns himself with, to quote Allen's characterization, "a very pragmatic and determinable intertextual relationship between specific elements of individual texts"

(101). If texts themselves are "webs" (to unpack the metaphor implicit in this Latin term), Genette argues that they also find themselves fixed within larger yet particular and unique webs of production and discourse. This peculiar ontology he denominates *transtextualité* (transtextuality), a term that importantly includes both the notion of a self-defined object one productively might designate as a text and also the "textual transcendence of textuality," the way in which text-ness itself, somewhat paradoxically, is made (if only partly) dispensable by the web of other texts. Such transcendence is multifarious and can only be understood in the most general of terms, perhaps best summarized by its result, as "all that establishes a relation, open or hidden, between a text and other texts."[4] The most important subcategory of the transtextual is the relation *hypotexte/hypertexte*, which would be, taking the widest view possible of the phenomenon, "every text derived from an earlier text by means of either a simple or indirect transformation" (7).

If this transformation is global, resulting in two quite similar texts, these two categories of transformation might be roughly summarized as "remaking" and "imitation," to be differentiated by the degree of resemblance that characterizes the relation between the first text or hypotext and the one that follows it in order of production, the hypertext, which can for that reason always be understood as "of the second degree."[5] Naturally, the terms "remake" and "imitation" do not indicate distinct categories as such, but constitute the end points of a continuum. It seems fairly clear that Brian De Palma's *Body Double* (1984) is an imitation of Alfred Hitchcock's *Rear Window* (1954), while Jeff Bleckner's *Rear Window* (1998) is a remake of the original. But is *Blow Out* (Brian De Palma, 1981) a remake or an imitation of Michelangelo Antonioni's *Blow-Up* (1966)? One could offer evidence for either position, but perhaps there is no point in attempting to make distinctions of this kind. It is important to emphasize a further point Genette makes. He acknowledges that hypertextuality in a global sense does not describe a restricted category of texts but is instead a "universal aspect" of textuality, for "all works are hyptertextual."[6] That being the case, he suggests that discussion of the phenomenon be confined to those instances that are "most in the light . . . [being] at once extensive . . . and declared, in a fashion that is more or less official."[7] A theoretical position that could easily become embroiled in unproductive discussions of categories thus becomes transformed into a critical approach useful for the analysis of individual texts. It can, as Genette suggests, take as its object "*every* connection *joining* a text B to a text A anterior to it" (emphasis added).[8]

Not discussed by Genette as such, the phenomenon of the cinematic sequel is an exemplary category of hypertextuality. As not in the case of remakes and adaptations, however, the resemblance between the two objects is not very close. In fact, sequels, we might say, are determined by a productive, because unstable, dialectic of similarity and difference. Because they must offer "something more," they cannot reproduce the hypotext precisely, and yet there must be enough that is repeated in the hypertext to signal their connection. Sequels are all by definition texts of the "second degree," connected to others that, in terms of production, have preceded them. The connection between hypotexts and hypertexts of this type is always, once again by definition, "extensive" and "declared." The question of "joining" (*unissant*) will require further nuancing because it involves the issue of textual borders. To anticipate, these are clearly both acknowledged and transcended by transtextual connections, turning the work into something that is simultaneously itself and not the whole of the larger entity in which it participates.

Although he does not use the term, Genette makes several important points about sequels, one of which is of particular interest here. Genette distinguishes between two categories, the *suite* (etymologically, that which follows and connects) and the *continuation*, both of which "designate the connection between something and something else that preceded it." For Genette, if a hypertext is a "continuation," that means that its hypotext had ended "at a certain place that did not conclude it." A "suite," in contrast, is not a textual response in the second degree to a work that finds itself unfinished, but fulfills a completely different function: ". . . in general to exploit the success of a work, often considered in its own moment as finished, by making it come to life again with new elements of plot."[9] A suite, not a continuation, is what we conventionally mean by the term sequel.

But the relation between these two forms of transtextuality is more complex than might at first appear to be the case. A continuation is a hypertext whose purpose is amalgamation with what precedes it (which is not, because unfinished, a text as such, but a text *in potentia*); the continuation completes what is anterior to it, constituting it as text, not as a transtextual series. Although it may be explained, as Genette does, simply by reference to context (the desire to add to a previous success), the suite may also be conceived in terms of its rhetorical effect, which is considerable. For if not a response to incompleteness, the suite renders incomplete what was thought finished, problematizing the very sense of completeness.

Yet the two relations Genette terms "suite" and "continuation" designate not discrete categories as such, but the end points of a continuum of possibilities. He warns: "one cannot bring to completion without beginning by continuing, and by dint of prolonging one often ends up bringing to completion."[10] To put this in a way relevant to the issue at hand, the sequel makes "come to life again" something that appeared "in its own moment as finished," turning the end into yet another beginning. But then the suite becomes in effect a continuation, moving inexorably toward its own end, inevitably replicating the finished structure it has opened by closing it yet again. Sequels reject an ending that they must, in whatever altered form, reimpose. They finish what they first strive to render unfinished.

In the Ends Are the Beginnings

Thematically, the succession of sequels is ideally suited for the dramatization of intentions whose goal, although approached again and again, is never reached. This seems in large measure, in fact, the "directorial vision" evident in the Godfather series: a perfect marriage of the essentially unfinished qualities of a transtextual suite and the gloomy view of human nature and striving characteristically adopted in the films of the Hollywood Renaissance. This was that initial period of poststudio filmmaking in the 1970s that historian Robert Kolker appropriately calls a "cinema of loneliness." Kolker's view is that the Renaissance films "carry on an ideological debate with the culture that breeds them, [but] never confront that culture with another ideology, with other ways of seeing itself" (9). Because they are unable to conceive of any way to challenge dominant beliefs and practices, "too many [of these films] only perpetuate the passivity and aloneness that has become their central image" (10). Can we ignore, however, the antipolitical politics of this perception about the human condition? Spiritual exhaustion and existential refusal constitute a potent challenge to the official American narrative of self-fashioning. In the Godfather series, Coppola dismantles this narrative piece by piece. One might argue that the Godfather films offer a devastating critique of two cardinal elements of the national mythology: that hard work, dedication to principles, respect for the values of moral probity, and commitment to the family, offers a sure formula for worldly success; and that the assimilation figured by the metaphor of the "melting pot" provides a certain path to full, legitimate *participation* in the national public life.

The three Godfather films conclude with increasingly desperate images of their protagonist Michael Corleone, who is indeed finally reduced to "passivity and aloneness": first shutting himself off from family connections, especially his wife Kay; then finding memory the only salvation for an unbearable present that sees him commit fratricide, destroying the moral integrity of the family with a gesture meant to make it safe; and finally, his hopes for reconciliation with his estranged wife and children aroused only to be horrifyingly dashed (in a tragedy for which Michael is responsible and that prompts a silent scream of complete spiritual devastation). Michael then endures the worst of human destinies, dying alone and seemingly forgotten. Yet the three films also end by presenting the elaborately choreographed evidence that Michael has triumphed. In each instance, the godfather (in the end *malgré lui*) proves able to eliminate those who would thwart or kill him, signaling his power to impose his will on the world by showing how he can, far and wide, violently shape events to his design. That power, however, is shown to be desperately empty and useless when, at the end of *Godfather III*, he must pay for it with the life of his innocent daughter, Mary.

Like the other productions in this cinematic tradition, the Godfather films follow the Hollywood model in dramatizing the ability of their protagonist to act, but they also simultaneously speak, in Kolker's apt formulation, to a "continual impotence in the world, an inability to change and to create change" (9). In Coppola's artful handling of sequeling, the "end" is emptied of its power to impose stasis. Its closure is no longer projected. The finale is not a reassuring indication that the protagonist can cease his efforts to retain his power. The suite of sequels becomes the perfect form to express the bitter illusion of accomplishment that is always failure, a theme characteristic of Coppola's oeuvre (compare *The Conversation* [1974], *Apocalypse Now* [1979], and even his script for Franklin J. Schaffner's *Patton* [1970]). In all these films, while the main character succeeds against all odds in his appointed mission, his accomplishments are shadowed by a larger, complementary sense of failure and the inescapable threat of entrapment or destruction. His career a complex intersection of success and failure, of ends that inevitably make way for new and increasingly disastrous beginnings, Michael Corleone becomes the very embodiment of the sequel of which he is the main character.

This pattern is set from the very beginning, providing a template for expansion and elaboration even before a sequel seemed a possibility. Just before his death in *The Godfather*, of natural causes, while pretending for his grandson's amusement to be the monster the film has decisively shown him not to be, Vito Corleone (Marlon Brando) confesses to his young son and heir Michael (Al Pacino) that he is both satisfied with and disappointed by his life. Although he never let big shots deter him from his path toward success, he is disappointed that Michael has joined the family business instead of living out the immigrant dream of second-generation success. Despite his Ivy League education and a war record that establishes him as 100 percent American, Michael has not become a senator, that is, a power broker who bestows offices and benefits, the legitimate reflex of the *padrone* role that Vito came to play in his own, restricted community, deriving influence and wealth from exploiting the mild social evils of gambling, sexual vice, and union racketeering.

As the film's opening sequence dramatizes, this shadow government came into existence because the Italian community, lacking established roots and hence political strength, could not otherwise protect itself from injustice or use the legal system to gain legitimate social ends such as naturalization papers for an eager immigrant. At the beginning of the film, Michael is the outsider. But even before Vito's death, loyalty to the family, especially his admirable desire to keep his father from being finished off after a botched assassination attempt, has pushed Michael into taking over as head of the Corleone crime family in the fact of his father's proud disapproval. Although he has sired one heir with the character and brains to continue the criminal empire he has built from nothing, Vito fails to launch that favored son into a daylight world of legitimate business and respectable society, entrance to which was always denied him (bought by the godfather's money, the senators invited to Connie's wedding do not attend, fearful to be associated with Vito in public; his power always finds this limit). Generational change ironically endorses not only the value of tradition (the son inheriting the father's virtues, dedicating himself to continuing his *moyen de vivre*), but also its discontents (an inability to escape the limiting past, which is another way of regarding tradition, so that a new start may be made).

If *The Godfather* concludes with Michael's masterful and triumphant assassination of his Mafia rivals, an uncooperative Las Vegas business partner, and his traitorous brother-in-law, he pays the considerable price of his sister's hatred and his wife's distrust. Michael finds it impossible to live, as his father did, through the expansive metaphor of the family, which can no longer designate the seamless connection between blood relatives and criminal henchmen, between running illegitimate businesses and offering friendship and assistance to those in need. The film ends with the famous shot of the office door shut on his orders in the face of his wife Kay, banishing her, as the acknowledged center of one family, from witnessing or understanding the role that, as godfather, her husband Michael plays in its now-closeted counterpart, as plans are finalized for moving to Nevada, where his business will, Michael improbably declares, become entirely legitimate.

The second film refuses the easy temptation to simply continue this action, offering instead a beginning that deconstructs the ending of the first, revealing as unexpectedly problematic Michael's assumption of Vito's role as both head of the family business and spiritual father of an extended family. *Godfather II* exploits to the fullest the capacity of the sequel to redefine its sequendum. In *The Godfather*, father and son move together to occupy the same diegetic and moral space, forming a bond that is only strengthened until the don's idyllic death. In the sequel, Vito and Michael are shown to inhabit social universes of related but increasingly divergent values. The second film repeats in its initial narrative movement the form of the first, but with a radical change of tone. Again Coppola begins with a public, family ceremony. But this time it is not a wedding party.

In *The Godfather*, the marriage between Carlo and Connie allows Vito to celebrate success in raising a family and seeing them off into adult life in the proper style. Offering the hospitality of his home to others, including business rivals, provides Vito with a legitimate opportunity to display his wealth and influence, which can be made manifest, among other ways, by the number of guests and the generosity of their bridal presents. During the festivities, moreover, the proud father, following tradition, enables others within the community to enjoy the benefits of his power to dispense justice and well-deserved favors (including making arrangements for someone else's daughter to marry the man of her choice). Attempting to locate the origins of its story in the impoverished Sicilian countryside, *Godfather II* opens instead with not only a funeral that memorializes the death of the father, who appears only as a corpse, but also the playing out of a vendetta that threatens to destroy the family completely and nearly does.

In a movement that reverses the idealized vision of the benevolent *padrone* in the earlier film, Vito's older brother is killed by a brutal and unforgiving Mafia don. Beseeched by the anguished mother to spare her younger son, the don refuses, has the mother killed, and attempts to do the same to Vito, who escapes. Grown to manhood, Vito will assassinate this man, extracting a righteous vengeance, ironically demonstrating that the don was correct in seeing the child as an eventual threat to his safety. But in his own assumption of the *padrone* role, Vito otherwise refuses to emulate this early model. Orphaned, Vito makes his way to America, where his desire for a new life comes to an unexpected, if temporary end, with a period of quarantine on Ellis Island.

But the dream of success, Coppola suggests, must be seen as fulfilled across a series of generations. From the image of the lonely, impoverished Vito, a stranger in a strange land singing plaintively in his cell a song from his now faraway home, the film cuts suddenly and startlingly to an image of his grandson, Michael's son Anthony, as he receives his First Communion. This cut evokes the relative rapidity of assimilation, the fulfillment of the American promise to reward hard work and ingenuity, the possibility of escaping a threatening or degrading past for a present that permits the preservation of some traditions (especially religion). The First Communion ceremony celebrates the entrance into full spiritual life, including both the increased responsibility for avoiding sin and the greater possibility of receiving a salvific grace. Anthony apparently enters the life from which Vito was excluded. The transition from the immigrant desperate to avoid annihilation to the second generation born to prosper in America enacts the national myth of assimilation and self-fashioning, dramatizing how full participation in communal life does not require the surrender of originary traditions (participating in a ceremony that his grandfather also passed through, Anthony enacts an unchanged pattern).

And yet the rest of the film demonstrates, in distressing, heartbreaking detail, how in the present this dream of transcendent success for Michael and his family has been thwarted, even as in the past Vito overcomes in true Horatio Alger fashion, his initial utter lack of resources, making a secure place for himself in the New World. Perhaps favored by his reception into the community of those who can be blessed by the body and blood of the Savior, Anthony luckily survives that same day, along with his parents, a vicious attack, as his house is riddled with bullets by two hired assassins. The walls and guards have not kept enemies out. A traitor lurks within, aiding those who wish the Corleones harm, and giving the lie to Michael's reiterated promise to Kay that the Corleone business would soon be completely legitimate. Michael must return east from Las Vegas to settle problems in the world he had ostensibly left behind for the Anglo-Saxon purity of Nevada, far from New York's Lower East Side where he grew up. Now a prominent figure in the world of American business, Michael also finds himself under investigation by the Kefauver Commission. He is forced to lie and blackmail foe and friend alike to ensure that the full extent of his criminal activities is not revealed to public gaze, but, inevitably, his reputation is besmirched in a way his father's never was.

If it traces the convergence, but then divergence, of the paths of Vito and Michael (in a sense recapitulating the first film), *Godfather II* problematizes generational change in another way as well. The passing on of the role of godfather, seemingly so natural and unchallengeable in the first film after the death of eldest son Sonny (James Caan), is seen as the root of a deadly jealousy that helps destroy the spiritual well-being of the Corleone family. Michael's older brother Fredo (John Cazale) is revealed as resentful that Vito favored Michael over him, and family enemies used this jealousy to plot Michael's assassination, which, although it fails, undermines Michael's claim to be heir to his father's power and influence. Disgusted to find herself married to an unrepentant gangster, Kay aborts Michael's child, and the couple separates. A further deal to legitimate the Corleone Empire by investing in the casinos and hotels of Battista's Cuba comes to nothing as Castro's revolution topples the corrupt regime. The potent metaphor of the family loses its ability to coordinate, and yet keep strictly partitioned, domestic and business life. Michael asks his mother if losing your family is possible even as you attempt to be "strong" enough to save it. She cannot understand the question, which is answer enough.

Michael finds himself trapped by a contradiction that his father, living in an immigrant culture only barely Americanized, never had to face. The past cannot be escaped for the full version of the new life that America promises, and yet at the same time the social structure that had given the past its vitality and value has crumbled. In the film's closing spectacle, Michael once again organizes an impressive destruction of the family's enemies. If at the end of *The Godfather* one of those who must pay for disloyalty and treason is Michael's brother-in-law, then at the end of *Godfather II*, Michael's brother Fredo has forfeited his life. Driven, so he thinks, to kill his brother to keep his family safe, Michael forces himself to watch as his henchman carries out the murder, assuming, like his father would (but for something his father would never have been in a position to contemplate), the moral responsibility for his actions. Now safe, yet (because?) isolated in his beautiful house, Michael turns his thoughts back to the family past.

The moment that memory chooses for Michael is a family dinner on 8 December 1941. On that day, the world of the Corleone family had changed, seemingly irrevocably, with the announcement of Michael's enlistment in the Marines, but this act of independence (joining mainstream America in a gesture reflecting Vito's hopes for his son's future) proved an illusion. The scene is the old family home (in New York), and those at the dinner, including Carlo, Sonny, and Tessio, all subsequently killed or executed in the Corleones' vendetta with the other families, recall the beginning of *The Godfather*. Attending, but not participating in, Connie's wedding, Michael firmly states his independence to the young woman, not an Italian, who he intends to marry ("That's my family, Kay. That's not me"). But *The Godfather* ends with the reinforcement, not the attenuation of family ties, as Michael is drawn into the family business in order to save his father's life and, afterward, to preserve his legacy. For Michael at the end of *Godfather II*, the December 1941 dinner surely represents the treasured past, with its poignant sense of irremediable loss, because Vito is not present and the family lacks its head. Tellingly, however, the scene also marks the road to independence subsequently not taken, the path that would have led to the living of a different life than the one that for Michael in 1959 has lost its center and meaning.

The film's viewer, perhaps, also looks back to a different past, because Fredo is present at that long-past dinner. In the scene evoked at the opening of *Godfather II*, Vito makes his way to America not because of a desire to begin a new life, but because the murder of father, mother, and older brother forces him to seek safety there. Having made a fortune both in a legitimate business (selling olive oil) and also in its illegal counterpart, Vito returns to Sicily accompanied by a very young Michael to take vengeance on someone who can now do him no harm. *Godfather II* ends with the climax of a horrifying vendetta, as Michael revenges, like Vito, a failed assassination on an enemy who no longer poses a threat. But this enemy is also his brother. *The Godfather* ends with the just elimination of a traitorous brother-in-law. But its sequel concludes with the more morally problematic execution of the brother who, Michael confesses, "broke my heart" when he loosed assassins on his own family.

Michael's spiritual distress at the end of *Godfather II* could be read as a form of stasis (a condition of suffering that precludes further moral development), but it might also be seen as the first step (contrition) along the road to spiritual rehabilitation. When, for business reasons, Coppola had to accept after many years of refusing an offer from Paramount to make a second sequel, he declined to consider numerous alternatives for continuation that avoided working out what might happen with Michael if he sought forgiveness and reconciliation. *Godfather III* begins with a sequence that images the failure of Michael's intention to join the larger American community and preserve his family: the Lake Tahoe compound is deserted and in ruins (its cemetery-like desolation presided over by an abandoned statue of the Blessed Virgin).

The first two films open with celebrations of significant events in family life staged at home: a wedding, a First Communion. The third shows that the home, located far from the community that supported it, has ceased to exist as anything but the distressing reflex of a family split apart. It is also, of course, the scene of the crime: the place where Michael and Kay, along with their children, were almost cut to pieces by machine gun fire and where the traitor was subsequently put to death for his complicity in the plot. The opening sequence of *Godfather III* emphasizes the boat house and the lake where Fredo was executed by Michael's bodyguard as they fished together. What plays over these images of loss and desolation is Michael's plea, in voice-over, that Kay and his estranged children attend the ceremony in New York where

Michael will be awarded papal honors for his work for and contributions to charity. During the ceremony, full of praise for his virtue, Michael thinks back to the day of Fredo's death. Later at the celebration he hosts in his own honor, his son Anthony makes clear that he will have nothing to do with his father's business and intends to pursue a career as an opera singer instead. Michael attempts to reconcile with Kay, but she accuses him of his brother's murder, and he has no answer for her. Only with Mary (Sofia Coppola) does Michael succeed, convincing her to remain the head of the charitable foundation he has created to manage the family's considerable wealth.

The remainder of the film traces Michael's futile attempt to find an heir, as the powerful criminal empire he had built from what his father had bequeathed to him forces him to return to the gangster role he is desperate to leave behind in his search for spiritual healing and complete legitimacy. But threat appears not only in the form of upstart wiseguy Joey Zasa (Joe Mantegna), who, although the inheritor of Corleone interests in New York, is resentful of Michael's business success in Las Vegas. To clear the field of competitors, Zasa plans the spectacular murder of Michael and his criminal associates, gathered, ironically enough, to mark the end of the Corleones' involvement with illegal business. Michael survives thanks to the courage and resourcefulness of the brutal young man who is his spiritual son, Vincent Mancini (Andy Garcia), bastard child of his brother Sonny. But more powerful enemies lurk in the background, who attempt to thwart Michael's attempt to invest the bulk of his funds in a real estate holding company the Vatican owns. In the end, with Vincent's help, Michael destroys those who oppose him, but not before they almost kill him and shoot his daughter Mary by mistake. As at the end of *Godfather III*, Michael retreats into the past, finding the insufficient comfort of haunting memories: dancing with Mary at the award ceremony, and in years gone by with his two wives, Kay and Apollonia, nurturing female figures who are all now denied him by death or rejection.

Glenn Man comments: "Try as he may, Michael cannot extricate himself and the family from the web of destruction woven into the past" (126). What Man does not recognize is that way in which the three Godfather films, reflecting the insufficient singularity of texts connected by the relation of sequel to sequendum, intermittently and incrementally dramatize Michael's failure to sever his connection to the environment that both nurtures and traps him, makes him rich and deprives him of the comforts of family life, provides the theater in which his courage and cunning can be usefully dramatized while destroying his soul. Michael's failure to disconnect is reflected in the textual form his story takes: a series of beginnings that lead to endings that are always already beginnings, limning the viciously circular outlines of the existential trap in which he discovers again and again the impossibility of change, the always receding remoteness of his object of desire.

Notes

1. But consider what Peter Biskind has to say under the heading "*The Godfather: Part IV*": "Why not? Maybe this was what Coppola was put on earth to do. He is reportedly thinking about it. It might be a look at the thirties and forties. . . . If the film were to be set in this period, De Niro could well play the lead, Vito Corleone redivivus. Rumor has it that a script is already finished" (*Godfather Companion* 181).

2. The script development for the final sequel was a contentious battle that lasted many years between Coppola, Puzo, and a series of writers the studio hired. Most of the proposed treatments did not connect closely to the main narrative line of the first two films. As Biskind remarks, "One of the mistakes made by the screenwriters who worked on scripts for *III* was abandoning the Corleone family and ignoring characters and clues provided by the first two films" (*Godfather Companion* 136). Coppola and Puzo designed the third film as a "close" sequel to the first two.

3. In a study with great relevance, *mutatis mutandis*, for the theorization of the sequel, *Pour une théorie de l'adaptation filmique*, Patrick Cattrysse discusses this principle of irreversibility (see esp. 2–15).

4. ". . . *transcendence textuelle du texte . . . tout ce qui le met en relation, manifeste ou secrète, avec d'autres textes*" (Genette 7). All translations in this chapter are my own.

5. ". . . *tout texte dérivé d'un texte antérieur par transformation simple . . . ou par transformation indirecte*" and ". . . *de texte au second degré*" (14, 12). For an intriguing and informative discussion of remaking that approaches the phenomenon from another theoretical perspective, see Verevis, *Film Remakes* (esp. 81–104).

6. ". . . *un aspect universel . . . toutes les oeuvres sont hypertextuelles*" (16).

7. "*le plus ensoleillé . . . à la fois massive*". . . *et declaré, d'une manière plus ou mois officielle*" (16).

8. ". . . *toute relation unissant un texte B . . . à un texte antérieur A*" (11).

9. ". . . *désignent la liaison d'une chose avec ce qui la precede . . . restée à un certain point qui ne la terminait pas . . . en general d'exploiter le succès d'une oeuvre, souvent considérée en son temps comme achevée, en la faisant rebondir sur de nouvelles péripéties*" (182).

10. ". . . *on ne peut terminer sans commencer par continuer, et à force de prolonger on finit souvent par achever.*" (182).

5

CLAIRE PERKINS

Sequelizing Hollywood

The American "Smart" Film

I N HIS INTRODUCTION TO a collection of essays originally written around a retrospective of 1970s American films at the 1995 Vienna Film Festival, Alexander Horwath suggests, "if you have come of age as a cinemagoer during the heyday of New Hollywood cinema—sometime between *Bonnie and Clyde* [1967] and *Taxi Driver* [1976]—you've probably experienced the main brands of post-1970s American cinema by necessity as less rich, less intelligent, less political, as retrograde" (9). Horwath here typifies the widely held position that regards the birth of the New Hollywood in the late 1960s and early 1970s as a "Renaissance" in American filmmaking. Expressed most consistently by Noel King and Thomas Elsaesser, this critical position understands the historical period as "a brief window of opportunity when an adventurous new cinema emerged, linking the traditions of classical Hollywood genre filmmaking with the stylistic innovations of European art cinema" (King qtd. in Neale 91). Generally regarded as an interim between the decline of the classical Hollywood studio system and the reassertion of a similarly conservative system the new formulaic blockbuster form of films such as *Jaws* (Steven Spielberg, 1975) and *Star Wars* (George Lucas, 1977) enabled, the Hollywood Renaissance is approached as a unique time

Figure 5.1. *Scarecrow* (Jerry Schatzberg, 1971). Courtesy Warner Bros/
The Kobal Collection.

by its supporters insofar as its experimentation and dissident ethos was
underwritten by a Hollywood keen to hit on a new formula for success
(see Schatz; Hillier; Balio, *American*). The cinema of "alienation, anomie,
anarchy and absurdism" (King 20) associated with directors including
Arthur Penn, Robert Altman, Monte Hellman, and Peter Bogdanovich
represented not just a change in filmmaking, but a radical transformation
of *commercial* filmmaking.

Insofar as it understands this era as a type of finite Golden Age—
"the last good time we ever had," in King's estimation[1]—the Renaissance
position has an unmistakably pessimistic undertone. In a recent article,
Steve Neale has challenged the dominance of the position in discourse
on contemporary American cinema, arguing that it produces "a partial
and misleading picture" of history (91). Citing the box-office success
of musicals (*Funny Girl*, William Wyler, 1968), war films (*Tora! Tora!
Tora!* Richard Fleischer and Kinji Fukasaku, 1970), and family-oriented

films (*The Jungle Book*, Roman Davidov, 1967) during the late 1960s and early 1970s alongside films such as *Bonnie and Clyde* (Arthur Penn, 1967) and *M*A*S*H* (Robert Altman, 1970), Neale challenges the perception that audiences were solely endorsing the violent and formally innovative Renaissance films. Furthermore, Neale attempts to diffuse the view that this era marked a revolutionary break with traditional ideological values by looking back to the breaches generally acknowledged to have been made by earlier American films such as *Anatomy of a Murder* (Otto Preminger, 1959) and *Psycho* (Alfred Hitchcock, 1960; 106–7). In this latter way, Neale combats the culturally pessimistic perception of the Renaissance as a finite and singular impulse. This particular challenge can be supported by a perspective that looks not back but *forward* to evidence of the impulse in later American cinema.

In recent years, several commentators have echoed the enthusiastic claims of the Renaissance theorists in their discussion of the changes in Hollywood during the 1990s and the emergence of a new group of innovative American filmmakers during this decade. Peter Biskind's *Down and Dirty Pictures: Miramax, Sundance and the Rise of Independent Film* (2004), Sharon Waxman's *Rebels on the Backlot: Six Maverick Directors and How They Conquered the Hollywood Studio System* (2006), and James Mottram's *The Sundance Kids: How the Mavericks Took Back Hollywood* (2006) all, from their titles, take an interest in the emergence of a critically and popularly successful "commercial-independent" strain of 1990s American cinema.[2] Focusing on directors including Quentin Tarantino, Steven Soderbergh, Paul Thomas Anderson, Spike Jonze, Sofia Coppola, Wes Anderson, Alexander Payne, and David O. Russell, these works recapitulate the broad critical interest that has been taken in these directors and their influence on American filmmaking over the last decade or so. With a common focus on the Sundance Film Festival as a platform, each book is broadly concerned with the way in which the popularly favorable reception of the formal and thematic innovations of these directors offered a perceived challenge to the dominance of the New Hollywood blockbuster form, effectively forcing the studio system to accommodate them via the establishment of "mini-major" arms such as (Disney's) Miramax, (Universal's) Focus Features, and (Warner's) Warner Independent (Mottram xxix).

Peter Biskind openly describes his account of this period as "a sequel, of sorts, to *Easy Riders, Raging Bulls*, my history of that exuberant, fecund decade, the 1970s, that gave us the so-called New Hollywood" (*Down and Dirty* 1). For Biskind, the key aspect of the 1970s legacy is the emergence of directors such as those mentioned earlier: "a loose collection of spiritual and aesthetic heirs." Mottram opens his book similarly, describing the "Pizza Knights"—a monthly film group comprised of a representative sample of these directors—as the "spiritual descendents of the so-called maverick filmmakers of 1970s Hollywood" (xv), and claiming that his book centers on the question: "are we returning to an age where formerly independent directors are using studio funds to further their own idiosyncratic vision? In other words, is this the dawn of New Hollywood Part II?" (xv). Furthermore, Horwath suggests in the piece already quoted that "during the past fifteen years many of the (few) important American films still had their reference points . . . in the culture of the Seventies" (10), and gestures toward a handful of these directors—Paul Thomas Anderson, Wes Anderson, Richard Linklater—along with some crossovers from the earlier generation—Robert Altman, Martin Scorsese, and John Sayles.

The concept of sequelization that Biskind and Mottram elaborate is largely founded in industrial terms. Both—particularly Biskind—are essentially concerned with the position of these directors in relation to Hollywood and in how they triggered a transformation of the 1980s studio model. Horwath, by contrast, is more interested in textual issues of transposition. The "reference points" he refers to in the 1990s films include personnel, aesthetics, and attitudes from the 1970s: New Hollywood as style and subject matter, he argues, is still locatable in films made after 1977. Biskind and Mottram's sweep of contemporary directors is also necessarily broad with a focus to the "larger" figures—Tarantino, Soderbergh, and David Fincher—whose films have been at the forefront of the industrial transformations. With an eye to Horwath's textual conceptualization, this chapter is concerned with the contemporary American "smart" film as a narrower and somewhat nebulous tendency within Biskind's broad "Sundance" generation on which to trace interests sequelized—continued, transformed—from the 1970s. Coined by Jeffrey Sconce in 2002 as a term to group several tonally ironic 1990s American films sharing a loose set of stylistic and thematic characteristics, the "smart" sensibility can be identified in many but not all of the films Biskind and Mottram are interested in ("Irony" 349–69). A distinctive type of stylistic "blankness" is the smart film's key formal trait, and the politics of the white, middle-class American family a major thematic concern. Considering this, it is perhaps Wes Anderson and Todd Solondz—directors who Biskind and Mottram respectively passed over—who best demonstrate the sensibility.[3]

"The Pathos of Failure": Crisis 1

In his 1975 article "The Pathos of Failure: American Films in the 1970s," Thomas Elsaesser gave what is still regarded as the definitive account of the transformations films such as *Two-Lane Blacktop* (Monte Hellman, 1971), *California Split* (Robert Altman, 1974), and *The Conversation* (Francis Ford Coppola, 1974) effected on Hollywood filmmaking in the 1967–75 era. One of the most enduring aspects of Elsaesser's piece is the way in which his summation of the unmotivated heroes and directionless journeys of these films anticipates what Gilles Deleuze describes as "the crisis of the action-image" in his *Cinema 1*, published in France eight years later. Elsaesser sees in these films aspects of metacinema familiar from the cinematically self-conscious European directors with which Deleuze is principally concerned. As a key characteristic, the waning of physical action is, for Elsaesser, the result of a search for a new form of narrative free from "the parasitic and synthetic causality of a dramaturgy of external conflict," the search "for a mise-en-scène that can take a critical stance" (283). The new form arises from the way in which the conventional, external motif of the journey is complicated by the protagonist lacking a corresponding internal drive. Elsaesser comments on how, in *Two-Lane Blacktop*, the journey is introduced in an offhand way—the potential goal of the race to Washington is "[toyed] with," inciting no real interest for either the characters or the film narrative. Intrigue is played down in other dimensions as well, most notably in the way action avoids the potential conflict between the male characters over the single female. As Elsaesser notes, all the points at which the spectator could potentially become absorbed by a plot are played down, resulting in an "anti-action" film (281).

This lack of drive infiltrates practically all of the Renaissance films as a stylization of despair or helplessness (Elsaesser, "Pathos" 287). Attitudes of obsession, guilt, and anxiety recur across their various scenarios, emanating from figures who are neither psychologically nor emotionally motivated. Unlike the protagonists of classical Hollywood, these figures have no "case to investigate . . . name to clear . . . woman (or man) to love [or] goal to reach" (281). For Robert Kolker, loneliness defines the era. The bitterness of a film such as *Night Moves* (Arthur Penn, 1975), he suggests, "comes from anxiety rather than anger, from a loneliness that exists as a given, rather than a loneliness fought against . . ." (19). Tracing images of paranoia, isolation, oppression, and claustrophobia in films including *The Parallax View* (Alan Pakula, 1974), *The Wild Bunch* (Sam Peckinpah, 1969), and *The Conversation*, Kolker describes the 1960s and 1970s as a type of *noir* revival, where these favorite themes of the 1940s cycle resurface after the more reassuring films of the 1950s (22–23). The emotional paralysis that permeates a film such as *Night Moves* renders any attention to details of an investigative plot useless: "the plotting becomes less important than the searching itself" (65). Other commentators also attend to this formal and thematic paralysis. For Christian Keathley, the Renaissance films are an explicit response to the Vietnam War: he describes them as a "post-traumatic" cycle that replays the war experience's defining realization of powerlessness. Themes of disaffection, alienation, and demoralization encode the "opening up of the interval between perception and action as a traumatic event" (296). The crisis of the action-image in these films is described for Keathley by the repeated fate whereby a character is left "not dead, but wounded and helpless" (297). The ending of both *Chinatown* (Roman Polanski, 1974) and *The Candidate* (Michael Ritchie, 1972) clearly represent the frozen state in which so many Renaissance figures are caught: between perception and action, or action and reaction; trapped, as Keathley describes it, "in the affection-image."

For Elsaesser, the rejection of personal motive in the 1960s and 1970s cycle of American films, along with their liberal outlook and unsentimental approach to American society, reflect a larger ideological rejection. By "essentially . . . manag[ing] to transform spatial and temporal sequence into consequence, into a continuum of cause and effect" ("Pathos" 280), classical Hollywood form posits a fundamentally affirmative attitude to the world based on faith in "the usefulness of positive action" (281). What Elsaesser witnesses in the Renaissance films' rejection of personal motive is a loss of this confidence, and thereby a larger rejection of purposive affirmation and moral pragmatism (281). Beyond issues of industrial similarity, it is the transposition of this textual and ideological effect to the contemporary smart film which is of interest here. As the model of "realism" which the Renaissance films put under erasure, the classical action-image is, for Deleuze, defined not by recourse to real events, but by a relation between milieus and behavior, or situation and action (*Cinema* 141). The key point of continuity between the two cycles is that both put this particular model of realism under erasure, and thereby mark two disparate points in the breakdown of the American cinema as a universal and triumphant model. Before examining how this sequelization takes place, however, we need to establish how the first Renaissance cycle achieves this breakdown.

Jerry Schatzberg's 1973 film *Scarecrow* is representative in many ways of the formal and thematic concerns of the Renaissance cycle. The film traces the journey of two drifters who meet in the opening scene while attempting to hitch a ride: Max (Gene Hackman) and Francis (Al Pacino), a sailor. Max, who has just gotten out of prison, is initially hostile to Francis—whom he calls Lion, after his middle name, Lionel—but soon asks him to be his partner in a car-wash business he is heading to Pittsburgh to establish. The film demonstrates the classic Renaissance journey insofar as this destination is vague and somewhat absurdly envisaged; the movement itself is the dramatic focus, marked out by three understated narrative developments. First, the two visit Max's sister Coley and, after getting into a fight while out with her and a friend one night, spend a brief time in prison. After they get out, they travel to Detroit en route to Pittsburgh so Lion can visit the five-year-old son he has never seen. When they reach the house he decides to telephone first and his former partner lies to him, telling him the child was stillborn. Soon after, Lion suffers a type of fit, descends into a catatonic state, and is hospitalized. In the final scene, Max buys a round-trip ticket to Pittsburgh, apparently intending to return and look after his friend.

In both the Renaissance and smart cycles, the crisis of the action-image is identifiable as a specific type of exaggeration, whereby the logic of the respective images is no longer simply a narrative device, but structures the characters' very reality. The crisis-image that emerges is not a straight subordination of the old sensory-motor schema, but a systematic deformation that simultaneously evokes and transcends its connective principles. Deleuze describes two forms of the action-image, the *Large Form* and the *Small Form*. The large form image is structured by the schema of Situation, Action, Modified Situation (SAS') that, very broadly, organizes the manner in which a situation (milieu) provokes responsive action that eventually modifies—or restores—the original situation.[4] The sensory-motor capacity of the small form image is, by contrast, founded on a reversed schema of Action, Situation, Modified Action (ASA'), whereby the situation must be deduced *from* initial action. The small form image is less stable insofar as the situation is "not given as an in-itself . . . [it] always refer[s] back to struggles and modes of behaviour always in action or in transformation" (Deleuze, *Cinema* 163–64).[5] Insofar as its journey structure displays some fidelity to this differential logic, the model of realism that *Scarecrow* "erases" is that of the small form action-image.

A film concerned principally with a journey will almost always reject the large form SAS' model by refusing the primacy of a milieu. A character may be forced out of a situation and onto the road by certain milieu forces but, once into the journey, action is the defining element: it is movement and transformation *from which* each new situation along the way appears, and not vice versa. Typifying Renaissance form, *Scarecrow* transposes this structural "index of lack"[6] to its narrative, which is not developed in close detail. Relying on the spectator's *deduction* of information, the action on screen is elliptical, with no clear establishment of where the characters are at any one moment, where they are heading, or what they are thinking or feeling. Each new location emerges from

their movement in an unheralded way and eventually gives rise to the
action of new movement as they continue on. Their movement itself is
depicted in dialogue-free montage sequences that show Max and Lion
clambering up or down the sides of trains, picking fruit at sunset, distributing notices on the windshields of parked cars, eating over a campfire.
The sequences are temporally indistinct: they form ellipses in the film
insofar as we are held at a distance from the narrative, not granted access
to the details of the situations, in much the same way as we know little
about either of the main protagonists, and where their various quirks
and attitudes emerge from.

The analogies Deleuze draws on to describe the classical type of the
small form image include a knotted rope, a broken line, and a skeleton,
each one describing how the action is still structurally encompassed,
but in an unpredictable way (*Cinema* 168). Insofar as each sequence in
Scarecrow appears discrete—the action cannot be determined by and in a
preceding scene—the film's *fidelity* to the small form image can begin to
describe the idiosyncratic character of its journey-form. However, only
with its distortion of the classical image is this new form fully realized.
For Elsaesser, the new journey-form represents American filmmaking
attempting to deal with the technical problem of just how to depict the
unmotivated hero as a new type of ideological protagonist ("Pathos"
287). *Scarecrow*'s opening scene offers a remarkably pure example of the
formal qualities of this type of journey. Like all road movies, the film
alternates between sequences of travel and periods of relative stasis in
the destinations reached. The opening scene confuses these sequences
in a way typical of the narrative as a whole: we meet Max and Lion *in
action*—on the road trying to hitch a ride—but this action consists of
nothing but waiting—the two characters merely pass time, Max almost
motionless and Lion clowning around on the spot in an effort to win
him over. As is typical in the small form image, action functions as an
index of lack insofar as it discloses a situation the film does not explicitly
establish (Max and Lion hitching). But stretching a handful of shots over
at least five minutes, action emerges as a more literal index of lack: it
functions not only as the suppression of a narrative situation, but also as
the suppression of the whole dimension of character motivation.

In contrast to the journeying heroes of the classical Hollywood
genre films, neither Max nor Lion have any real goals beyond getting
a ride. Their (indirect) movement toward Pittsburgh functions to dis-
guise their real lack of motivation, as do the peculiar façades of commitment both display, such as Lion obsessively carrying with him the lamp
intended for his child and Max keeping compulsive track of his funds.

Their arbitrary destination is propped up by Max with a combination of clichéd dreams (the car wash will have a deep freezer full of steaks and a radio playing the hit parade) and absurd fixation (it has to be in Pittsburgh because his money is in a bank there). Their forward movement is neutralized, consistently failing to bring about situations that challenge and eventually realize character desire. Action is, in this way, ineffectual: an independent variable that seems to exist quite apart from the journey itself. Action loses all ability to link logically to a situation: each new situation is not *disclosed* as somehow preexistent but is *created* anew in each instant, existing only in and of itself *as* a continuous type of action. As Deleuze suggests on the specific crisis of the small form action-image: "ellipsis ceases to be a mode of the tale . . . it belongs to the situation itself, and reality is lacunary as much as dispersive" (*Cinema* 207). When *Scarecrow* literalizes the crisis of the form by having Max purchase a round-trip ticket in the last scene, committing to a perfectly circular form of movement, we can see the "necessary and rigorous" line that anchors the sensory-motor dimension of the small form image severed altogether.

"Joint Custody Blows": Crisis 2

In *A Cinema of Loneliness*, Kolker (asking the reader to suppress chronology for the sake of imagining the relation of the fictions) observes how Gene Hackman as Harry Moseby survives *Night Moves* only to emerge "older, more frightened, and even more lonely, as Harry Caul in . . . *The Conversation*" (68). Although these attitudes are represented in a fundamentally different way, our interest in finding a specifically textual type of sequelization to films such as *Scarecrow* and those Kolker refers to can be supported by observing the way that Hackman emerges older, more frightened, and lonelier again twenty-six years later, as Royal Tenenbaum in *The Royal Tenenbaums* (Wes Anderson, 2001). This coincidence in Hackman's performances gestures toward the way in which the anxiety-based attitudes that are largely stamped out of studio-based filmmaking in the late 1970s and through the 1980s reemerge in the 1990s smart film. Sconce encapsulates the transposition by which this occurs when he suggests that the critique of bourgeois taste and culture that the anxiety in both cycles represents is borne out in essentially different terms: in his estimation, the shift is from an activist emphasis on the social politics of power in 1960s and 1970s "art cinema" to an ironic concentration on the personal politics of power, communication and emotional dysfunction in the later, smart cycle ("Irony" 352).

Both thematically and formally, this shift is clearest in the respective approaches of each cycle to characterization and genre. Where the Renaissance films tend to cast their apathetic protagonists as unattached drifters or obsessive loners, the similarly anxious figures of the smart film are securely tethered to a family, house, and career: generically, the shift can be broadly determined as a move from the road movie to the family (melo)drama. The fear and loneliness no longer belongs to the outlaw or drifter but to alienated professionals, suffocated housewives and disaffected teenagers, and the violent outbursts and escape motifs of the first cycle are translated into the smothered, insular themes of adultery, divorce, and abuse. This generic movement indicates how the formal crisis of action in the smart film is enacted on a fundamentally different image from that of the Renaissance crisis. Both cycles are more concerned with the observation of character behavior than with a strongly attenuated plot, but the family setting of the smart film means the characters are less likely to be thrown together in an attempt at flight and transformation than to be struggling with a configuration that is eternal and familiar. As we have seen, the small form inclinations of the Renaissance image stem principally from the fact that the earlier films do not begin with meaningfully constructed milieus: the story comes from the forces implicit in the action we see, not in the history we do not. By contrast, the portraits of dysfunctional American families that the smart film depict evoke the Large Form action-image (SAS') insofar as they rely heavily on its initial step of establishing a milieu as a situation whose forces bear down on the protagonists (Deleuze, *Cinema* 141).

Noah Baumbach's *The Squid and the Whale* (2005) can be described as a "fast-moving series of short, pointed vignettes" (Scott) depicting the immediate aftermath of parental separation in an intellectual Brooklyn family in 1986. Based on his own childhood experience, Baumbach's film examines how each member of the Berkman family—Bernard (Jeff Daniels); Joan (Laura Linney); Walt (Jesse Eisenberg), 16; and Frank (Owen Kline), 12—deals with the change to his or her life. The internal tension with which the film is essentially concerned is established from the competitiveness of the family tennis match that opens the film, where Bernard and Walt play Joan and Frank. Postseparation, these battle lines are maintained, with Walt supporting his father's new life "across the park" and taking on Bernard's pompous literary attitudes as a way of dealing with other people, and Frank siding with Joan, who has had affairs, and quickly begins dating his admired tennis coach, Ivan (William Baldwin). Grounded by a pedantic joint custody arrangement whereby the boys spend exactly half their time with each parent, *The Squid and the Whale* traces, among other things, Walt's doubtful relationship with

Figure 5.2. *The Squid and the Whale* (Noah Baumbach 2005). Courtesy Samuel
Goldwyn Films/The Kobal

his classmate Sophie and crush on his father's student Lili, who Bernard
himself starts dating when she moves into his spare room; Frank's "acting out" by drinking, swearing, and masturbating in public; Bernard's
slight, rejected attempt to reconnect with Joan; Walt's plagiarism of a
Pink Floyd song and subsequent trip to an educational psychologist; and
Bernard's eventual collapse and hospitalization from alleged exhaustion.
The film ends with Walt rejecting his father for the first time, leaving
him alone in hospital and claiming he wants to "even things out" and
stay with Joan some more.

   The Squid and the Whale expresses the very essence of smart narrative action in that its story consists of a series of moments that appear
at once dense and incidental, and which succeed one another quickly
and unpredictably. Similarly to the Renaissance films, the smart cycle
is not concerned with a traditional three-act structure tracking the purposive development of a plot. Conversely to the earlier cycle, however,
the smart film does not suppress information about its characters and
context; techniques including voice-over, montage, titles, and music are
commonly used throughout the narrative to often exaggerated effect,
establishing and embellishing details in a swift and detailed way. This

information-heavy approach indicates the cycle's reliance on the Situation or milieu of the Large Form action-image. The trappings so easily rejected by the Renaissance characters—job, home, school, parents—in favor of obsessive flight (literal or figural) are the very substance of the milieus sketched in the opening sequences of the smart film. Characters are introduced not in terms of their individual quirks—as Max and Lion are—but in terms of their milieu: the smart protagonists are inherently *connected*, part of a situation that restricts their movement and, cinematically, recasts the possibility of action.

The first three sequences of *The Squid and the Whale* all involve all four members of the Berkman family: they play tennis, drive home through the leafy streets of their Park Slope neighborhood, and eat dinner together. In each sequence, the forces implicit in their family milieu become more visible. The effect of this in the dinner sequence gives some insight into why Sconce describes the "awkward dining shot" as one of smart cinema's stock techniques ("Irony" 364). These sequences—and expressive examples can be found in *The Royal Tenenbaums*, *The Ice Storm* (Ang Lee, 1997), *Storytelling* (Todd Solondz, 2001), *Happiness* (Todd Solondz, 1998), *Welcome to the Dollhouse* (Todd Solondz, 1995), *Donnie Darko* (Richard Kelly, 2001), *The Safety of Objects* (Rose Troche, 2001), *Your Friends and Neighbours* (Neil LaBute, 1998), *Punch Drunk Love*, (Paul Thomas Anderson, 2002), and *Magnolia* (Paul Thomas Anderson, 1998)—establish the milieu and its pressures by expressing the dynamic of the family unit, where everyone has a role to play and there is usually an undercurrent of conflict. Demonstrating a significant insularity, the conversation usually involves issues internal to the milieu: work, school, family interaction. When external issues are raised it is principally to illustrate the dynamics of the unit. In *The Squid and the Whale*'s own example, the relative quality of Charles Dickens's works comes up as dinner discussion, but primarily to articulate, with tremendous economy, the relationship between the teenage Walt, his arrogant father, and his candid mother. As one review describes, this scene is an early sign of how Walt is morphing into his father, and Linney nicely underplays Joan's horror at watching her son become the enemy (Longworth). Meanwhile, Frank—the younger son—is distracted by the cashew he has just put up his nose.

In his discussion of the Large Form action-image, Deleuze illustrates the SAS' schema by exclusive reference to American genres, including the documentary, the psychosocial film, *film noir*, and the Western (*Cinema* 143–46). In each example, the image develops slightly differently, but each genre is nonetheless "solidly anchored" in a milieu that acts as the "Encompasser": "the milieu and its forces incurve on themselves, they act on the character, throw him a challenge, and constitute a situation in which he is caught" (141). In the genres Deleuze mentioned, the milieu often has a quality of openness: the situational forces of the Fordian milieu, for instance, are framed by the constant presence of the land and the immanence of the sky. Gesturing back to the genre of the family melodrama, the smart film presents a converse and exaggerated Encompasser in that, as Douglas Sirk has commented on the earlier genre, everything "happens inside" (Elsaesser, "Tales of Sound and Fury" 52); the milieu is peculiarly *stifling*. The smart film amplifies this effect again by squaring its closed family units into clearly separate entities. The titles of *The Safety of Objects* introduce the various families as tiny, titled groups depicted inside their fenced premises. And, like other films dealing with numerous proximate and interconnected families—*Happiness*, *The Ice Storm*, *The Chumscrubber* (Arie Posin, 2005)—the film expresses the relation between these separate units in terms of suspicion, hostility, and open competitiveness. The families of the smart film tend to regard themselves as individually *empowered* units—something simultaneously encouraging and encouraged *by* their carefully divided proximity.

Baumbach literally described this specific type of empowerment in a conversation with Phillip Lopate, where he suggests that the sense of separation and insularity conveyed in the Brooklyn location of his film reflects that felt by the Berkmans, who tend to regard themselves as "somehow smarter and better" than other families. In *The Squid and the Whale* this quality is most overtly articulated in the faux intellectualism of Bernard and Walt—who divide the world into philistine and nonphilistine—but Baumbach claims he is trying to represent the way that *all* families regard themselves as somehow smarter and better than others, and the way that this has less to do with education per se than with a quality created by the insular family unit. The smart film's articulation of this attitude is one element that affects its treatment of the classical action-image. Insofar as the family unit puts itself into a type of exile from the neighbors it regards itself as superior to, the family shifts from being an entity that is simply closed to being, in Baumbach's words, an outsider. As Elsaesser has commented on the family melodrama, the characters are each other's sole referents ("Tales of Sound and Fury" 56), and their sense of self is inevitably understood in terms of the unit. The smart family milieu expresses a curious force that, typically against their will, casts its members as quasi-aristocratic *types*: the Tenenbaums, the Berkmans. These milieus make limited claims to universality: they are hyperbolically local and obsessively detailed, and it is as though the sheer weight of their history and detail is more powerful than the characters, who are finally unable, or unwilling, to effectively modify them.

As an amplified Encompasser, then, the family milieu functions as a stifling situation from which its characters cannot extricate themselves. In Deleuze's specification, the *action* (A) in the SAS' structure of the Large Form image consists of the characters' responses to the milieu forces that bear down on them. This action, however, cannot happen before they become capable of it: a "big gap" necessarily exists between the initial situation and the action that finally modifies it (*Cinema* 154). Action, when it occurs, is driven by the power of actualization through which the character(s) "acquire a new mode of being" (141), and the sensory-motor advance of the form hinges on the condition that it is *only* at this point that they are able to effectively modify or restore the initial situation. In the smart film, the hypermilieu impacts severely on the characters' potential for this type of purposive actualization.

The divorce theme of *The Squid and the Whale* offers a literal example of how this proceeds. The film's vignettes can be read almost entirely in terms of contrasts between the new and old situations, where the characters' navigation of the postdivorce situation is meted out in small, and larger, discrepancies from the historical family milieu. Bernard struggles to replicate the family home—claiming that getting a place like Joan's was important for him and that he is going to cook and run the house as the boys are used to—but, initially, both sons can focus only on differences: the further distance from school, what will happen to the cat, their father's unwelcome "surprises" of a ping pong table, a poster of a tennis pro who Frank dismisses as an "asshole," and a tiny, absurd writing desk designed for a "leftie." Some discrepancies are confronted (Bernard feeding the cat generic food instead of Purina) and some we merely observe (the ease with which Bernard always finds a park directly outside his new house rather than having to search endlessly as he does in Park Slope). The physical restriction of the family—represented most fully in the figure of Bernard, who is constantly driving back and forth between houses with the boys, loitering on Joan's doorstep while waiting for them or double-parking in the street—poignantly expresses the manner in which all four Berkmans are inhibited in their potential to develop a new mode of being. Joan is most active in her efforts to establish this, but her attempt has shadows of the historical milieu cast all over it: her relationship with Ivan is belittled by a jealous Bernard ("why is your mother dating all these jocks? Very uninteresting men," he comments to Frank) and her publishing success palpably traversed by both Bernard's and Walt's resentment. Walt's own effort to establish a relationship with Sophie develops entirely in "Berkman" terms: he seduces her with empty literary clichés and promptly breaks up with her on his father's advice that it is good to "play the field" at his age. Even Frank's desperately *anti*-Berkman, philistine-like behavior (drinking, masturbating) cannot avoid a precocious self-awareness: "do you think that you and I are philistines?" he matter-of-factly asks a visibly taken-aback Ivan, after a conversation with his father.

This restricted potential for character actualization necessarily impacts on the causal schema of the Large Form action-image. The textual sequelization we are tracing here between the Renaissance and smart cycles rests on a conception of the erasure of a classical model of realism by way of an exaggeration or amplification of its indices. In the Renaissance cycle, the structural index of lack is transposed from a narrative device to the suppression of motivation. As suggested, this broadly amounts to a stretching-out of sensory motor form: action slows down to the point where it can no longer link or disclose situations. In the smart cycle, the milieu is amplified to the point where it inhibits rather than triggers character actualization. In an inverse experimentation to the Renaissance cycle, the effect of this can be characterized as a certain acceleration of sensory-motor form.

In his own discussion of the breakdown of the action-image in the American Renaissance cycle, Deleuze comments on how chance becomes the sole guiding thread in these narratives, meaning "sometimes the event delays and is lost in idle periods, sometimes it is there too quickly" (*Cinema* 207). This schema offers a fitting description of the differing forms of experimentation between the Renaissance and smart cycles. A film such as *Scarecrow* is clearly dominated by "idle periods," which obscure its "events"—the fight which lands Max and Lion in prison, Lion's fit—adding up to the impression that little really occurs. By the film's end, however, organic change has unmistakably occurred in the characters, who have effectively acquired a new mode of being: Max, most clearly, has learned the importance of human contact and made a friend whom he plans to look after, tempering his early-stated position that he does not love or trust anybody. The smart cycle exhibits little of the Renaissance idleness: as the suggested swift-moving series of vignettes, the films are marked by the rapid and detailed introduction of several characters who are almost immediately involved in a disparate series of events. In a precise inversion of the earlier cycle, much appears to happen to the characters, but these encounters do little to change, or actualize, them.

In the smart film, then, the "event" is "there too quickly." This phenomenon is clearest in the films that are founded on the cycle's general interest in issues of chance and coincidence—*Donnie Darko*, *Magnolia*, *The Sweet Hereafter* (Atom Egoyan, 1997)—where the event is not impelled by the protagonists at all but happens *to them*, and tends to occur early: a falling jet engine, a bus crashing into a lake. The "coincidence" films highlight the way in which action in the smart film is never something the protagonists really become capable of. Insofar as these narratives do not trace the actualization of hero's power, no "big gap" exists between the initial situation and a form of definitive action that will modify it. Rather, the gap exists between the action—or series of actions—and the *modified* situation, and the defining characteristic of the form is that the degree to which this gap is filled at all is always ambiguous. In classical terms, the action (A) occurs too early, and the majority of the narrative is an examination of a modified situation that has not been purposively or adequately built toward. In *The Squid and the Whale*, character action attempts to respond to the claustrophobic milieu forces early in the narrative, with the "family conference" at which the separation is announced and Bernard's subsequent move happening within the first ten minutes of the film. The accelerated schema is described by Walt—at least from his perspective—in the scene immediately following the conference. He confronts his mother in the bathroom, asserting that "this is a great family" (Situation) and "I don't know why you're screwing it up" (Action). Within this logic, the overwhelming part of Baumbach's film is concerned with the physically modified situation as a discrete series of examples; it is, in the terms of the film's tagline, an examination of how "joint custody blows" (Situation').

By altering the distances implicit in the classical Large Form schema, *The Squid and the Whale* comments on the implausibility of the form as a model of realism. The absence of any one, definitive point of action promotes an anticausal conception of life as an unpredictable and continuous flow, with several small moments building one on another rather than moving forward. Insofar as the outcome of one vignette rarely leads logically into the premise of the next, the smart characters seem to run in place, and the end scenarios of the films suggest that, while some characters may find redemption, many do not. Varying directorial styles and critical interpretations cast this in different ways. The interpretation of *The Squid and the Whale* as Walt's recognition of his parents as "neither gods nor monsters but as screwed-up, very foolish adults" (Denby) suggests that the film's collection of disparate experiences *does* produce a certain sense of insight, for Walt at least. Part of the reason this is so marked, however, is that it is starkly contrasted to the concurrent lack of change in his father, who responds to Walt's attempts to break away with typical blustering pomposity, promising that he will put some new posters up in his son's room, and lend him his first edition of *The Naked and the Dead* "as a present." This type of character blindness and superficiality is a signature effect of smart directors such as Solondz and LaBute, whose protagonists never achieve any level of recognition through their experiences, and simply continue on in their willful and destructive patterns.

For characters such as Walt, the effect is more complex. After he leaves his father in the hospital, he runs through the streets of New York to the Museum of Natural History, and the film ends on his silent contemplation of the squid and whale diorama, which an earlier sequence has revealed terrified him as a child. His stare could be interpreted as a triumphant conquering, but this possibility is rendered ambiguous by the sequence, which cuts from a close-up of his blank look to a long shot from behind, which dwarfs him in relation to the enormous display. Recalling in some ways the blank, paralyzed stare that ends many of the Renaissance films, this moment again refers *The Squid and the Whale* back to the family melodrama, which, as Elsaesser notes, most often "records the failure of the protagonist to act in a way that could shape the events and influence the emotional environment, let alone change the stifling social milieu" ("Tales of Sound and Fury" 55). Without the catharsis of direct, externalized action, the conflict, and even the redemption, of smart characters necessarily turns inward, where it cannot escape the terms of their situation. Elsaesser suggests that the protagonists of the family melodrama "emerge as lesser human beings for having become wise and acquiescent to the ways of the world" (55). Walt's stare indicates how the smart film also confers a negative identity on its characters: if they recognize anything, it is typically merely their powerlessness in the face of their world.

In his work on the smart film, Sconce alludes to the cycle as a generational phenomenon, observing how many of the directors at the heart of this type of filmmaking belong to Generation X. For Sconce, this marks the cycle as one tendency within the broader 1990s "irony epidemic," where the strategies of disengagement exhibited in the films are an explicit response *against* the earlier generation: "a means of non-participatory engagement with [baby] boomers and their domination of the cultural and political landscape" ("Irony" 355). Sconce's position can go some way toward illuminating the concept of sequelization that this chapter has attempted to advance. Whereas the Renaissance and smart cycles have been likened on the basis of broad industrial and critical similarities, the textual dimension of their sequelization, once closely examined, is clearly borne out in entirely transpositional terms. Indeed, in this analysis, "sequelization" takes a precisely reversed form: the crisis of sensory-motor style is enacted on two converse images by way of two broadly opposed movements. These patterns of difference belie the generalized idea of "continuation" on which sequelization tends to be founded in the discourse of cinema studies. If the smart film, as a facet of the "Sundance" generation, offers something like "New Hollywood Part II," then its "secondness" and its sequelization are necessarily highly differential ideas.

Notes

1. King's introduction to *The Last Great American Picture Show* is titled, " 'The Last Good Time We Ever Had': Remembering the New Hollywood Cinema."

2. The term "commercial/independent" comes from R. Barton Palmer. In an article on *Blood Simple* (Joel Coen, 1985), Palmer describes two notions of "independence": those unwillingly marginalized by market forces, and those seeking the ground of creative freedom. A text such as the Coens', he suggests, appeals complexly and simultaneously to both "[their] makers, by exploiting their independence and producing a "different" product, often paradoxically strive thereby for a more central place within the institutions of commercial filmmaking" (6).

3. Biskind makes only two brief references to Anderson (*Down and Dirty* 21, 387). Mottram defines his "Sundance Kids" as a uniquely West Coast phenomenon, excluding directors such as Solondz and Hal Hartley because "they have remained camped out on the East Coast, largely avoiding entanglements with the studios" (xxii).

4. For full detail on the five laws that define the Large Form action-image see Deleuze, *Cinema* 141–59.

5. For full detail on the two laws (indices) defining the Small Form action-image see Deleuze, *Cinema* 160–77.

6. Deleuze uses this term to describe how an action discloses a situation that is not given because "the situation is not given for itself, the index here is an index of lack; it implies a gap in the narrative, and corresponds to the first sense of the French word *ellipse*" (*Cinema* 160).

6

JOYCE GOGGIN

From Remake to Sequel

Ocean's Eleven and Ocean's Twelve

I
N *OCEAN'S TWELVE* (Steven Soderbergh, 2004), the sequel to *Ocean's Eleven* (Soderbergh, 2001), one of the cast members remarks: "I want the last check I write to bounce." This one line sums up much of the economic and, by extension, aesthetic dynamics that drive the initial *Ocean's Eleven* (Lewis Milestone, 1960), as well as its remake and sequels, including *Ocean's Thirteen* (Soderbergh, 2007).[1] Although the notion of a bouncing check may appear, at first glance, to have little to do with the economics and poetics of remaking and sequelization, this chapter shows that the two may be related in important if surprising ways, suggesting significant parallels and contradictions.

Perhaps the most obvious connection between a bouncing check, the Ocean's films and this segment of the Hollywood film industry is their mutual connection to money, seriality, and goods that are infinitely reproducible and whose value is taken to be particularly low. As contemporary filmgoers and film scholars know, remakes and sequels remain a much-maligned category, invariably criticized as a form of lassitude on the part of directors and producers who opt out for a known commodity, banking on viewer familiarity with the "original" to guarantee a presold product. Summarily then, the remake is often understood as "evidence of

Figure 6.1. *Ocean's Eleven* (Steven Soderbergh, 2001). Courtesy Warner Bros/
The Kobal Collection/Marshak, Bob.

Hollywood being an 'aesthetic copy-cat,'. . . of 'cultural imperialism' and
'terroristic marketing practices' designed to block an original's competition in the U.S. market" (Verevis 3).

Before proceeding to a discussion of these received notions of
remakes and sequels, and how the Ocean's films both reinforce and critique such limited views, I would like to rehearse briefly where such
arguments come from. The notion that remakes and sequels are always
primarily about money rather than aesthetics reposes on pessimistic,
postlapsarian ideas about art, rife with the suggestion that there was
once a Golden Age when artistic production was "original" and free from
vulgar commercial motives. Current cultural output, therefore, necessarily pales by comparison, being nothing more than watered-down drivel,
mass-produced with the basest of profit motives in mind. This view of
popular culture confirms Max Horkheimer and Theodor Adorno's worst
nightmare—that films no longer even pretend to be art and that "business is used as an ideology to legitimize the trash they [the cultural
industries] intentionally produce" (95)—to draw the obvious conclusion
that we are destined to regret our lamentable plight while gobbling up
inane remakes of old movies, as investors increase their profits.

Has artistic production not always—to a greater or lesser extent—
been caught up in the problematics just outlined? Certainly, as Marc

Shell so eloquently demonstrates in *Art & Money*, economics and aesthetics have been intimately connected at least since coins have been stamped with portraits of emperors, and the Holy Spirit was represented in Byzantine paintings in gold leaf (6–56). Money played an obvious role in the Renaissance, where artists' careers were made possible by wealthy patrons, and money was the prime motivator in the robust seventeenth-century Dutch art market, where paintings of gamblers and money changers were popular items, often sold to finance important careers. Such genre paintings, like movies, were collective efforts in which several studio artists undertook various figures or still life elements in the same paintings, which were then sold to down-market customers (see Goggin, "Making Meaning Happen" 43–52; Israel 548–49).

The novel, an aesthetic genre that once provided a social pleasure that film would later supply, likewise emerged through the market which it narrated, and in which it was sold as a product for mass consumption. Daniel Defoe, author of the first modern novel, was an economist whose works such as *Robinson Crusoe* (1719) made it abundantly clear that he was sensitive to the relation of literature to money. This important, founding connection between the novel, economics, and profit came to its fullest expression in the serialized novels of the nineteenth century, most of which were vehicles for peripatetic marriage romances, many of which were remarkably similar, and constituted remakes and sequels of themselves. The result was a booming market in serialized, sequelized fiction that instrumentalized branding, product placement, and the professionalization of writing, through which writers such as Charles Dickens turned an enormous profit (see Hughes and Lund; Patten 122–42).

Although the separation of art and money is arguably a constructed binary that has been enthusiastically and repeatedly deconstructed since the early 1980s, postromantic ideas about the absolute value of "originality," and the importance of keeping aesthetics unsullied by finance still hold considerable sway. Given the persistence of objections to remakes and sequels as soulless commercial artifacts, perversely lacking in "originality," the only effective response is one that takes into account the cultural, industrial, historical, and narrative concerns at the heart of remake and sequel production. Only by stepping back and asking how we got this way can we hope to reevaluate cinematic remakes and sequels in any way that makes sense of them for what they *are*, as opposed to everything they *are not*. This is especially important because the unabashed remake and its close cousin, the sequel, have constituted the dominant mode of artistic production since the late twentieth century, a trend that got underway, along with Andy Warhol's soup cans, in the 1960s (see Dryer).

What is arguably new about the market in remakes and the production of sequels that got started at the end of the twentieth century is that these cultural products showcase themselves as such. Moreover, they are generally uninterested in aligning themselves with "literariness" or some other manifestation of "high culture," but rather take their "inspiration" from other movies and television shows, hence films such as *Popeye* (Robert Altman, 1980); *The Brady Bunch Movie* (Betty Thomas, 1995); *Cape Fear* (Martin Scorsese, 1991); *Mission: Impossible* (Brian De Palma, 1996); and *Ocean's Eleven, Twelve,* and *Thirteen.* This is important because, as Pamela Falkenberg has argued, in the past filmmakers and marketers emphasized a film's "art" status in an attempt to hide its commercial strategies because, "under capitalism, art is precisely that commodity whose exchange value depends upon its denial of its status of a commodity" (qtd. in Forrest and Koos 16). Clearly, because Falkenberg wrote these words two decades ago, things have changed. My task here will be to get at what has changed and why, by studying the Ocean's films as a prime example of the kind of cinematic remakes and sequels that have been made since the beginning of this century, and which flaunt their status as one more product in a specific line or brand, rather than attempting to conceal it.

My argument makes these observations a key component of my underlying premise: namely, that romantic and postromantic notions of originality and commercial innocence are no longer relevant. Originality is, and has always been, a construct, and aesthetic production (be it in painting, sculpture, theater, or literature) has always been intimately linked to mercantilism, commerce, the market, and, more recently, the financial market. Given their preoccupation with finance in both plot and location, the Ocean's films are appropriate texts through which to consider Hollywood self-appropriation and self-promotion as a product line. These films are, moreover, of particular interest because they boldly thematize both their lack of originality and their interest in money and the market as cultural phenomena—indeed, as their very subject matter. In terms of their plot, for example, all of the Ocean's films center on a heist in which an enormous sum of money is stolen from a casino or, in the last two films, from a casino owner. But while the motor that drives the slim plot behind all of the Ocean's films is stealing money, these films also represent how the market has worked in tandem with Hollywood since the 1960s when the first Ocean's film was made, and particularly where the circulation and investment of money is concerned.

Significantly, the "original" *Ocean's Eleven* is based on a short story by Hollywood writers George Clayton Johnson and Jack Golden Russell, who had the city of Las Vegas and Vegas entertainers—Frank Sinatra, Dean Martin, Sammy Davis Jr., Joey Bishop, and Peter Lawford—in mind when they wrote it. Since that time, George Nolfi, Brian Koppelman, and David Levien have written *Ocean's Twelve* and *Thirteen* as vehicles for the Clooney Rat Pack, fully (self-) conscious of all the nostalgia, as well as the economic and cultural issues, such a gesture implied. In other words, the *Ocean's Eleven* remake, and the sequels it now spawns, openly serve to publicize popular stars rather than as adaptations of some revered, high-culture antecedent. What this means is that autoreflexivity in these films, which is ultimately the promotion of the famous stars who act in them, becomes nothing less than their aesthetic texture, architecture, and function. Perhaps the most blatant example is Julia Roberts's redoubling role in *Ocean's Twelve* as Tess Ocean, who is now called on in the narrative to *pretend to be* Julia Roberts.

Hollywood and Vegas

The Ocean's films have their Las Vegas location to thank for the better part of glamour, and Hollywood producers know that they can bank on this eccentric and specialized urban center to provide instant visual and visceral excitement.[2] In fact, Hollywood discovered early on that the bright lights of Las Vegas instantly spelled money and excitement, hence, for more than half a century now, the two cities have been engaged in what might be called a positive feedback loop based on copromotion. Importantly, the lucrative relation in which these two highly specialized centers are engaged is also influenced by a managerial peculiarity that Las Vegas shares with few other gambling centers. This unique feature is the city's propensity to mirror, at any given time, the vision of an entrepreneurial genius who, for the duration of his tenure as Vegas kingpin, imparts a particular shape to this former desert outpost, while structuring the messages it broadcasts, particularly through Hollywood film.

The first of these Las Vegas visionaries was Bugsy Siegel, who turned Vegas into a desert resort and getaway spot where the general public could rub shoulders with Hollywood stars. During Siegel's reign, Ria Langham went to Las Vegas to divorce Clark Gable and appeared in the press gambling and romping as she waited out her six-week Nevada residency requirement. The ensuing publicity turned Vegas into the "Divorce Capital of the World," and in 1941 *Las Vegas Nights* (Ralph Murphy) became the first film to capitalize on this kind of glamour and invest in Vegas-Hollywood synergy. This low-budget production heralded a decade in which the town went from being a playground to the stars and a glamorous setting for press photos, to a popular location for a new kind of romance, involving the cinematic manipulation of a complex galaxy of cultural signs such as cowboys, gangsters, hoods, streetwalkers, show girls, and compulsive gamblers.

Just as Bugsy Siegel left his mark on the 1930s and 1940s, Las Vegas of the 1960s was stamped with the style of Howard Hughes, who owned the Silver Slipper, the Desert Inn, and the Frontier. Hughes produced *The Las Vegas Story* (Robert Stevenson, 1952), specifically to flaunt the town's heavy investment in neon, which made Vegas a "naturally" sensational setting. It was also in the 1960s, under Hughes's direction, that the production show policy took off, and the Sands, also owned by Hughes, became the favorite haunt of Dean, Sammy, Joey, and Peter—the members of Frank Sinatra's Rat Pack. The Sands became the setting for the first *Ocean's Eleven*, a virtually plot-free heist film expressly created to showcase the Rat Pack and about which there was nothing particularly "original." According to one critic, *Ocean's Eleven* "functioned as a celebrity travelogue that provided Las Vegas with the cachet and glamour of Hollywood as a playground for the rich and famous, focusing primarily on the aura of Frank Sinatra and his cronies" (Gottdiener, Collins, and Dickens 71).

Hardly flaunting itself as a culturally significant production, the first film in the Ocean's series served as a sort of remake of the Rat Pack's own production shows. Given that the members of the Rat Pack also performed in casinos on the strip while making the movie, filmgoers were treated to an early frisson of postmodern self-consciousness and the fictionalization of "real life," as in the last segment of the film where Sammy Davis sings into the camera. The camera departs from the Hollywood norm by breaking down the fourth wall, with Davis, filmed in front of the Sand's marquee, announcing a performance of the Rat Pack, and uncannily conflating the cinematic with the real. In keeping with a trend to narrative aesthetic production that would increasingly and unabashedly flaunt its own means of production (in this case, Hollywood and the economics of promoting the stars it created), the first Ocean's film stood at the cutting edge. The film's characteristic self-conscious humor was supplemented with cameos by stars such as Red Skelton, who appeared as himself, and Shirley MacLaine, whose ad-libbed line to Dean Martin—"I'm so drunk I don't think I could lie down without holding on"—was a typical Dean Martinism at the time.

The Hughes decades were followed by a drab, faceless corporate period in the late 1970s and 1980s, in which the town was known almost exclusively as the world center for bad taste. About this time Steve Wynn, then a young slot and keno manager, showed up determined to give Las Vegas a facelift by developing casino-hotels in themed family parks, such as Treasure Island and the Excalibur. Wynn was also determined to give the place a little class, which he did by building casinos as simulacra, or remakes, of culture capitals such as Paris, New York, Venice, and Bellagio. To make space for his megalomaniacal dreams, Wynn also devised a plan to clear the path for progress and make money at the same time. The magnate's strategy for accomplishing both is what reporter Jeff Simpson has called "one of Las Vegas' most impressive spectacles—[the] hotel implosion." Since Wynn's entrepreneurial debut, an impressive list of casinos has been imploded and captured on videos sold everywhere in Vegas. His greatest hits include the Dunes (1993), the Hacienda (1996), the Old Aladdin (1998), El Rancho (2000), the Desert Inn (2004), and most importantly, in 1996, the forty-four-year-old Sands, which had opened in 1952 and was once home to Frankie, Dean, Sammy, Joey and Peter.[3]

Wynn's entrepreneurial profile appears in *Ocean's Eleven* (2001), and its sequels *Ocean's Twelve* and *Thirteen*, as the Terry Benedict character (Andy Garcia). Like Steve Wynn, Benedict comes from humble beginnings, collects art, is obsessed with security and surveillance, and, most importantly, he implodes casinos and makes events out of the implosions. The fictional vault in *Ocean's Eleven* hints at Wynn's obsession with heightening security measures. In his latest hotel-casino, Wynn Las Vegas, players are issued radio frequency identity (RFID) chips, which make it easier to "identify counterfeit chips, keep track of markers, rate players for comps, and deter casino cheats" (see Goggin, "Casinos and Sure Bets"). Wynn's explosive approach to economic management is also dramatized in *Ocean's Eleven* in a pivotal scene in which Benedict detonates an old casino, replicating Wynn's now famous implosion events. More significantly, this acknowledgment of the film's "real-life" setting and character (Las Vegas and Steve Wynn) and its constructed self (as remake of the first *Ocean's Eleven*), recalls the self-conscious positioning of Sammy Davis in the first film, thereby effectively adding a further dimension to the process that the initial *Ocean's Eleven* set in motion. Interestingly enough, the *Ocean's Eleven* remake also contains an embedded narrated segment, which itself contains embedded narratives of attempted heists in Las Vegas in the 1950s, 1960s, and 1980s: the mafia years, the Hughes era, and the corporate strip, respectively. The *mise en abyme* structure of this segment again self-consciously draws attention to the "real" Las Vegas, its legal and criminal economies, and its close ties to Hollywood. In other words, this is a Hollywood film that remakes Las Vegas in three microsequences that hint at the structure of the Ocean's films as a whole.

Gambling, Speculation, and Aesthetics

While *Ocean's Eleven* (1960), the remake, and its sequels market Las Vegas and Hollywood stars, they also adapt and represent particular aspects of

the postproduction economy in which they were made, namely speculation, finance, and gambling. This is to say that as these films were being
made the ostensible divisions between speculation, finance, and gambling
were rapidly eroding, and these closely related economic practices began
circulating wealth, risk, and chance in similar ways. One example of this
is the boom in the casino industry and, of course, flimflamming casinos
is the comic plot device that drives these Vegas films. This section, then,
investigates the relation between the financial economy, often described as
a casino economy, and how it relates to the Ocean's films as well as to Hollywood and the economic practice of producing remakes and sequels.

To establish the groundwork for this investigation, we need to
return briefly to recent monetary and financial history. Money, the medium in which the financial market is visualized, underwent a significant
change in 1933, when the United States severed paper money from the
gold standard for domestic trade. In 1971, Richard Nixon drove through
a policy that constitutes one of the most significant monetary transformations in history by cutting money loose from the gold standard for
international trade within the United States. At this point, paper money
began to circulate definitively, and on its own, without the indexical
safety net of specie to back it. Hence, as Brian Rotman has pointed out,
paper money no longer makes any pretence of being redeemable for the
amount of precious metal that it would formerly have guaranteed, so that
"a dollar bill presented to the U.S. Treasury entitles the holder [only]
to an identical replacement of itself" (89). This is to say that money no
longer represents the supposedly more stable gold standard, but rather
serves as a remake of itself without the pretence of referring to a more
material antecedent.

In a similar vein, Jean Baudrillard argued that the Twin Towers at
the World Trade Center in New York City were the perfect icon of the
US financial economy because the towers reflected the role that paper
money took on in 1971, at roughly the same time as the towers were
being built (Baudrillard, *Simulacra* 75–79; see also Rotman 88–97). Like
paper money, the towers referred to and reflected nothing save their own
identical twin. "The most interesting thing about them," writes Gary
Percesepe, "was that there were two of them, and the way they were
positioned, not exactly next to each other, but north and south [each] at
the perfect angle in relation to the other [. . .] they seemed to echo one
another other, an exercise in architectural repetition."

Parallels to what Baudrillard would call duplication without representation, of which money and postmodern architecture are examples,
abound in the Ocean's films precisely because they are all, in some way,
a remake or a sequel. To develop just one example, the deregulation of

money has made possible a deregulated financial market, in which such economic constructions as derivatives and notoriously risky junk bonds are traded (incidentally, Wynn financed the construction of the Mirage casino in 1989 with junk bonds, bringing together gambling and finance in seemingly perfect symmetry). If money, and instruments of credit such as those just mentioned, always inform and even dictate aesthetics, argues Mark C. Taylor, then understanding manifestations of contemporary culture such as the remake and sequel is impossible without taking into consideration current developments in the financial markets. Understood in this way, the Ocean's films are all more or less explicitly a commentary on the economy that spawned them, and they make no attempt to represent anything outside of themselves, but rather endlessly duplicate Las Vegas and famous stars, who frequently play themselves, such as Bruce Willis in *Ocean's Twelve*. This accounts for many similar scenes in *Ocean's Eleven*, such as the one in which George Clooney asks Brad Pitt if his delivery was too fast, or the closing scene of *Ocean's Thirteen* in which Clooney advises Pitt to settle down and have a few kids. In other words, these films are openly self-reflexive and expect that audiences will enjoy moments at which this self-consciousness is foregrounded.

Moreover, part of how the market informs contemporary culture is the growth of a strong relation between Las Vegas and Wall Street, which both serve as metonymies of the financial practices that take place in them. This also applies to the mode in which these two centers represent themselves, which constitutes an aesthetics of finance, including digital displays of "derivatives, virtual currencies, and e-money" (Taylor 8). While the visual aesthetic of money was still in the process of becoming evermore prominent in our daily lives, "financial markets began to resemble a postmodern play of signs indistinguishable from the digital signs on display along the Vegas Strip" (8). According to Taylor, this is why one cannot "understand the Wall Street of the 1970s and 1980s" without Las Vegas, and particularly the period since then, wherein "playing the market [has become] a new form of mass entertainment," much like a trip to the desert gambling capital (184, 207).

The logic of the "real world" market likewise asserts itself in *Ocean's Eleven* in several ways. First, it remakes the supposed "original" 1960 film that, as explained earlier, is no more original or authentic than the gold standard ever was. The only thing that is perhaps in some sense "authentic," is the pretence under which this logic operates. However, even in the film, Danny Ocean and his friends are no dupes to specious logic and know that robbing a casino is better than a bank because (as Ocean explains), unlike banks, casinos are required by law "to hold in reserve enough cash to cover every chip played on the floor" at any given

time. What this ostensibly means is that casinos are now more effective
in producing the *illusion* of security than banks, while the faster moving,
more risky, and exciting Wall Street threatens to supersede Las Vegas as
a financial entertainment capital.

The idea that the "real" economy has become more risk-based than
a casino is also hinted at in *Ocean's Twelve*. In this sequel, Terry Benedict
puts the finger on Ocean and his band of thieves for the $160 million
they originally stole from him, plus interest over three years bringing
the balance—"assuming that Benedict gives prime plus one"—up to $190
million. This is a calculation of which we are repeatedly reminded in
the film along with the "fact" that the money is being held "in escrow"
until the Ocean's crew (each of whom owes precisely $17.34 million: as
Linus, played by Matt Damon, quips "the interest just kills you") can
compete with François Toulour, played by Vincent Cassel, to steal a
priceless Faberge egg. By talking about stolen casino money in financial
jargon and assuming that it accrues interest like any other money, the
characters assume that bankers, casino owners, and thieves are all more
or less in the same business—they just have different offices.

Signs and Things

The value of sequelization and remaking—or rather the hierarchical
assumptions underpinning their contemporary production—is further
played out in the Ocean's films in terms of architecture. I therefore
turn briefly to the question of architecture and how it expresses the
financial systems that underwrite it in order to look at a broader semiotic
issue, which is also at stake in the Ocean's films. The explicitly financial architecture that gives Vegas its unique style, and which likewise
gives the former desert watering hole its distinctive Hollywood appeal,
is also powerfully present in the architecture of Times Square. Here at
the epicenter of the financial economy, the Reuters building is covered
eight stories deep in a digital NASDAQ sign displaying real-time market
activity, revolving and hovering on "a semblance of the only headquarters
that NASDAQ has" (Taylor 190).

While this trend in contemporary architecture certainly has a lot
of glitz, it is also a high-water mark in the history of commercial design
as it turns buildings into giant surfaces on which to advertise. Signs,
therefore, become all-consuming and buildings more or less disappear
behind signage that signifies the market, itself part of an illusory, self-reflexive economy that endlessly trades on, and inflates, itself. Therefore,
the buildings at Times Square have become signs, much in the semiotic
sense of the term, and take their place in a market that is based on the

play and manipulation of other signs, so that the signifier is, in effect, temporarily fused with the signified, in a potentially endless process of self-reflexive redoubling.

But the merging of architecture with signage is an innovation that Las Vegas pioneered long before architects such as Frank Gehry were designing buildings for Time Square. By the mid-1940s the Young Electric Sign Company, known as Yesco in Vegas, had created the city's trademark Vegas Vic, an enormous cowboy who would later be joined by Vegas Vickie. However, the real boom in Las Vegas sign architecture got underway in the 1950s as a means of pulling motorists into casinos from the city's strip, itself an innovation in the drive-through urban planning that would come to define the postmodern city. As architects Venturi, Brown, and Izenour explained in *Learning from Las Vegas*, the city chose not to follow but to transcend the Universalist principles of modernist architecture, in terms both of the buildings, which became giant signs of themselves as well as of the city. Las Vegas therefore adopted the symbolic, the particular, and the presentational, a trend that relinquishes "any pretence of representing reality, instead presenting possibility" (Firat 115). And this of course, is the perfect setting for the Ocean's remakes and sequels that celebrate gambling and the financial market by way of an aesthetic practice that mobilizes stars such as Brad Pitt as semiotic markers, always referring back to themselves, rather than representing any form of external reality. One excellent example of this is the scene in *Ocean's Eleven* in which Pitt is introduced. Here Pitt is implicitly playing the role of Ricky Jay, a "real life" cardsharp and magician-cum-movie star, who began in Hollywood by coaching stars in poker moves for gambling films. While fans in the know will immediately get this self-conscious nod to Ricky Jay and his unique persona, the scene also serves to authenticate Pitt's stardom because he is set off against the "real life" celebrity of the (lesser) television stars—Joshua Jackson, Topher Grace, Holly Marie Combs—whom he is attempting to teach just enough poker skills for them to be believable in a Hollywood movie.

This trend to promoting signs for things naturally impacted on cultural production outside of architecture as well. As early as the 1956 film *Meet Me in Las Vegas* (Roy Roland), viewers are explicitly invited to enjoy MGM's "Goldmine of Entertainment," that is, not the representation of a love story, but rather a spectacle of wealth and MGM's advertisement thereof. In other words, at this juncture, with the help of Hollywood, Las Vegas began representing itself through a blatant manipulation of signs of itself, which viewers were expected to enjoy for the simple reason that it made a lot of money. This same trend also manifests itself in the city's relation with Elvis Presley whereby, according to one author, Las Vegas in the 1990s "had merged with Elvis into a double sign, with the enter-tainer posthumously multiplied as the definitive Las Vegas entertainer by hundreds of impersonators" (Gottdiener et al. 73). In this case, the dead performer who, ironically enough, electrified audiences in *Viva Las Vegas* (George Sidney, 1964), becomes more important as a sign than as a per-son, and continues to proliferate and circulate in the bizarre play of signs that constitutes the postmodern financial economy of which Las Vegas is a part (see Anderton and Chase 5–13). Not to be left out of the loop, *Ocean's Eleven* featured Elvis impersonators and the film's end credits roll to a remixed version of Elvis's "A Little Less Conversation."

More generally speaking, this kind of self-consciousness, predicated on constant autoreflexivity, is the logic that informs all of the Ocean's films throughout: it constitutes their form, style, function, and continued production. Hence, what began as one narcissistic, self-promotional Las Vegas movie that banked on the popularity of the town's own Rat Pack, became a vehicle for the promotion of a gang of stars whose leader, George Clooney, was (in 2006) reportedly set to invest in a casino (Las Ramblas) in Vegas. In broader terms, therefore, the Ocean's sequels pres-ent themselves at first glance as signs of an "original" that turns out *not* to be an originating narrative in any traditional sense. Moreover, although one might say that the new films in the series are actually bizarrely faith-ful to the promotional intention of the original *Ocean's Eleven*, what they represent at the macrolevel is the capitalist logic of Hollywood, and the financial machinery that drives contemporary mainstream film.

Taylorizing Leisure

As described earlier, the Ocean's movies were, and continue to be, pro-duced as the gambling industry, and particularly Las Vegas, became increasingly important to the greater economy. Along with Las Vegas, economic developments such as deregulation, privatization, and a deraci-nated dollar, have resulted in a financial market that is progressively more abstract and is increasingly understood as a part of the entertainment industry, along with Vegas and gambling. In short, we are now living in what economists have referred to as casino capitalism, a "system" in which gambling is a major industry, and wherein governments and economists have long given up the pretence that a line exists between speculation and gambling.[4] This is significant because gambling—like the remake and sequel—serializes leisure time as the gambler engages in a continuum of wagers, over and over again.

Serialized leisure is, moreover, Taylorized leisure: that is, time that has been parceled out, mass-produced, and rendered uniform (see

Garite). As such, leisure comes to form the complement of the Tay-lorized labor performed by factory workers and, in a postproduction economy, by anyone employed in the information, entertainment, and countless other industries that deal in nontangibles. Although the term comes into being with the management theory of Taylor, the thinking that it instrumentalized began much earlier with mercantilism and the development of the art market and the inexpensive copy in the seven-teenth century (see Giesz). In terms of narrative, the novel form, divided into convenient chapters designed to fill the limited leisure time of those who work, got underway in the eighteenth century and is followed by the serialized novel of the nineteenth century. These novels were expansive and meant to stretch out over readily affordable episodes that ended in cliff-hangers, producing a needy, if not addictive, audience (see Goggin, "Nigella"). This publication strategy shaped buyer habits, desires, and needs to meet the production cycle of an industrialized society, and one that was increasingly becoming Taylorized. Serial publication, as sug-gested earlier, favored the remake and the sequel as popular romantic plots were reproduced in varied settings, and generations of novelistic characters followed one another into the reader's experience and enjoy-ment of fictional worlds. This is, of course, precisely how the Ocean's films work, as a remake of one mindless 1960s movie is followed by what threatens to be an endless series of brilliantly packaged sequels of approximately the same length, in which the same actors return to pick up the last cliff-hanger where it was left, and entertain us with an ongoing Vegas story that occasionally changes setting.

The Taylorization of labor and leisure also coincides with Sig-mund Freud's discovery of what he called the pleasure principle, which he characterized as "an economic point of view" on the human psyche ("Beyond" 1). For Freud, the human psyche is regulated by the pleasure principle, which strives to reduce "unpleasurable tension," and this it accomplishes through the "avoidance of unpleasure or the production of pleasure" (1). From this postulate Freud goes on to explain psychic responses to the frequent failure of pleasure to dominate experience and how we are driven to reenact these experiences in a manageable form, thereby gleaning pleasure from the sensation of having corrected an unpleasurable experience from the past. We remake such painful lacks and experiences in fantasy form, repeating them endlessly until the pain and its pleasurable resolutions begin to form recognizable sequels in our lives (see Goggin, "Gaming/Gambling").

The drive to remake and create sequels is directly related to certain aspects of economic practice that developed alongside of industrializa-tion. In a society that has grown up with Freud's economic model of the human psyche, we now expect cultural products such as narratives, films, video games, and television shows to reach a (partial) conclusion and begin again, like a hand of cards in an evening of poker. Moreover, as Georg Simmel (612–42), Walter Benjamin (481–503), and Gerda Reith (138–55) have shown, the experience of gambling itself is distinguished by sustained, serial gestures and episodes, which begin again as soon as bets are placed. As a form of Taylorized entertainment, gambling, which involves repeating sequences, is an entirely fitting topic to adapt to other forms of serialized entertainment such as the Ocean's movies. What is more, the Ocean's films not only mimic Las Vegas in the way that they, as remakes and sequels, belong to the production modes of both industrial and postindustrial capitalism, but also in the way that Vegas remakes other cities such as Paris and Venice, as well as Hollywood themes as in the MGM Grand casino.

Furthermore, as previously explained, as Las Vegas was becoming a regular location for Hollywood cinema, the world economy was growing ever more complex as a result of industrialization, while transactions became increasingly abstract and risk based. The result is that the present, postproduction, finance-based economy is now virtually indistinguishable from the workings of a casino. This development is evidenced in the way that the economy expresses itself through a particular flashy aesthetic style, reflected in the signage that financial institutions have borrowed from Vegas casino culture. Appropriately then, the market also communicates through Las Vegas, and films about Vegas, which are among some of the economy's most eloquent expressions.

These films also remake the velocity and the futurity that David Harvey associated with modern economics, based on the speed at which transactions can be completed, and the concomitant need to predict future market scenarios (285–307). This kind of futurity is also shared by gambling, an activity that is very much about present-ness, as the past and future coincide in the turn of a card. In other words, because of the excitement of anticipation, the gambler's attention is always fixed on what *will* happen, rather than what *has* happened. Similarly, the Ocean's films reproduce the in-the-moment-ness of gambling both thematically as each film implies the next and in terms of trademark self-conscious humor predicated on stars' awareness of their own time-contingent popularity and how the films function as a vehicle thereof. And while they construct this kind of "nowness" through the hype of Las Vegas, gambling, and popular culture icons, these films also return repeatedly into themselves for source material, bringing the past repeatedly into the present, hence the cameo roles Henry Silva and Angie Dickinson play from the original *Ocean's Eleven* in the remake. The "nowness" that the Ocean's series projects and on which it banks is, in this way, a reflection of the temporality of the gambler and the related futurity that the market demands.

Sequels and Conclusions

This closing addresses an issue that has been suspended to this point, namely, what a sequel is and whether we can safely say that *Ocean's Eleven* is a remake, and whether all of the supernumerated films that follow are also sequels? For Linda Hutcheon, sequels are tantamount to "never wanting a story to end," whereas remakes are about "wanting to retell the same story over and over in different ways," and this logic seems to apply nicely to the Ocean's sequels, which are numbered to imply that each film is yet another installment of the same story (9). According to Thomas Leitch, a sequel continues "the story of an earlier film by bringing a new set of characters" to the serialized story line, or by "inventing new adventures for characters established by an earlier film," and in "the age of the VCR" a big part of this is directed toward "creat[ing] an appetite for the original film" (41). By Hutcheon's definition, then, sequels are about never wanting the fun to end, while for Leitch part of the fun is creating a market both for the sequels and for what he calls "the original film."

In her *Sight and Sound* review of *Ocean's Twelve*, Liese Spenser suggests that the trouble with the film is that it is a "knowing sequel to [a] remake." She hastens to add, however, that by "flashing sparkle at the audience like an expert conman, Soderbergh makes the hardest job of all—following a hit film with a probable hit sequel" look easy (64). By this I take her to mean that, although impressively glitzy, *Ocean's Twelve* is somehow one step too far removed from the "original," and that the director knows this and does not care because he is a con man who is only after making a "hit sequel." Here again, the notion of an "original" and the genuineness that originals are supposed to guarantee still persists, much as the collective memory of the gold standard still unconsciously informs our view of money. But what *Ocean's Twelve* as a sequel also seems to suggest is that, like finance, the films have gone global, and so what was formerly thought to be a binary opposition between Las Vegas and the rest of the world, has been deconstructed and can be felt equally in the glamour capitals of old Europe. In other words, no longer does any place exist where notions such as "authenticity," "originality," and "genius" have been left untouched by late capitalism's propensity to create simulacra.

To return to the metaphor of a bouncing check that began this chapter, a check that bounces is one that has no funds to back it and, if one may draw an analogy between funds and plot, then one could say that the Ocean's movies, and the stars in them, bounce endlessly from one meaningless caper to the next in a potentially endless progression of sequels. But this would hardly do these films justice. Although the Ocean's films are Hollywood vehicles for stars, they are also prime examples of the dominant mode of aesthetic production that informs contemporary culture. In other words, these films rehearse themselves in an endless catalog of cute self-conscious gestures, each one being an infinite texture of the same, so as to perfectly mirror the lead up, beginning in 1960, to the current postproduction economy with which the producers threaten to keep step as they discuss *Ocean's Fourteen*. More important, the Ocean's movies provide a rich archive of contemporary styles, tastes, culture, and, of course, financial practices—in short an archive of those things that make us who and what we are. Simply writing these films off, to stay with the metaphor, as fluffy sequels with no content, intended only to make money, is to miss the point entirely. The significance of these movies as aesthetic products is that they typify the culture and history that produced them and have, therefore, a great deal to tell us about the way we live now.

Notes

1. *Ocean's Thirteen* (2007) was in production at the time of writing.

2. Although *Ocean's Twelve* includes segments in Las Vegas, it was, of course, shot in various locations including Amsterdam, a city that tolerates soft drugs and has an extensive red light district that illuminates postcards and tourist Web sites. As such, Amsterdam is another Sin City and signals much of the same kind of excitement as Vegas, while lending the sequel an international and "global" feel. In *Ocean's Thirteen*, George Clooney and his stable of actors return to Las Vegas along with Toulour, the French thief from *Ocean's Twelve*.

3. As a sentimental gesture, Warner Brothers now includes documentary information and footage of the Sand's implosion with the DVD as a tribute to the casino that served as the location of *Ocean's Eleven* (1960).

4. I use the term "system" here in the loosest, most schizophrenic and deconstructed sense of the term possible. With *Casino Capitalism*, Susan Strange popularized the expression and the notion that the economy works like a casino. More recently, Kurt Anderson has argued that the US government has "in effect, turned the US into a winner-take-all casino economy."

7

INA RAE HARK

Decent Burial or Miraculous Resurrection

Serenity, Mourning, and Sequels to Dead Television Shows

I N *GALAXY QUEST* (Dean Parisot, 1999), the extremely knowing parody/
paean to aficionados of science fiction television, the fans within the
text receive proof that their show's fictional world has been made
flesh, so to speak, and their aid is solicited to help the heroes accom-
plish their mission and defeat the enemy; said enemy is ultimately dis-
patched onstage at a science fiction convention in full view of the adoring
throngs. What more could the most devoted follower of a long-cancelled
television program ask for? The filmmakers have the answer: they want
their show back. So the film concludes with the credit sequence of the
resurrected "Galaxy Quest," revealing that all the original characters are
back after their eighteen-year absence, Chen's real-life alien girl friend is
playing herself, and once-dead "redshirt" Guy is playing a new character,
the security officer who provides comic relief.

How should we refer to this reincarnated version of the show? Is it a
spin-off, a sequel, a continuation? Indeed, how do follow-ups to cancelled

Figure 7.1. *Serenity* (Joss Whedon, 2005). Courtesy Universal Studios/The Kobal Collection.

television shows relate to the concept of sequels at all because television series are just that, serial narratives expected optimally to provide sequels every week for one season and several seasons after that. Most moderately successful, hour-long dramatic television shows have far surpassed even the longest-running film franchises, such as the twenty-plus James Bond movies, in duration. As the film industry becomes ever more interested in cranking out multiple installments, this distinction begins to blur, as a recent article in *Time* on the third *Shrek*, *Spider-Man*, and *Pirates of the Caribbean* films pointed out:

> [Money]—rather than the itch of some gifted writer or director to make an original statement—is the reason these movies get made. Audiences don't demand art here, just terrific entertainment. The first *Shrek* served that up in style; so did the first *Pirates*. But the

second and third time around, the studio's need for a sure thing is matched by the moviegoer's desire for a familiar one. *For all the skills on display, sequels are made primarily to satisfy the consumer's addiction for the same old, some new. Isn't that called TV?* (Corliss, emphasis added)

Richard Corliss's comments raise the question of whether we can even speak of a sequel to a television program when television series by their very nature are sequelized. Is renewal for another season the equivalent of a film gaining a sequel? Are "spin-offs" with at least some members of the original cast a sequel? What about "reunion" television movies many years after the program has been cancelled, or one-shot television movies or miniseries made to wrap up dangling storylines left by an abrupt cancellation, as in the case of *Farscape: Peacekeeper Wars* (Brian Henson, 2004) or the five Alien Nation television movies that ran from 1994 to 1997 as a follow-up to the series that was cancelled after one season from 1989 to 1990? Defunct series also live on in licensed tie-in novels and more recently in graphic novels sometimes written by the original showrunners, such as the "season 8" of *Buffy the Vampire Slayer*, Joss Whedon is writing for Dark Horse comics. And, of course, fans keep their favorite characters alive in fan fiction and fan videos.

The questions become even more complex when a television show jumps to the medium of commercial cinema for its continuation (see Hark). The vast number of television-inspired films, we may safely say, are not sequels but remakes for the big screen with different actors playing the original characters. The past two decades has seen myriad of these, most forgettable, but some fine movies in their own right, such as *The Fugitive* (Andrew Davis, 1993) and *The Addams Family* (Barry Sonnenfeld, 1991). Often a film remake of a long-dead series goes on to have its own filmic sequels, such as *Charlie's Angels: Full Throttle* (McG, 2003). (For an extensive discussion of these films, see Verevis 37–57.)

Far less common, however, is for an established series to make a feature film with its regular cast during the television run. A somewhat frequent practice for low-budget filmmaking in the 1960s, producing such gems as *McHale's Navy Joins the Air Force* (Edward Montagne, 1965), it has virtually ceased in recent years, usually relegating such projects to made-for-television movie specials or direct-to-DVD releases. Still, there are exceptions, such as the *X-Files* movie (Rob Bowman, 1998) or *South Park: Bigger Longer & Uncut* (Trey Parker, 1999). Rarer still are feature films with the program's original cast made a considerable time after the show's cancellation, and it is these that we can perhaps most confidently describe as sequels. The most celebrated and successful examples, of course, are the six films featuring the cast of the original *Star Trek* and the four featuring the cast of its spin-off *Star Trek: the Next Generation*. An example of a series of movie sequels far more prominent than the television original are the three Naked Gun comedies from 1988 to 1994, based on the little-seen Police Squad series that was cancelled after just six episodes in 1982.

What this proliferation of various sorts of continuations of cancelled television shows demonstrates is that as an open-ended, recurring form of storytelling, television programs never seem conclusively finished. That is why they are not just shows or programs, but *series*. Audiences often may highly desire and anticipate the sequel to a film, but such sequels more often than not are received as surplus, as more of a good thing that has, however, reached a satisfying conclusion, should no sequel follow.[1] By contrast, more episodes of a departed television show are received as natural, making up for a deficit that its cancellation has brought about. Indeed, if a television show leaves the airways unexpectedly, or in mid-season, or with a cliffhanger unresolved, viewers often react not only as if they have suffered a loss, but as if they have suffered a bereavement. Viewer and entertainment media discourse surrounding such cancellations frequently evokes paradigms of death and resurrection. Moreover, this is experienced not as a quiet death in fullness of years, surrounded by loved ones, but as a sudden violent extinction of someone in his or her prime. Behavior of the most devoted fans will closely resemble that of people who are working through the process of mourning, often matching point-by-point the famous Elisabeth Kübler-Ross "Grief Cycle"—of shock, denial, anger, bargaining, depression, and testing—although many fans never quite get around to the final phase, acceptance.

This chapter explores how the sequel to a "dead" television show can either facilitate acceptance or trigger more unresolved cycling through the stages. For some viewers, if a sequel wraps up dangling plotlines and serves as the characters' valedictory to them, it can function similarly to the final funeral rites for a loved one whose death contains ambiguous elements, its causes uncertain. In other words, the sequel brings closure. For other viewers, closure is the opposite of what they desire or are willing to accept. Because television shows, unlike living beings, can in rare circumstances come back from the dead, they will settle for nothing less than resurrection and depend on the sequel as the first step in the return of the show and its characters to renewed, serial life.[2]

My case study here is the Joss Whedon–produced "space western" *Firefly*. Running on the FOX network from September through December 2002 and cancelled due to poor ratings after fourteen episodes (including the two-hour pilot) had been shot and eleven broadcast, *Firefly* certainly looked about as dead as a television show can be. However, Whedon was obsessed with continuing it in some form, confessing, "I don't deal with grief very well and I don't deal with loss" ("Relighting"). Coupled with strong DVD sales of the complete series and the desire of Universal Pictures to sign him to a movie deal, Whedon's persistence resulted in a feature film sequel, *Serenity*, which reunited the entire cast and was released in the fall of 2005. This chapter looks at the dual function of *Serenity* as decent burial and miraculous resurrection by examining fan discourse about it on the Internet, especially on the dedicated *Firefly* fan site, fireflyfans.net. I read the narrative of the cancellation and return of the Firefly universe as industry practice against the themes of the series and film themselves because *Firefly/Serenity* happens, ironically, to be obsessed with death, burial, and resurrection.

"Can't more be done? It cannot die."
—Poster at fireflyfans.net

The grieving process for dying television shows has a certain consistency across fan communities. A chronological look at some thread titles on the general discussion board at fireflyfans.net from October 2002 through January 2003 illustrates it well:

Any hope for Firefly? 10/14

Well, here comes a fatal blow . . . 10/19

Save the Show! 11/2

Anybody know any Nielsen families they can bribe? 11/15

How many of you have written FOX? 11/26

So much for a great show. Firefly gets the axe. 12/13

I just can't believe it. 12/13

Savefirefly.com 12/14

Remember Babylon 5 . . . keep pestering them 12/15

Pissing off FOX may make things worse 12/15

SIGN THE ONLINE PETITION TO SAVE FIREFLY 12/18

Boycott FOX!!!!!!!!!!!!!!!!!!!!!!!!!!!! 12/20

UPN has passed on Firefly 1/11

How about HBO? 1/15

Firefly on the big screen? 1/15

FIREFLY: THE VIRTUAL SEASON 1/26 ("Archive")

One brave poster even offers up a four-part "Necropsy" for the show, but he is reaching the acceptance stage far too quickly for most on the board members, who attack him roundly. As ratings fall and rumors of cancellation appear, fans insist that such a high-quality show could not be cancelled on the basis of mere numbers. (The hardest point to make to a grieving television aficionado is that it is a business, and failure to make a profit will doom even the greatest work of televisual art.) Many launch attacks on the Nielsen rating system, claiming that it underrepresents viewers of cult shows and fails to account for Tivo/DVR viewings, while at the same time even the smallest upward spike in those despised ratings is seized as evidence that the show's death is not inevitable.

But the shock and denial phases pass quickly in fandom. Most characteristic of fan grieving is the cycling between anger and bargaining. To the dedicated viewer, no show's demise occurred because it was "sick." There are no coroner verdicts of death by natural causes here; beloved shows are always murdered, with network executives as the usual suspects. Fans speculate wildly about network motivations to cause a show—in which the network has after all invested quite a lot of money—to fail. Accusations of sabotage abound. And in the case of *Firefly*, circumstances provided more fodder for such conclusions than usual. It was known that after FOX saw the two-hour pilot, "Serenity," they almost decided not to pick up the show and instead asked Whedon to write a new, one-hour first episode over a weekend. The result, "The Train Job," convinced FOX to put the show on the air, but the buzz of failure was already attached to it. By not airing "Serenity" first, the network did not allow viewers a proper introduction to the characters and the overall story arc that *Serenity* the film would resolve. Furthermore, for several reasons, not least its hasty composition, "The Train Job," as Keith R. A. DeCandido observes, "didn't do the job" a first episode must: "Give the show an opportunity to make that good first impression [and] give viewers sufficient reason to tune in the following week" (56).

Other causes for fan anger may have resulted from bad business decisions or unavoidable circumstances rather than malice. Friday at 8.00 P.M. was not the ideal timeslot for a show appealing to the young, cult crowd and the fact that all FOX's shows are disrupted during the fall premiere season because they carry the Major League Baseball playoffs also did not help the ratings. But even Whedon felt that he had not been given a real shot for success: "Second of all, don't think for a second that I have given up on this show. I think it has been mistreated shamefully, but the FOX network has indicated that they would not stand in the way (which they can) of my finding a new home for the show," he posted on the Official Firefly Board after the cancellation (qtd. in "Haken"). Anger against the network was a prevalent theme of Internet conversation in the days and weeks that followed the cancellation, epitomized by a fan coinage adopted by many: to rename the network FUX.

Energies were directed more positively into bargaining, as fans brainstormed the various ways that Whedon might indeed keep the *Serenity* flying. Cancelled series are occasionally picked up by another network or given an extra season. Because fan efforts at saving the show inevitably accompany such decisions, there is easy slippage in the minds of devotees to fan efforts causing the show to be given a second chance. Some of this can be a *post hoc ergo propter hoc* fallacy, but displays of support surely do not hurt. An ad in *Variety* was purchased in support of *Firefly*, online petitions were created and signed, various networks emailed and snail mailed, but in the end none offered *Firefly* a new home and a second season.

Yet even after going off the airwaves, *Firefly* survived in the DVD sets, and a 2004 post by "Sidaris," someone who had just finished viewing the series, recapitulated the entire grief cycle that the board had undergone two years earlier:

> I have not felt so right about something in a long time, as I have in watching *Firefly*. This was something special, something never done before. This is something that should not have died so young, but have lived to a ripe old age. I don't understand why more options haven't been explored. Why has Joss not brought the show to UPN or the WB, SCI-FI or ABC/CBS/NBC? Any of them. . . . Why not even HBO, where anything could go on this show. I don't understand it. FOX is obviously not the right place to be with this show, so let's go somewhere else! Joss isn't some newbie director, he created *Buffy* and *Angel* two of the biggest shows in history! I don't understand why everyone gave up.
>
> I know some people, some people who may be able to help, I am not giving up on this show. All of you want to help, so let's

do it. This show was something more then [*sic*] just another great show that was cancelled, and I think not only we know that, but the entire cast and crew of *Firefly* know this. With all the piss-poor reality shows clogging our airwaves, and the mildly satisfying sit-coms, we need a show like this in our lineup. Anyone with half a brain would know this show is not just a half-assed attempt, but this is something bigger then [sic] all of us.

Watch the show, watch the special features, you'll see that no one wants this show to die. We have to bring it back, and do more then [*sic*] just sign a petition. Let's work with people we know, and figure out a way to bring this back to life in any way we can.

Life is too short to let an opportunity like this pass us by. Joss, if you see this, please, pull some strings, do something, anything to bring this show back to us. *Firefly* is not just a show, but a way of life.

Board veteran "SergeantX" updated "Sidaris" in a rueful post that acknowledged the triumph of the upcoming film but mourned the lack of full resurrection as a television series:

Everyone involved knows how good it was and that's why, despite being turned down by every single broadcast outlet, they've refused to give up. So we've got a movie being made, and the potential for a trilogy. To pull that off required a deal with the devil (Fox) that, reportedly, precludes any televised version for at least five years (Jewel Staite was quoted as saying that the stipulation was for ten years). It's bittersweet inspiration to see an artist in Joss's position putting so much on the line for a work he clearly loves. It's equally disheartening to know that it won't be in the format it was designed for. The movies will be wonderful, I have no doubt, but they won't be the same as getting a weekly fix for the many, many seasons *Firefly* deserved. (See "Archive")

"At what point does this stop being CPR and become necrophilia?"
—Whedon on the *Serenity* DVD

In crafting a movie sequel to *Firefly* that could serve both as decent burial and springboard for possible miraculous resurrection in the form of more films, Whedon had the advantage of working with an original whose " 'verse" replayed that cycle over and over. Set 500 years in the future, the television series posited that the Earth had become "used up" (or as the teacher in *Serenity* explains it, "Earth that was could no longer sustain our numbers, we were so many"), compelling humanity to create new Earths by terraforming uninhabited planets and moons in a distant solar system and colonizing them. Central planets occupied by the rich and powerful became gleaming futuristic techno-utopias; the less affluent were shipped off to scrubby, desert-like moons on the outer rim, adopting the lifestyles, dialect, and dress of the Old West. But many found that the independence and self-determination of life on the outer worlds was a satisfactory trade-off for the hard-scrabble living conditions. Then the central planets decided that they wanted to have governing authority over the entire human population and suggested that all worlds join into one giant Alliance. The Independents resisted and future humanity restaged America's Civil War, keeping the states' rights issue but removing the issue of slavery.

Firefly's protagonist, Malcolm Reynolds (Nathan Fillion), fought on the side of the Independents and was one of the few survivors of the two-month siege of Serenity Valley, the battle that forced the Independents to negotiate surrender after half a million total deaths on both sides. Stranded for a week amid the dead and dying, Mal and his right-hand Zoe (Gina Torres) were the only ones of their original platoon to escape. Now a man without faith or forgiveness, he seeks the only independence he can still muster, captaining a Firefly-class cargo spaceship for legal and illegal transport, focused only on the mantra "keep flying" because, as the show's theme song declares, "I don't care / I'm still free / You can't take the sky from me." The ship, like the pilot episode and the film sequel, is named *Serenity*. In a scene deleted from the pilot, when curious passenger Dr. Simon Tam (Sean Maher) asks Zoe, now first officer for Captain Reynolds, why he would name his vessel after such a horrible experience, she replies that once you have been in Serenity Valley, you never leave, you only learn how to live there. Physically alive, Mal is dead in his soul, and the overall plot arc of the series was to have shown his spiritual resurrection, a task that *Serenity* the movie accomplishes.

The catalyst for Mal's redemption takes the form of another symbolic rising from the dead. In the pilot "Serenity," Simon smuggles his sister River (Summer Glau) aboard in suspended animation, naked in a box that simultaneously suggests womb and coffin. A prodigy who has been the subject of terrible medical experiments on her brain, River was to have been part of a cadre of psychic supersoldiers available to the Alliance. One of the side effects, however, has been to make her highly unstable mentally, and her protectors aboard the *Serenity* always have to be wary of dangerous psychotic outbursts. The plot of the film centers on the efforts of the Alliance to reclaim River through the skills of a ruthless, deep-undercover agent known only as the Operative (Chiwetel Eijofor). It turns out that River's condition is not due solely to the procedures she endured but also to classified information she read from the minds of an audience of high officials brought to admire the scientists' results. That is why the Alliance will stop at nothing to retrieve her and why only coming to terms with the confusing welter of thoughts she gleaned will cure her insanity.

The mystery is solved when Mal and his colleagues undertake a dangerous journey to the planet Miranda, whose name has surfaced in River's vexed brain. Although the official story has it that this was a failure of terraforming that resulted in a few hundred casualties, Miranda turns out to be full of advanced cities that would rival any on the central planets. Millions of people had clearly settled there, but the crew arrives on a world that is one vast graveyard, full of decomposing bodies. When they discover a recording made by the exploratory team sent to find out why Miranda had fallen silent, they learn that it was the site of an Alliance attempt at social engineering, utopian in purpose but gone horribly wrong. Have-nots from the outer planets had been lured there with the promise of advanced technology to rival that of the gleaming cityscapes of Alliance stronghold Ariel—the matching allusions to *The Tempest* are no accident. To ensure that their rough-and-ready ways did not disrupt communal order, however, the Alliance covertly flooded the ventilation systems with the gas Pax, designed to inhibit aggression and, implicitly, rugged individualism. But Pax instead turns into a recipe for *requiescat in pace*. It shuts down all initiative whatsoever, and the people die *en masse* of thirst and hunger, sitting in chairs or lying in beds they cannot quite motivate themselves to get out of. Only one in a thousand survive, but that is because on them the gas has the opposite effect, turning them into mindless beasts motivated only by aggression: these are the fearsome rapist-cannibal-flay-you-alive Reavers who savage a planet from which the crew members of *Serenity* barely escape at the opening of the film and hold the space between Miranda and the rest of the inhabited worlds. Posited on the television series as men who lost their minds from living for too long in "the black," semimythical bogeymen the Alliance feigns not to believe in (and nonracist equivalents of the marauding Indians of the classic Westerns Whedon is invoking), they turn out to be a direct result of Alliance governance. Psychic River has picked up images of this charnel house from the government bigwigs brought in to view her part in yet another ill-advised Alliance science project. They are what have driven her mad and the Alliance will do anything to stop her before she reveals the truth of the Miranda disaster.

The parallels between Miranda and Serenity Valley are instructive. The Pax experiments were run prior to the idea of Unification being advanced by the central planets and can be seen as an attempt to forestall the resistance that the Independents would put up, leading to the civil war. Both places become vast landscapes of the unburied dead, and if Mal and his fellow survivors of the battle do not turn into monsters, they are bitter, crushed, and broken—"the people history stepped on," as Whedon called them. While neither the Reavers nor the surviving Independents have technically been resurrected, their former selves have died to be replaced by beings whose humanity has been compromised. Sometimes, the film is telling us, decent burials may be preferable to existence as one of the living dead.

Other dead worlds surface in *Serenity* when the Operative destroys any and all who might provide Mal and his friends with sanctuary, most devastatingly Haven, where former *Serenity* denizen Shepherd Book (Ron Glass) is discovered dying. With his final words he urges Mal to regain his lost faith, not necessarily in God and Christianity, but to believe in something once more. Mal's body survived Serenity Valley, but his spirit is trapped there. The last act of the film allows for its resurrection and the ability for him no longer to be stuck there as if in purgatory. Mal resolves to go, and the crew members agree to accompany him, to the massive guerrilla communications station run by "Mr. Universe" (David Krumholtz) and broadcast the incriminating video made by the last Alliance survivor on Miranda throughout the solar system. After a fierce battle with pursuing Reavers and the Operative, and helped by words from beyond the grave that Mr. Universe has programmed into his android "companion," Mal launches the signal. The Operative realizes that the cause he has served so ruthlessly was unworthy of the damnation he has incurred by believing in it; he spares the *Serenity* and her crew and the need to silence River becomes moot.

Within its diegetic world, *Serenity* offers both decent burials and miraculous resurrections. Besides Book and Mr. Universe, Wash (Alan Tudyk), the ship's pilot and Zoe's husband, dies during the film. Whedon includes a quiet funeral ceremony and shots of each of their graves back on Haven. Mourning rituals have always figured prominently in his works, the most notable example being "The Body," the episode of *Buffy the Vampire Slayer* that dealt with the death and burial of Buffy's mother Joyce. Two of the last *Firefly* episodes, "Heart of Gold" and "The Message," shot as the inevitability of cancellation loomed, conclude with funerals.

River, on the other hand, is restored to sanity and takes over Wash's duties as pilot, completing her journey from corpse-like girl in a box to whole human being. After being "violated" to pass as a Reaver vessel, *Serenity* itself is nearly destroyed during the final battle and its own repair and rebirth conclude the film. The final exchange between Mal and River in the cockpit contains images of life emerging from trouble and despair. The first rule of flying, the captain confides, is love, which keeps a ship in the air when it ought to fall. River notes the worsening storm they see around them. "We'll pass through it soon enough," he replies.

As a sequel, *Serenity* serves the same double function. It wraps up most of the major hanging plot threads from the television series, giving viewers a sense of closure after the show's abrupt midseason demise. It also clears the way for further stories featuring the surviving crew, a possibility because Whedon and the cast had all signed options for a three-picture deal if box-office revenues dictate.

"Take me out, to the black / Tell them I'm not coming back" —Lyrics to *Firefly* Theme

As with the launch of *Firefly*, the release of *Serenity* was not smooth. Universal had originally scheduled it to premiere in April 2005, a few weeks ahead of the last Star Wars prequel, *Revenge of the Sith* (George Lucas, 2005), but they were unsure how to market the space-western hybrid with no established stars that was a sequel to a cancelled television program with which the general movie audience was unfamiliar. So they instead decided on marketing the film via word-of-mouth from its small but fiercely dedicated fan base of Browncoats (the name given to the Independent Faction who fought against the Alliance in *Firefly*, and subsequently adopted by dedicated followers of the series). To that end, they previewed it on several days throughout the summer all over the United States and in the United Kingdom, ahead of a 30 September release. Most screenings sold out, and the Internet was abuzz with chatter about obtaining tickets, meeting fellow fans at the theater, and evaluating the film's rough cut. "Whedon flock ready for 'Firefly' resurrection" wrote *The Hollywood Reporter*'s Anne Thompson after the massive turnout for the sneak previews.

But, as spoilers about the cast deaths started to filter out, the marketing plan developed a downside. More so than Book, Wash was a central character on *Firefly* with a huge fan following. He was the deadpan joker in Hawaiian shirts who played with plastic dinosaurs, the everyman who also happened to be a whiz as a pilot and the ordinary guy the beautiful woman warrior Zoe had fallen for and married. Some fans became so upset by his random death just after he had miraculously landed the severely damaged ship that they said they would boycott the movie. One review thread that berated Whedon for this choice had the title "Joss, I'm Calling You Out" ("Archive"). Other fans began a letter-writing campaign urging Universal to recut the film so that Wash lived. Just as there had been denial about the reality of cancellation, so Wash's death was transformed into something that might not really happen. As poster "Auraptor" wrote:

> But I wanna just add that I don't think Wash's death was a good move . . . period. I'm more than bit annoyed at the whole idea. It made no sense. It leaves Serenity w/out a pilot, Zoe w/out a husband and leaves a huge hole in the make up [sic] of the crew. His comedic ability and antics will make any future projects greatly lacking. Part of me hopes this has been a cruel plot twist by Joss just to see how fans would react, and that when the BDM [big damn movie] premiers [sic], Wash really doesn't die. Well, one can wish, right?

Having gotten their miraculous resurrection against all odds, many fans were in no mood to leaven their joy with Whedon's patented sudden character deaths and rituals of mourning.

Critics outside the fan community had generally positive reactions to the film; it currently has an aggregate 81 percent "fresh" on the Web site rottentomatoes.com. More than a few pronounced it superior to *Star Wars: Episode Three—Revenge of the Sith*. Others thought that it would indeed fulfill the fans' dream of even more sequels. Tom Long of the *Detroit News* made both claims. Headlined "Energized 'Serenity' screams franchise," his review's first paragraph says: "A blast of sci-fi energy that makes you realize how good the 'Star Wars' movies could have been, 'Serenity' mixes space cowboy hijinks, Big Brother paranoia, meteor-fast quips and slamming action sequences into an absolute feast for fantasy lovers."

But resurrection into a franchise to succeed Star Wars and Star Trek was not to be. *Serenity* opened with a disappointing $10 million weekend and faded fast. In its six week run in US theaters, it grossed only $25.3 million, well below its $40 million budget and nowhere near the $80 million domestic gross Universal required before considering a sequel. Although fans again complained about studio mishandling of marketing and advertising, the fact was that the film drew in virtually no one who was not already a part of the *Firefly* fan base. Whedon's "post-Civil War Western in space" premise, no matter how skillfully executed, did not speak to a broad, mainstream audience, either on television or in theaters.

Box-office admissions are countable without using representative samples from which to extrapolate, so the argument that the television ratings underestimated the *Firefly* audience could not be made in respect to the anemic grosses. Indeed, the 4 million or so viewers Nielsen credited as *Firefly*'s 2002 viewership looked to be just about the same number of people who bought tickets to *Serenity*.

In the end, the outcome of *Firefly*'s miraculous resurrection into the sequel film *Serenity* had been predicted by the television episode the cast was filming when they got the cancellation notice. In "The Message" (never aired on FOX but included on the DVD set and broadcast when *Firefly* was shown on the Sci Fi channel during the summer of 2005) a feckless young man named Tracey, who had served in the war with Mal and Zoe, has his body shipped to them, requesting that they return it to his home world for burial. It turns out that Tracey is in fact not dead, only in a drug-induced state that mimics death. He has agreed to be a "mule" for some revolutionary new, experimental human organs, with his own to be reimplanted when they reach the buyer. He double-crosses his employers to make more money from a rival cabal, but he is found out and has to flee. The crew members come up with a ruse to save him from the deadly pursuers, but Tracey thinks they have betrayed him, too, and his reckless actions thereafter force Mal to shoot him. The episode ends with *Serenity* delivering the now really dead Tracey to his family for a decent burial. The causes of the apparent and actual deaths are different, but the fate of Tracey and the fate of the *Firefly* 'verse end up being the same.

Although many of the fans accepted the closure they received from the film and moved on, the bargaining stage for the twice-dead *Firefly/Serenity* still lives on at sites all over the Internet. In August 2006 fan "11th Hour" began a message board just for discussing ways to revive the show. The initial post proclaims:

> If there's money to be made, a studio will make a production. It's true that the box office returns for *Serenity* were lower than hoped for. (There are several legitimate arguments regarding the promotion, or perhaps insufficiency thereof, which can be made in that regard . . . but that's another thread topic.) The thing is that there are now far more *Firefly/Serenity* fans now than there were last year when *Serenity* was released. *Serenity* itself created those new fan[s] . . . plus the word of mouth of existing fans and very real *Firefly* and *Serenity* DVD sales that continue quite well on Amazon.
>
> The reason why fans have a legitimate hope for sequels is that the cast all signed 3 picture contracts with Universal for *Serenity*.

Their contracts all have a built-in clause for a trilogy.

Joss wants to tell more stories of the 'Verse, he has stated that he has hundreds of yet untold stories. The cast love playing their roles, and they genuinely enjoy working together. The fans of course will respond immediately to more incarnations of the 'Verse. Though *Serenity* did not make huge profits when it was released, and low numbers were the story for all movies released during that same time, *Serenity* did receive overwhelmingly great reviews and many awards.

So here's where it's at:

• Joss wants to do more.
• The cast want to do more.
• The fans are aching to have more.
• The production itself was widely acclaimed.

The ONLY thing missing from the above formula for green lighting a sequel is "Great box office returns." That's it. Just comes down to getting bigger audience numbers . . . connecting more with main stream audiences. A studio wants to make money. They are not going to say "no" to a profitable franchise. The thing is, *Serenity*'s profits weren't that bad, and the movie has climbed into profit with the DVD sales. But the returns weren't in the blockbuster range, and Universal has to think how best to utilize their wonderful new acquisition: Joss Whedon.

Universal is most likely biding its time and seeing how things develop after the release of *Serenity*. If the fan base keeps growing, if the DVD sales stay strong, if the merchandise keeps selling, then there will be good reason for them to mount another production in the future. Again, they are a business and they want to make money.

Once they see that the audience numbers justify another investment, Universal will be glad to press that green light.

New ideas continue to be posted toward this end, wistful magical thinking undeterred by the realities of the economic structure and profit requirements of huge media conglomerates. As I complete this chapter on 13 April 2007, poster "MartinT," having just finished his first viewing of the series on DVD, writes: "And if we do a list of signatures and show them how much we want it back I think we have a big possibility to affect. If we have thousands of names they can't just ignore us."

Other fans convince themselves that the only way to ensure a return of the 'verse is for them to finance more sequels themselves. A poll on the fireflyfans.net home page asks "How much are you willing to contribute

annually to produce the 'Firefly' series or have another movie made?"
The amounts range from $10 to "over $100," with 27,000 pledges, 40
percent in the latter category. New models for media dissemination have
also caught the eye of *Firefly* resurrection entrepreneurs. A Web site
for "Firefly Season 2: On Demand—Seeking Independence from the
Network Alliance" claims to represent "an independent production company and core group of Browncoats . . . currently pursuing the rights to
continue the series from FOX and make it available to the fans, either
directly or via another broadcaster." Its business prospectus reads:

> The Firefly Season 2 Project:
>
> Captain Mal and the crew of Serenity need *your* help to stay
> flying.
>   We are looking to push the envelope of episodic television
> by offering Season Two of *Firefly* in a groundbreaking new format.
> Each episode (or the entire season) would be made available for
> purchase in Standard or Hi-Definition.
>   It's possible that subscribers may choose one of three play-
> back options; monthly DVD deliveries, TV On-Demand using
> your cable or satellite provider, or computer viewing via Stream-
> ing Download.
>   It's also possible that a box set of DVDs would be available
> at the end of the season.
>   In order for our plan to be successful, we need to take stock
> of the Browncoat recruits that support our cause. It will only take
> a minute, is strictly confidential, and each profile will take us one
> step closer to victory!

If the notion of obtaining the rights is naïve, and the profiling could
indicate some sort of scam, the business model probably would make
sense to many fans still holding out hope for another iteration of the
'verse. In the future, dead television shows may well come back to life
in this manner.

The example of *Firefly* fans demonstrates the broader truth that
television series become part of people's quotidian reality, and losing
them can set off emotions very similar to those that accompany grief
and mourning. Depending on the individual viewer, this loss can be felt
as similar to a good friend moving to another city, or losing a job, and
to the more intensely devoted, it feels like the death of a loved one.
And because television shows have on rare occasions been resurrected,
getting stuck in cycling back and forth among the stages of mourning

than to reach acceptance and closure is even easier. That *Firefly* did not stay dead the first time, but rose again in its sequel, leaves cruel hope lingering that striking the right bargain will revive it once more, despite all empirical evidence that it is now really dead and buried. If the fan posts I have quoted seem at times to be from people suffering from serious delusions, I can only point out what Freud himself said about the work of mourning: "It is almost remarkable that it never occurs to us to consider mourning as a pathological condition and present it to the doctor for treatment, despite the fact that it produces severe deviations from normal behavior. We rely on it being overcome after a certain period of time, and consider interfering with it to be pointless, or even damaging" ("Mourning and Melancholia" 203–4).

Notes

1. Movie series conceived of from the beginning as multipart narratives, such as the Star Wars, Lord of the Rings, and Harry Potter films, are exceptions.

2. Examples of both sorts of coping mechanisms occurred recently on the message board, "ExIsle," devoted to general media discussion with a bias toward science fiction and fantasy. One thread, started by "Drew," "Cancelled Shows that Need Closure," asked members to list programs that belonged to that category. Another, begun by "ScottEVill," titled "Straight-to-DVD Movies of Cancelled (and Living) TV Shows," asked "What other shows, live or dead, would be good candidates for straight-to-DVD releases?" Both lists included *Firefly*.

8

PAUL SUTTON

Prequel

The "Afterwardsness" of the Sequel

IN A REVIEW ARTICLE OF *Batman Begins* (Christopher Nolan, 2005), published to coincide with the film's U.K. release, film critic Kim Newman begins by noting the fact that "of course Batman, the iconic comic-book character, has 'begun' many times" ("Cape Fear" 18). He then proceeds to detail the various ways in which Nolan's film borrows from a whole range of earlier sources, reproducing, despite his opening comments, a traditional trajectory of legitimization and origin; ultimately, he suggests, the article is "an attempt to give credit where it's due."[1] It is unsurprising that many of the reviews of *Batman Begins* are similarly concerned with these questions of foundation, derivation, and legitimacy, as are many of the principal figures involved in the production of the film. Critic David Grove, for example, proposes that "as the name suggests, it represents a new beginning in the film franchise, not another sequel" ("Christian Bale" 198). And Christian Bale, who plays Batman, comments, "this is an origin story, not a sequel," adding, "You could say it's a prequel—it feels like a prequel—because we don't have the pressure of following anything that's already been created" (qtd. in Grove, "Christian Bale" 202). The film's status as a possible prequel is contested too, however, with Christopher Nolan himself explaining, "I don't see this film as either a sequel or a prequel to the other films. It

Figure 8.1. *Batman Begins* (Christopher Nolan, 2005). Courtesy Warner Bros./ D.C. Comics/The Kobal Collection/James, David.

just sort of exists in its own very different universe" (qtd. in Jordan and Gross 23).

Despite Nolan's attempt to separate the film from its precursors—as much a question of economic prudence and shrewd or careful marketing after the critical and commercial failure of Joel Schumacher's final Batman outing, *Batman and Robin* (1997)—for many commentators it is nonetheless seen as the fifth film in the franchise that began with Tim Burton's *Batman* in 1989. Burton's sequel, *Batman Returns* (1992), was followed in 1995 by Joel Schumacher's *Batman Forever,* which produced its own sequel, *Batman and Robin,* two years later. Certainly the critical response to *Batman Begins* defines it in opposition to this earlier cycle of films: "Eight years after *Batman and Robin* buried a once-booming franchise under a deadly avalanche of fan backlash, toy-dictated story lines, nippled Batsuits, and director Joel Schumacher's relentlessly campy aesthetic, Warner Bros. and *Batman Begins* director-co-writer Christopher Nolan are betting $180 million that audiences are ready for more. Or ready to start fresh, at any rate, with a total reboot that essentially ignores the four previous installments" (Russo 68).

The "originary" status of *Batman Begins* in relation to the previous four films is repeatedly stressed, " 'There are fans of the other movies, but we're not going for that,' Bale says. 'In my mind, this is the first one' " (qtd. in Russo 68). Burton's 1989 film, as Will Brooker explains, introduced a "new Batman [. . .] clearly defined as other than the TV series and [. . .] akin [. . .] to the better-known graphic novels of the mid-1980s" (191), both of which had been preceded by a feature in the 1960s, *Batman* (Leslie Martinson, 1966), and two cinematic serials during the 1940s, leading back to Batman's moment of comic strip origin in May 1939 (see Brooker; Kempster; Newman, "Cape Fear"). As Brooker stresses, however, Batman began as the amalgam of several earlier cinematic sources such as *The Bat Whispers* (Roland West, 1931) and *Dracula* (Tod Browning, 1931). That this should be so is in no way surprising given that cinema has always "adapted, copied, plagiarised, and been inspired by other works" (Mazdon 47). In exploring the "many faces" of Batman, Brooker makes a similar point, arguing that "Batman has [. . .] a cultural existence which has to a large extent been freed from its roots in an original text" (185). The question of the origin of *Batman Begins* lies at the heart of the film, not only in relation to its diegetic concerns with cause and effect, evidenced in the traumatic triggers contained within it, but also in relation to the film's own position as variously, a sequel, a prequel, or a stand-alone film.

The definition the *Oxford English Dictionary* gives for "prequel" is straightforward: "a book, film, etc., portraying events which precede those of an existing work." On this basis *Batman Begins* may be considered a prequel because it describes events that come before any of the four previous Batman films in the current cycle; however, it is also, to a degree, a remake, because it remakes aspects of the Batman origin story contained in Burton's 1989 *Batman*, although it is also true that *Batman Begins* ends by returning the spectator full circle to this same film, either closing the series perhaps or establishing the possibility of a direct remake of Burton's "original" *Batman*. Importantly, all of the principals in *Batman Begins* have signed for two or three possible sequels (see Grove, "What the Butler Saw" and "Writing Batman"; Jordan and Gross). Of course given the previous incarnations of Batman on film, in some senses any film is always at one level a remake of those earlier films. Given that *Batman Begins* has as an explicit aim the goal of renewing the franchise begun with Burton's 1989 film one could even argue that at one level it is remaking the franchise itself.

The status of *Batman Begins*—as variously prequel, sequel, or stand-alone film—is clearly something of a vexed question, and this difficulty of designation interests me here. Thus this chapter argues, as a means of theorizing the significance of the prequel specifically (although within the broader context of the remake), that it is structured by the logic of "afterwardsness," that it possesses a peculiar dual temporality that enables it to both precede and follow the film or films to which it is a prequel. The prequel, then, despite its precedence, is able to effectively remake the film or films to which it is in fact structurally and narratively anterior. Not insignificantly, Christopher Nolan, the director of this high-profile prequel, had previously directed a Hollywood remake, *Insomnia* (2002), and he is perhaps most well known for the film *Memento* (2000), arguably a theoretical meditation on, and practical exposition of, the very notion of "afterwardsness." However, before addressing the question of "afterwardsness," a brief account of the *Batman Begins'* narrative is first required.

Batman Begins

Batman Begins opens with a young Bruce Wayne (Gus Lewis) playing Finders Keepers with childhood sweetheart (and subsequently Gotham City's assistant district attorney), Rachel Dawes (Emma Lockhart). As they play, Bruce falls into a dry well shaft, disturbing the bats that dwell in the adjacent cave, who swarm past the terrified boy. As he screams in terror the film cuts to the adult Wayne (Christian Bale), awakening from a nightmare into the equally nightmarish world of a remote Chinese prison. In a series of flashbacks that recall the temporal dexterity of Nolan's *Memento*, the prologue to *Batman Begins* shifts the viewer back and forth between Wayne's childhood, the defining moment of his parents' murder and his foiled attempt at revenge, as well as his self-imposed incarceration and his training at the hands of the crime fighting League of Shadows, led by the mysterious Ra's Al Ghul (Ken Watanabe). This introduction establishes both the motives behind Wayne's becoming Batman and the means by which he is physically and mentally able to do so. The advice of his trainer and mentor Ducard (Liam Neeson) that "theatricality and deception are powerful agents; you must become more than just a man in the mind of your opponent" points to the direction that Wayne will take in his construction of the Batman while also signaling the importance of the mythic, the symbolic (when Commissioner Gordon asks, "Who are you?" Wayne, as Batman, replies, "Watch for my sign") and of course the cinematic. Identity, the film stresses, is ultimately performative.

On his return to Gotham City, Bruce Wayne begins to explore the operation of the criminal underworld, headed by Carmine Falcone (Tom Wilkinson) and supported by a largely corrupt police force. A chance encounter with a trapped bat leads Bruce back to the well that he tumbled into as a boy. The cave that he discovers, and in which he finally purges his fear of bats, becomes the Bat Cave, the "unconscious" beneath the "conscious" Wayne Manor. Working in "Applied Sciences" for Wayne Enterprises allows Bruce to conceive and develop, with scientist and former board member Lucius Fox (Morgan Freeman), the equipment that the previous four films in the recent Batman franchise have taken for granted. As Batman begins to emerge, his adversaries begin to come into sharper focus too. It becomes evident that while Falcone stands for all that is corrupt in Gotham City, Dr. Jonathan Crane (Cillian Murphy) and Ra's Al Ghul represent Batman's real foes. Disrupting the receipt of a shipment of drugs, Batman serves up Falcone for arrest by Commissioner Gordon; he also discovers that part of the shipment, a fear-inducing hallucinogen, is being diverted to Dr. Crane. Batman's nocturnal crime fighting begins to affect Bruce Wayne's life, and after Fox advises him to devise some kind of "cover" to account for his activities, Wayne adopts the second of his "theatrical" deceptions, playing the role of billionaire playboy. In the meantime Rachel Dawes has also become suspicious of Dr. Crane and while investigating him is kidnapped and drugged. Batman rescues her from Dr. Crane's Arkham Asylum base and discovers that Crane has pumped the hallucinogen into Gotham City's water supply. Discovering that the League of Shadows, under Ducard's leadership, plans to drug the entire population of Gotham City by vaporizing the spiked water supply and sending them into a frenzy of fear induced self-destruction, Batman succeeds in overpowering Ducard (after the partial release of the drug in the depressed "Narrows"), and so prevents the citywide release of the toxin. With Wayne Manor destroyed in the "purging" fire the League of Shadows set, the film ends with discussion of its reconstruction—"improving the foundations in the South-East corner"—and the further construction of Batman himself, as Commissioner Gordon discusses with him the dangers of escalation and the emergence of a new criminal mastermind, the Joker: "Now take this guy: armed robbery, double homicide, has a taste for the theatrical like you; leaves a calling card."

As this descriptive account of *Batman Begins* demonstrates, the question of Batman's origin (as an effect of traumas suffered by the young Wayne) makes up a large proportion of the film, prompting one reviewer to suggest that "with its *bildungsroman*-like focus on the early life of Batman's unmasked alter-ego, it could happily be called *Bruce Wayne Begins*" (Lawrenson 40). As the film makes abundantly evident Bruce Wayne is, of course, as much a masked figure as Batman, a development in character that renders both Wayne and Batman far more complex than in previous versions (for an exploration of the various masks in play in *Batman Begins*, see Mugleston). This concern with identity in relation to memory and trauma is certainly one that Nolan himself is adept at exploring, with much of his earlier work, most notably *Memento* exploring precisely these issues; as Newman remarks, "The Nolan of *Memento* and *Insomnia* is at home with extreme psychological states—this might complete a Three Colours of Neurosis trilogy by following memory loss and sleeplessness with phobia" (Rev. of *Batman Begins*). This concern with "extreme psychological states" is what makes *Batman Begins* such an unusual blockbuster, marrying the independent intelligence of Nolan's smaller scale projects—*Following* (1999) and *Memento*—with the big-budget Hollywood summer blockbuster. Trauma and memory are central to the articulation of the psychoanalytic concept of "afterwardsness" and to the theory of cinematic spectatorship that has been developed in relation to it. Before looking specifically at the prequel, the following section offers a brief account of "afterwardsness" and the spectatorial paradigm based on it, referred to elsewhere as "afterwardsness in film."[2]

"Afterwardsness"

That a sequel should follow on from or be the continuation of an earlier film seems self-evident; however, from a psychoanalytic perspective such fidelity to the logical niceties of causality and linear temporality is frequently brought into question. Grappling with (and ultimately rejecting) the seduction theory, Sigmund Freud used the term *Nachträglichkeit*, generally translated into English as "deferred action," to describe a temporal structure that involved the rewriting of past events in the light of subsequent experience. Although never explicitly theorized in Freud's writing, this notion gradually came to underpin the mechanics of trauma and its symptomatic representations. The delay in the appearance of a traumatic illness was an effect of the temporality of deferred action: an event becomes traumatic not at the moment of its occurrence but only afterward, later, once additional knowledge or understanding precipitates a recognition of that earlier event *as* traumatic. This temporal structure effectively undermines traditional causality, repositioning an originary event as secondary, as "after the fact," so to speak. As one critic has noted, "in place of the quest for the truth of an event, and the history of its causes, *Nachträglichkeit* proposes, rather, that the analysis of memory's tropes can reveal not the truth of the past, but a particular revision prompted by later events, thus pitting psychical contingency against historical truth" (Radstone 86).

The term "afterwardsness" derives from the psychoanalyst Jean Laplanche's reworking and retranslation of Freud's term and as Laplanche himself has argued it is through the effects of a certain kind of "afterwardsness" that the term has come to take on contemporary significance (it was Jacques Lacan's interest in the term that provoked others to reinvestigate and to rearticulate or retranslate it). "Afterwardsness" for Laplanche is a profoundly significant psychoanalytic concept because it "is not simply one mode of temporality among others (the temporality of the causality of the trauma), but [. . .] the temporal structure which determines the emergence of temporality itself" (Osborne 90). In his account of psychoanalytic subjectivity, Laplanche argues that identity comes from the other, results from "a primal 'communication situation' between adult and child" (101); it is an ongoing encounter in which the child receives messages (or signifiers) from the adult other which it is unable to decode or translate. Because these messages derive, in part at least, from the adult's unconscious they are, Laplanche suggests, inherently enigmatic (to both the adult and the child). Furthermore, the imbalance between the adult and the child, in terms of development and knowledge, and the enigmatic quality of these messages produces "a primal [demand] 'to-be-translated' " (Laplanche 259). This, for Laplanche, sets in motion the formation of the child's own unconscious, which emerges "out of the untranslated (indeed, untranslatable) elements of the message[s] which inevitably remain" (Osborne 106). These untranslated elements are, however, "endlessly *re*translated as they enter into new contexts of significance, encounter new signifiers" (106); they are in effect subject to the temporal logic of "afterwardsness." As is especially evident in the case of Bruce Wayne/Batman, which will become clear later, the emergence of the child's subjectivity occurs, then, through a process of what Laplanche refers to as "autotranslation," the continual de- and retranslation of these enigmatic messages. The temporality of "afterwardsness" makes it ideally suited to explorations of narrative causality and to considering how stories are recounted and the past remembered. Having articulated the basic structure of "afterwardsness," we now consider the importance of memory for cinema and to stress its particular importance for sequels and prequels.

Cinematic Memory and "Afterwardsness"

The cinematic apparatus itself relies on memory for its effects. Describing childhood memories in cinematic terms, one critic has noted, "Psychologists tell us that reported early childhood memories usually take a camera's-eye view. We don't remember scenes from the perspective of a child: we visualise a movie with the child/self as actor. We recall a memory that has been reworked, polished, burnished, edited, and yet we continue to feel its authenticity" (McCarthy 22).

In technical terms our capacity to watch a film was originally believed to rely on what one might almost call a kind of memory: retinal persistence. This describes a process in which the reaction of the eyes to transitory stimulation is prolonged beyond the moment of stimulation. Cinema, as a mechanical system based on the projection of luminous images and designed to represent movement, was believed to be subject to the exigencies of this theory. Recent theories of perception have sought to disprove or at least reposition this account of cinematic continuity, proposing instead that the spectator is also subject to the *phi* effect. Nonetheless, the notion of persistence endures in accounts of cinematic perception. Current research, for example, posits the "*après coup* effect" (literally, the "afterwardsness" effect) to explain how apparent movement can be attributed to static objects, "If one looks for some time (say, one minute) at a regular movement—the classic example is that of a waterfall—and then moves the gaze to a static object, that static object will seem to be moving in the opposite direction" (Aumont 29).

The perception of movement in film is clearly the result of several complex unconscious and instantaneous processes. Reference to research in this area demonstrates the importance for cinematic perception of some kind of persistence of effect beyond an initial stimulus. Thus some have argued that perception is simply an "occasion for remembering [. . .]. There is for us nothing that is instantaneous. In all that goes by that name there is already some work of our memory" (Bergson qtd. in Doane, "Technology's Body" 10). As such some have suggested that the "human experience of perception hence pivots upon a temporal lag, a superimposition of images, an inextricability of past and present. To that extent it is a perverse temporality, a non-linear temporality" (Doane, "Technology's Body" 10). I refer to this research because the notion of a stimulus producing a prolonged after effect (*après coup* effect) invokes the terms used by Freud to describe the structure of *Nachträglichkeit* or, in Laplanchean terms, the effect of "afterwardsness." However, it is also, "Undeniable that memory [. . .] plays an important role in the act of *spectating* (the act of watching a film). For example, in order to construct a narrative form and comprehend the characters's [*sic*] actions, the spectator must be able to recall faces, places and situations from one segment of a film to another" (Lefebvre 479).

Memory is an active function of cinematic spectatorship, a necessary process if a film is to be viewed in "narrative" terms (regardless of whether the film itself is a narrative film). Spectators generally impose some form of narrative onto a film in order to comprehend it. Even a nonnarrative film will be narrativized by its spectator in terms of a technical narrative. Thus, for example, a film might be described in terms of rhythmic editing or graphical matching even if no narrative is apparent or immediate, and frequently such a response will be retrospective, analytical. In the case of sequels and prequels, which extend a preexisting narrative, memory is undeniably central to their effects. As one commentator has suggested, "Memory is essentially a process that constitutes the composition of the film's events during its projection, never ceasing to rearrange these events, relating them to each other, giving them their entire perspective" (Esquenazi 18, my translation).

This process of reconstitution is subject to the temporal logic of "afterwardsness," demonstrating also the absolute centrality of memory for the cinema. But memory is also as we have seen always a retrospective construction that is produced by deferred action, afterward. As Sarah Kofman argues, "In memory, the past only emerges as a distortion [a misrepresentation]. The meaning of our experience always emerges by "deferred action." . . . Memory is always already imagination. Meaning does not become in the present but is constructed afterwards" (96, my translation; emphasis in original).

The sequel invokes the spectator's memory on two levels, first in the context of the film being viewed and second in relation to the film that the prequel follows. While one could argue that all film because of its fundamental intertextuality produces similar effects, I maintain that the sequel represents a conscious and therefore more immediate and direct instance of this. The prequel operates in a broadly comparable fashion but the temporal relation between cause and effect is rendered more complex. Prequels and sequels demonstrate the paradox that "only in a culture of the copy do we assign [. . .] motive force to the Original" (Schwartz 141). The original is only significant as an original in its relation to a copy, just as an originary trauma only becomes a trauma through the temporal logic of "afterwardsness."

"Afterwardsness" in Film

To return to Laplanche's proposition that identity formation is the product of an attempt to de- and retranslate traumatic enigmatic messages or signifiers that come from the other one might well contend that this process extends to the domain of the cinematic. Thus one may argue that a similar process occurs during cinematic spectatorship, producing an active, performative spectatorship that is also constitutive of a performative cinematic identity. These (traumatic) memories, enigmatic signifiers, the de-translated remnants of one's cinema history are perhaps retranslated and remade, engendering a remaking of oneself around these fragments in a process of "autotranslation."

One might surmise that the cinematic spectator develops a specifically cinematic unconscious on the basis of the "repression" of the (enigmatic) messages received via the screen (enigmatic because interpretation, understanding may not be immediate but subject rather to delay or deferral). This "repression" occurs as a result of the sheer volume and traumatic intensity of the visual and aural stimuli encountered, which cannot be immediately ordered, understood, de- and retranslated. These enigmatic messages, structured by the temporality of "afterwardsness," provoke the spectator into a process of reconstruction or retranslation what might be described as a form of remaking.

The effect of the sequel is to produce a similar process of reconstruction; however, in the case of the sequel the messages are anything but enigmatic because the sequel is designed precisely to provoke the spectator into recollection and retranslation while at the same time providing pleasurable repetition. The sequel repeatedly reminds the spectator that repetition is a fact of everyday (cinematic) life; indeed it celebrates this fact through visual reminders and often comic dialogue. John McClane (Bruce Willis) memorably lamented in *Die Hard 2: Die Harder* (Renny Harlin, 1990), one of the earliest of the contemporary blockbuster sequels, "another basement, another elevator; how can the same thing happen to the same guy twice?" While the notion of origin (the "original" film) is a presence within the sequel, its significance is perhaps even more overt in the case of the prequel. The apparent temporal complexity the prequel appears to bring into play foregrounds the question of origin to a greater degree. The prequel claims originary status for itself while at the same time remaining a literal sequel. Hollywood has produced several high-profile, big-budget prequels in recent years, films such as *Superman Returns* (Bryan Singer, 2006) and *Casino Royale* (Martin Campbell, 2006), which operate at one level as sequels while at the same time proclaiming themselves to be franchise-renewing originals. These films reveal, in their very assertion of originality, the impossibility of such a contention. The sequel may be seen to produce a conscious "afterwardsness" effect for its spectator but the prequel is the effect, in a cinematic context, of "afterwardsness" itself.

The idea of a spectatorship of "afterwardsness" or of "afterwardsness" in film, is then to express the very dynamism of the spectatorial experience, to speak of the reconstructive and creative aspect of spectatorship. My proposition is therefore that the adoption of the causal and temporal structure of "afterwardsness" gives rise to a spectatorial paradigm whereby spectatorship does not involve passive reception and subject positioning, but is seen, rather, as a fluid process in which identity may be performed, enacted. In this account, (cinematic) identity is destabilized, becoming a continually de- and reconstructed performance, a kind of remaking. This process of spectatorship recreates or remakes the films it "remembers," while at the same time enabling the "auto-translation" of the spectating subject (see Sutton, "Afterwardsness in Film"). The sequel and the prequel are perhaps privileged examples of this process because such a mode of spectatorship is almost a structural necessity, an effect of their temporal relationship to each other and to any perceived original or originals.

"Afterwardsness" and the cinema both share a common concern with temporality. They also share a common interest in memory and are both bound to a particularly Laplanchean notion of translation. Film has always been thoroughly intertextual and has always sought to remake or (re)translate itself for differing generations and different nations. My proposition, then, is that spectators remake films as part of the very process of spectatorship and that beyond the actual cinematic experience they carry a remade and remembered "film" with them. This view of spectatorship takes "afterwardsness" as its motivating force. Not only is the spectator left with memories from, and of, the film after it has ended, but any number of (frequently traumatic) enigmatic signifiers or messages may have been unconsciously recorded, requiring subsequent de- and retranslation, demonstrating a prospective as well as retrospective dimension to spectatorship. The final section of this chapter now turns to the prequel and returns once again to *Batman Begins*.

Batman Begins, Again . . .

As a prequel then, Nolan's *Batman Begins* returns the spectator to the period in Bruce Wayne's life before he becomes Batman, to his childhood and the *locus classicus* of Freudian psychoanalysis. "Afterwardsness" is central to this return, not only as that which describes the temporality of trauma, but also as that which accounts for Wayne/Batman's subjectivity. Thus Batman emerges as Wayne's "autotheorization," the result perhaps of the bats, that as enigmatic, untranslatable signifiers, first "implanted" when Bruce Wayne encounters them as a child, are subsequently de- and retranslated (remaining occasionally untranslated, repressed) at various moments in the film. This happens in China when training with Ra's Al Ghul and at Wayne Manor when he reencounters first the single bat and then a swarm of them in the cave, the point at which he is finally able to retranslate them for himself, into the persona Batman. As Osborne notes, "these untranslatable (or 'de-translated') fragments, are, however, endlessly *re*translated as they enter into new contexts of significance, encounter new signifiers. It is through this process of de-translation and re-translation that temporality enters the picture, as the movement of a process of translation which is 'at once a taking up and a leaving behind' " (106).

As Wayne negotiates this process of "autotranslation," he "takes up" the identity of Batman and "leaves behind" a version of Bruce Wayne. Wayne's unconscious in this account is formed, in part, as a result of his encounter with the bats as a child; they represent the repressed "enigmatic message," which requires continual de- and retranslation (around which his identity coalesces). When he becomes Batman, Wayne finally achieves a retranslation that fits its context; perhaps the context of Wayne's return to a corrupt Gotham City produces this retranslation, preceded by the various retranslations that have been leading up to it. The question of origins, explored earlier, is especially important here because "origin" ultimately comes from the other. The translation of enigmatic messages is ultimately the de- and retranslation of messages without origin.

This process of de- and retranslation describes both the remaking within the film but also the temporal in terms of the logic of "afterwardsness" that is at work, the same "afterwardsness" that the spectator perhaps experienced in his or her encounter with the film. For the spectator *Batman Begins* renders the untranslatable of the earlier films translatable; it provides a new context of significance for the emergence of Batman while at the same time retranslating or remaking the four previous films of the Batman cycle. Thus *Batman Begins*, which charts the before of these earlier films, afterward effectively remakes them.

To conclude, these films ultimately complicate the textual relation that exists between the various incarnations of Batman, whether between the graphic novels and their film adaptations, the singular adaptation and its sequel, the filmic "original" and its remake, or the prequel and its sequel, while at the same time foregrounding the fundamentally inter-textual nature of film. The mutability of these texts and their shift-ing relations produces for the spectator an encounter that is marked by temporal confusion and instability but which requires of that spectator a level of engagement that is productively reconstitutive in its effects. In conclusion and in the spirit of the bidirectionality of the temporal-ity of "afterwardsness," I reference the latest extension to the existing Batman "series," the sequel to *Batman Begins*, which was released in the summer of 2008. Directed once again by Christopher Nolan, *The Dark Knight* (2008)[3] continues on more or less directly from the final scenes of *Batman Begins*, reintroducing the figure of the Joker and providing an experience of literal "afterwardsness" for the spectator that involves not only a sense of temporal continuity, but also produces inevitable comparison with Burton's *Batman* and its sequel *Batman Returns*. The spectator of *The Dark Knight* is once again drawn into a multifaceted filmic relationship that plays repeatedly with the temporal complexities of the film form, in the context of a film that is arguably not only a sequel but also an adaptation and a remake, yet retains its own singular identity. Ultimately, the effect of the sequel on *Batman Begins* is to secure further its originary status, to reconstitute its "afterwardsness," and, as Schwartz has reminded us, its singularity.

Notes

1. That Newman's article, titled "Cape Fear" and published in the July 2005 issue of *Sight and Sound*, reproduces the title from a June *Premiere* article, "Caped Fear," is somewhat ironic; the pun that both articles use refers of course to a film that was itself remade: *Cape Fear* (J. Lee Thompson, 1961) and *Cape Fear* (Martin Scorsese, 1991).

2. See Paul Sutton, "Afterwardsness in Film," "Afterwardsness in Film: Patrice Leconte's *Le Mari de la Coiffeuse*," "Cinematic Spectatorship as Procrastinatory Practice," and "Remaking the Remake."

3. One should note that the graphic novel from which the latest Batman film is almost certainly adapted is entitled *The Dark Knight Returns*; the "return" stressing the temporal dimension rather more explicitly than the film title allows for.

9

DANIEL HERBERT

Circulations

Technology and Discourse in *The Ring* Intertext

HE RING. THESE WORDS EVOKE numerous metaphors. *The Ring* as a circle, as a system of circularity, of cycling, and of recycling. Hence the Japanese film *Ringu* (Hideo Nakata, 1998) is derived from the 1991 novel by Koji Suzuki.[1] A series of film sequels and prequels followed *Ringu*, including *Rasen* (Jôji Iida, 1999), *Ringu 2* (Hideo Nakata, 1999), and *Ringu 0: Birthday* (Norio Tsuruta, 2000). In 1999, *Ringu* was remade in South Korea under the title *Ring* and known in English as *Ring Virus* (Dong-bin Kim). Hollywood also remade *Ringu*, in English and with an international cast in 2002 as *The Ring* (Gore Verbinski). Further still along the circle, a sequel to the Hollywood version followed in 2005, directed by *Ringu* director Hideo Nakata, yet it held almost no direct intertextual connection to the Japanese *Ringu* series.

As a system of recycling, *The Ring* evokes the entire wave of Hollywood remakes of Asian films, which has become a significant trend within the global cultural industries. Following the enormous success of *The Ring* at the US box office ($129 million) and across the globe ($120 million), Hollywood apprehended a steady stream of Asian films and

Figure 9.1. *Ringu/Ring* (Hideo Nakata, 1998). Courtesy Omega/Kadokawa/ The Kobal Collection.

remade them, a process largely orchestrated by Roy Lee at Vertigo Entertainment. However, *The Ring* not only indicates new levels of interaction among Japanese and Hollywood players; but it is also vital to remember that the South Korean *Ring Virus* followed *Ringu* by merely a year. After years of troubled relations between Japan and South Korea, this remake marks an important instance of cultural exchange. Furthermore, new connections have also appeared between Hollywood and South Korea. Hollywood reacted to the recent boom of South Korean blockbusters by initiating remakes of a number of hits, such as *Il Mare* (Hyun-seung Lee, 2000), *My Wife is a Gangster* (Jin-gyu Cho, 2001), and *Oldboy* (Chan-wook Park, 2003). Since 2001, more than twenty Hollywood remakes of East Asian–produced films have been made or are currently in production.[2] In combination, *Ringu*, *Ring Virus*, and *The Ring* thus constitute a circuit of economic, semiotic, and cultural exchange, however imbalanced, among players across the Pacific. This constellation of texts, this *"Ring* Intertext," maps a transnational and macroregional space. This composes another metaphor, geographic as well as economic and cultural—*The Ring* Intertext as the Pacific Rim.

Considered this broadly, *The Ring* Intertext literally and figuratively illuminates forces of transnationalism and globalization, specifically through communications technologies. As Arjun Appadurai argues, electronic media serve as a primary component of globalization, transforming the geographies of culture and imagination (3–4). Similarly, David Morley and Kevin Robins argue that new global media transcend national borders and realign cultural identities (1–2). In this respect, *The Ring* Intertext is overdetermined by mammoth social forces, even as it represents these forces within specific narrative and aesthetic parameters. Moreover, for the purposes of analysis in this chapter, the compound term "communications technologies" may be productively divided into constitutive parts, *discourse* and *technology*. These terms signify the taut lines of connection and contestation throughout *The Ring* Intertext, articulating a new Pacific Rim cultural configuration and revealing the struggle for power within it.

This struggle for power manifests itself in two polarities that pervade *The Ring* Intertext as well as its broader economic, cultural, and discursive circumstances. First, the Intertext reveals tensions between technophilia and technophobia. The fluctuation between these poles finds a basis in the historically circumscribed economic and political relations among Japan, Korea, and the United States. The different modes of technophilia and technophobia these films exhibit demonstrate the asymmetrical power relations that inflect this cultural formation, specifically as the texts reveal anxieties about history and identity.

The second polarity that pervades *The Ring* Intertext is a dichotomy between logophilia and logophobia, terms Michel Foucault described in his essay "The Discourse on Language." There he posits that the apparent love for discourse in Western culture covers a deeper fear of discourse (228–29). This logophobia is a fear of the uncontainable proliferation of discourse; it is a fear of inarticulation. It manifests itself in the desire to censor, to monitor, to delimit, and/or to halt discursive proliferation. Alternatively, logophilia refers to a predilection for and a taking pleasure in the creation of texts, textual proliferation, and textual dissemination; it is the joy of putting into discourse. The polarity between logophilia and logophobia seen in *The Ring* Intertext pervades the relations among East Asian and Hollywood players as well as the contemporary institutional conditions of transnational remakes more generally. The dialectic between these two polarities, between technophilia/technophobia and logophilia/logophobia, gives shape to *The Ring* Intertext and significantly inflects the contemporary transnational-transtextual space of Hollywood and East Asian cinema.

Ghost in the Shell:
An Economy of Technology in *The Ring* Intertext

Ringu begins with a horror film cliché. Two teenage girls, home alone at night, gossip about an urban legend. Rather than a tale of ghosts or murderers escaped from prison, however, their story is about a killer videotape. The premise is simple—anyone who views this videotape dies seven days later. One girl admits she has seen the tape and now fears for her life, and as the scene plays out the girl dies mysteriously. This dramatic device—the killer videotape—derives from the novel *Ringu*, by Koji Suzuki, and the premise runs throughout the filmic versions of the narrative. Here in the first film, the narrative follows Reiko Asakawa, a female reporter, as she watches the tape and tracks the video to its source in an attempt to save her own life. She discovers that the tape is cursed and houses the malevolent soul of a dead psychic girl. *Ringu* thus locates terror in technology by conflating the spiritual and the mechanical. Similarly, the film *Pulse* (*Kairo*, Kiyoshi Kurosawa, 2001) depicts a world where computers house malevolent spirits and the South Korean film *Phone* (Byeong-ki Ahn, 2002) features a haunted, killer cell-phone.

This method of denigrating media technologies is not new. Jeffrey Sconce has observed the spiritualization of media since the mid-1800s, as in the case of the "spiritual telegraph" through which the living attempted to communicate with the dead (*Haunted* 12–13). Analogously, Geoffrey Batchen notes that the invention of photography was attended by ruminations about its close relationship with death (166–67). These early sentiments of "haunted media" resonate directly with *Ringu* and its remakes. As these films portray the ghostly inhabitation of a videotape, they articulate different temporalities in relation to technology and in the context of horror, combining "modern" rationalism and "premodern" superstition.

This characterization resonates with the differential histories of technological exchange among Japan, South Korea, and the United States. Of course, these relations are infinitely complex and fraught by intense struggles for power that continue to raise anxieties. Indeed, for Japan and Korea, modernization and technological progress was, and in some respects remains, associated with Westernization and the imperial power of the United States. Furthermore, Korean industrialization was associated not only with Western incursion but rather Japanese colonial domination, as Japan forcefully corralled Korea into its national/imperial economic infrastructure (Cumings 148–54, 162–75). However, technology also provided the means for Japan and South Korea to exert power across the globe during the second half of the twentieth century as both nations underwent economic "miracles" based predominantly on technological development. In these respects, the relational development of technology across the Pacific Rim is marked by the uneven spatial deployment of modernity and evokes an intense struggle for cultural power.

These tensions are intricately connected with constructions of cultural identities, as can be seen across a wide variety of Japanese films. As a prominent example, *Gojira* (Ishirô Honda, 1954) articulates these issues within its historical frame. The film fluctuates ambivalently between technophilia and technophobia in ways that correspond with tensions between the United States and Japan around nuclear technology. Because this film downplayed the issue of nuclear testing when it was "remade" as *Godzilla* (1956) for theatrical release in the United States, it demonstrates further how asymmetries of power inform cultural characterizations of technology across the Pacific Rim. More recently, the processes of globalization have transformed the lines of connection across the region and realigned the associative relations between technology and identity. Ian Conrich argues that *Tetsuo: The Iron Man* (Shinya Tsukamoto, 1988) and its sequel, *Tetsuo II: Body Hammer* (Shinya Tsukamoto, 1992), illustrate a "new wave of Japanese horror cinema" that dramatizes "postindustrial" fantasies (95, 100). The protagonist in this film obliterates traditional boundaries between human and machine in fantastic fashion, and he ultimately forms a cybernetic synthesis of the two categories. Furthermore, Eric Cazdyn reads the cyborg narratives of both *Tetsuo* and *Ghost in the Shell* (Mamoru Oshii, 1995) as allegories for the transition from national sovereignty to globalization (242–43). He argues that the films' representation of fluid relations between human and machine evokes the mobility of a transnational identity.

These associations, transformations, and tensions among temporalities, technology, and identities pervade the greater cultural configuration. Morley and Robins describe how the West distinguished itself from Japanese technological modernity through a discourse of "techno-orientalism," which denigrated the Japanese as overly mechanized and inhuman (168–73). They illuminate the discursive chain of associations that posits "if the future is technological, and if technology has become 'Japanised,'" then the syllogism would suggest that the future is now Japanese too" (168). Alternatively, Koichi Iwabuchi argues that Japan's immense global cultural impact has been largely through culturally "odorless" consumer technologies that do not necessarily bear associations of "Japaneseness" (27–28). As examples, Iwabuchi mentions "VCRs, computer games, karaoke machines, and the Walkman" (24). Furthermore, Paul du Gay et al., show how Sony as a company and the Walkman as a technology fluctuated between signifying Japan and the global (69–74, 77–80). These characterizations mark important tensions between national specificity and transnational abstraction and indicate how technology and its representations interact within a struggle for cultural power and identity across the Pacific Rim.

The Ring Intertext reworks this matrix of forces within its narrative and aesthetic strategies. These texts depict the "haunting" of imaging technologies, specifically dramatizing technospiritual threats to the human subject. This occurs within an apparent polarity between premodernity and (post)modernity. Just as importantly, this crisis raises questions about the relation of the individual subject to a transnational space of technological flows. Negotiating the split between technophilia and technophobia, the characters combat threats to their identities, between differential temporalities and from external domination, through the mastery over technology.

Early in the narrative of *Ringu*, the film associates imaging technology with terror and the erasure of identity. The female reporter Reiko discovers that, a week before their deaths, her niece and several of her classmates snuck away to a cabin. During her investigation, Reiko finds Polaroid photographs they took during their trip. In some photos the teenagers appear happy as they stand near the cabin. Yet other photographs depict the teens with their faces distorted, warped out of legibility. The Korean and Hollywood remakes of the film replicate this device, and it also recurs in one of the Japanese sequels, *Ringu 2*. Within the logic of the narrative, this warping occurs because the teenagers watched the videotape. As visualized in the photographs, the teens' identities were distorted by their experience with another imaging technology, the cursed videotape. Later, the protagonists, Rieko in *Ringu*, Sun-ju in *Ringu Virus*, and Rachel in *The Ring*, verify that they too have been cursed after watching the videotape by photographing themselves, and indeed these images depict their smeared faces. The characters become monstrous as a result of technology as seen through technology.

This effacement corresponds with another device in the films, the hair that covers the female ghost's face. Within each of the films, the ghost is rendered particularly creepy by the long, oily black hair that drapes over her face and obscures her features, making her unknown and perhaps unknowable. As both the photographic warping and the draping hair remove clear markers of individuality, these devices both raise anxieties about identity. Moreover, when contrasted with one another, these tropes mark a temporal divergence between premodernity and modernity. As a convention, long black hair covering the faces of female ghosts has a long history in East Asian visual culture. More recently, the ghost-story masterpiece *Kwaidan* (Masaki Kobayashi, 1964), among others, features this device prominently in one of its folkloric narratives. As the ghosts throughout *The Ring* Intertext feature this inky hair, they similarly evoke premodern East Asian culture.[3] This association is reinforced by the ghosts' originating from a distant rural area where cultural traditions presumably remain "untainted" by modern city life.

However, rather than immutably aligning *Ringu* and the others with "tradition," the past, and with Asia, saying that *The Ring* Intertext negotiates divergent historical temporalities and cultural spheres, which threaten stable conditions of identity, is more accurate. The films manifest this negotiation by conflating the videotape and the vengeful female ghost by haunting a modern technology with a terror of the past. Furthermore, as the Hollywood remake of *Ringu* faithfully retains the iconography of the dark-haired female ghost seen in *Ringu* and *Ring Virus*, the Hollywood film repositions this visual trope within the context of transnational culture. In *The Ring*, the girl who eventually becomes the antagonist was adopted by unsuspecting parents before she became a malevolent spirit. Where her adoptive parents got her remains a mystery, but the film insinuates that she came from some distant place, from "elsewhere." However, although *The Ring* maintains the sense of the ghost's distance from contemporary culture, the film disassociates the iconography of the dark-haired female ghost from premodernity and East Asia. Replicated across the Pacific Rim and between East and West, the ghost's lack of identity marks her transnational legibility. She becomes a transnational figure, a figure of transnationalism.

A scene from *Ringu 2* reinforces the connection between the hair and imaging technologies as threats to identity. As a male reporter reviews footage of an interview with a girl who died from the videotape curse, her head shakes back and forth. The videotape player slips out of the reporter's control and the girl's head shakes ever more violently on the screen. The girl's face disappears, covered by her black hair and obscured by the videographic blurring, combining premodern and postmodern visual conventions in one cinematic moment. As with the warped photographs, this scene suspends the identity of the individual through her relation to technology. This presents a picture of transnational identity inasmuch as it displaces, suspends, and abstracts the surface markings of identity while contending with diverse historical experiences with technological modernity.

The Ring Intertext also dramatizes media technologies penetrating the human psyche. *The Ring* explains that the killer videotape resulted from the ghost exercising her psychic will on the technology, a concept appearing previously in *Ringu 2*.[4] The film shows the child Samara as she is tested in a mental institution. Because she is known for having psychic abilities, doctors seek to record Samara's extrasensory talents, which appear as bizarre images on sheets of plastic film that resemble X-rays. The protagonist finds that the cursed tape was produced in the same way, as imprints made by the child's mind on the imaging technology. The *Ringu* novel presents the inverse of this situation. When the protagonist views the cursed videotape, the tape inserts itself directly into his mind. The novel describes the experience as "strange—something

Figure 9.2. *The Ring* (Gore Verbinski, 2002). Courtesy Dreamworks/The Kobal Collection/Morton, Merrick.

was stimulating his five senses, some medium besides the sounds and visions that appeared as if he were suddenly recalling them" (Suzuki, *Ring* 80). Earlier in the viewing, the male reporter watches "concepts in the abstract, etched vividly into his brain," as if no technology or medium were involved at all (77).

Such characterizations demonstrate a deep concern with the relation between technology and subjectivity. *The Ring* Intertext presents the possibility for psychic projection on technology, making it malleable to the will of the subject, a direct reflection of the subject. Yet, the texts also warn of technology overcoming the subject, erasing his or her subjective individuality. This corresponds with the ambivalent split between technophilia and technophobia because it proposes that human and machine might interact in some transcendent fashion, yet one that threatens to erase the human entirely.

Situated firmly within the horror genre, *The Ring* Intertext tends toward technophobia. The association of technology with terror reaches its peak when the cursed tape kills the protagonists' male companion, the Ryuji Takayama—Choi Yeol—Noah Clay character. In the *Ringu* novel, Takayama dies as a result of terrible hallucinations in a mirror (Suzuki 264–65). In all the film versions, however, the television flickers to life on its own and gains the man's attention. The screen shows the top of the well where the psychic girl died, and shockingly, the video shows her crawling from this rim. She walks with uncanny jerks and twitches toward the screen; in fact, in *Ring Virus* and *The Ring* her movements align with the videographic technology, as flickers on the tape displace her closer to the screen's edge. When she reaches the lip of the screen she crawls into the "real world." Inexplicably, she kills the man with her sheer frightfulness. The girl is made present from the past, making the past present; she is ghostly and yet manifested through technology into the space of reality. Unable to reconcile the apparent contradictions of this figure, the man dies in a state of horror.

However, *The Ring* Intertext intersperses technophobia with technophilia, and the horror of these films is countered by the protagonists' positive engagement with technology. Paul Young notes that the reporter Rachel regularly and productively uses the Internet during her investigation throughout *The Ring* (229). Likewise, as part of her examination of the cursed video, Rachel and her ex-husband Noah review it in a professional video editing booth. As Rachel looks over the tape frame-by-frame with Noah's assistance, the camera languishes over the machine's many knobs and buttons. Noah demonstrates his technical mastery as he adjusts the controls and glides over the images, through them, and rests on them. Ultimately, his technological savvy allows the characters to ponder the meaning of the video's content. Nevertheless, he succumbs to the curse of the videotape at the end of the film whereas Rachel does not; she manages to survive through the technological tricks Noah taught her. Earlier, the characters believed they would escape the curse by recovering the girl's bones from the well in which she died. However, this laying to rest does not assuage the evil in the girl's soul and her perpetual wrath kills the man. Rachel escapes this fate through her use of technology; she survives because she made a copy of the tape and showed it to Noah. Moreover, at the end of the film she makes yet another copy to proliferate in order to save her son who had also viewed the tape. In this regard, technology provides the resolution to the film's central crisis about technology. Here, *The Ring* Intertext depicts a certain technophilia that counters the pervasive representations of technophobia. Fundamentally important is that the technological solution that the films offer facilitates the mechanical reproduction of a text.

Signs of Empire? Discursive Proliferation and Constraint across *The Ring* Intertext

The cinematic remake constitutes a split subject. Jennifer Forrest describes how, at the beginnings of cinema, a conflation of two types of filmic repetition existed, the dupe and the remake, a conflation of *mechanical* and *textual* repetition (92–93). The two types were not legally distinguished until 1905, and both were derided at the time as forms of economic and/or artistic theft (Forrest 93, 99–100). The integration of film into the US copyright apparatus made the remake possible because laws eventually associated film narratives with copyrighted, written sources (110). This troubled origin reveals the close relation between cinematic remaking and film distribution as related but distinct forms of filmic repetition and dissemination. This also indicates how the remake functions textually and intertextually; torn from its basis in a technology of mechanical reproduction, the cinematic remake exists as a mode of *textual* reproduction.

Issues of textual repetition and dissemination resonate with great intensity across the Pacific Rim, as a polarity between logophilia and logophobia shapes the discursive interactions across the region. These tensions manifest themselves overtly in negotiations around textual commensurability and incommensurability, a division that consistently threatens to reinforce oppositions between East and West and hierarchies of cultural power. In fact, this inflects the very definition of logophobia, as Foucault states: "there is undoubtedly in *our society*, and I would not be surprised to see it in *others*, though taking different forms and modes, a profound logophobia" (228–29; emphasis added). Foucault invokes the notion that discursive patterns and tendencies find a limit at civilizational boundaries. Indeed, these boundaries might help to define one another. Situated in this way, the lingual/civilizational other poses one of the greatest agitators of logophobia, as it arises from the potential meaninglessness of discourse, the "violent, discontinuous, querulous, disordered even and perilous in [discourse]" (229).

Roland Barthes provides a pronounced example of this issue in *Empire of Signs*, stating, "The dream: to know a foreign (alien) language and yet not to understand it: to perceive the difference in it without that difference ever being recuperated by the superficial sociality of discourse, communication or vulgarity; to know, positively refracted in a new language, the impossibilities of our own . . . in a word, to descend into the untranslatable" (6). Japan serves as the basis of this fantasy, but, as Barthes readily admits, he apprehends Japan not in reality but rather as "an unheard-of symbolic system, one altogether detached from our own" (3). This epitomizes a semiotic Orientalism inasmuch as the totalized difference of the discursive other provides a better understanding of the native language. Analogously, Noël Burch draws upon Barthes's approach in his analysis of Japanese cinema (13–14). Deriving part of his argument from characteristics of the Japanese language, Burch argues that the narrative and aesthetic tendencies of Japanese cinema purpose-fully deconstruct those of Western cinemas (37, 89). For both Barthes and Burch, Japan constitutes a coherent discursive entity, the alterity of which underpins their respective clarifications of discourse in general. In these cases, the division between logophobia and logophilia corresponds with the delimitation of discursive/cultural boundaries; the logophobic fear of meaninglessness, embodied in the discursive other, propels the logophilic drive for meaning and the greater resolution of discourse.

In creating such dualities, Barthes and Burch engage in what Naoki Sakai calls a "schema of cofiguration" (34–35, 50–59). As a tendency of translation, cofiguration entails the clarification of one's native or familiar language in the process of learning another, foreign language (34–35, 51). Such a practice has the pitfall of constructing or augmenting problematic alignments between language and nation as well as language and ethnici-ty, an issue that troubles constructions of "Japan" in particular (16, 43–44, 60–61). As a corrective, Sakai argues that understanding translation as a heterolingual mode of address undermines constructions of supposedly homogenous lingual, ethnic, and national communities (3–10). Hetero-lingual address "assumes that every utterance can fail to communicate because heterogeneity is inherent in any medium, linguistic or otherwise" (8). Thus Sakai maintains a productive tension between logophobia and logophilia, yet in such a way that it transcends boundaries between lan-guages and cultural groups. This intervention is particularly important to understanding *The Ring* Intertext, as it fluctuates between logophobia and logophilia and obscures divisions between East and West as well as among Japanese cinema, South Korean cinema, and Hollywood.

The narratives within *The Ring* Intertext dramatize this vacilla-tion between logophobia and logophilia. The *Ringu* novel emphasizes the textuality of the cursed tape by characterizing its content as a form of writing. It describes "a frayed bundle of lights, crawling around like worms, which finally formed themselves into words. Not the kind of captions one normally saw on film, though. These were poorly written, as if scrawled by a white brush on jet-black paper" (Suzuki 76). This description evokes an experimental film that has been hand-painted with India ink. More important, it situates the tape as a legible text, yet one emerging from an undifferentiated mass of illegible nonsigns.

In the films, the videotape serves as the visual enigma that the narrative works to resolve. In *Ringu*, the images on the tape defy imme-diate comprehensibility; characters float across the screen and spell out "eruption," a woman combs her hair in a mirror, and the top of a well stands isolated among trees. These images bear no explicit meaning and no logic clearly connects them. Nevertheless, in this film, as in *Ring Virus* and *The Ring*, the protagonist deciphers the meaning of the images in order to trace the tape to its source. Reiko and her ex-husband research newspapers to find that the woman in the mirror died by throwing herself into a volcano. They trace her to an island where they uncover the woman's personal history (she had a child who was later killed and thrown into a well). The images on the tape thus connect directly with historical reality and in deciphering the tape's code the characters draw these connections.

In *The Ring*, the tape similarly recodifies and represents reality through operations of condensation and displacement. The tape depicts disparate images of situations that the characters cannot interpret yet which they encounter later in reality. For instance, it shows a high-contrast black-and-white image of a ladder leaning against a white wall. Later, Rachel and Noah's investigation leads them to a farmhouse on an island. They find that the girl Samara was held in a loft in the roof of a barn and that an extremely tall ladder provides the only means of accessing this bizarre prison. As they climb, the images of *The Ring* clearly reference the image from the cursed videotape.

As seen in these cases, *The Ring* Intertext dramatizes acts of interpretation. The characters' movement through the narratives requires their making sense of visual texts. They learn the meanings behind images; they learn to read them. Initially, these texts appear as nonsensical nonsigns and raise the specter of logophobia. This drives the characters' logophilic search for meaning, and thus *The Ring* Intertext vacillates between these poles to propel the movement of its narratives. Just as important, when considered intertextually, these narratives also resonate with Sakai's notion of heterolingual translation. As transcultural remakes, *Ring Virus* and *The Ring* function as literal and figurative acts of translation. The production of these films demanded the literal translation of *Ringu*'s script and dialogue. Furthermore, Constantine Verevis argues that the process of repetition and transformation that occurs in cinematic remaking resembles that of translation (82–84). In this light, the alterations that the South Korean and Hollywood films made to *Ringu*'s narrative can also be viewed as translations. Notably, the trope of the cursed videotape occurs within each of these films and spans across them. Each of the films translate differing visions of the potentially meaningless and untranslatable, and in this respect *The Ring* Intertext offers dramatizations of heterolingual address across linguistic, national, and cultural zones. These dramatic renderings of logophobia and logophilia efface rather than reinforce these traditional boundaries, realigning a transnational cultural formation across the Pacific Rim.

Yet in addition to dramatizing acts of interpretation, *The Ring* Intertext also illustrates tensions regarding discursive control and containment. Through the trope of the cursed videotape, the narratives map logophilia and logophobia onto divisions between local and global, domestic and exotic. In the *Ringu* novel, the protagonist finds the cursed videotape in the lobby of a resort, on a shelf alongside numerous other videos. All the titles mentioned are Hollywood films, including *Raiders of the Lost Ark* (Steven Spielberg, 1981), *Star Wars* (George Lucas, 1977), *Back to the Future* (Robert Zemeckis, 1985), and *Friday the 13th* (Sean S. Cunningham, 1980; Suzuki 64–65). Here, the nonlabeled cursed tape becomes associated with foreign or global media. Similarly, as noted earlier, the films associate the tape with a geographic "elsewhere." Yet *Ringu*, *Ring Virus*, and *The Ring* more strikingly associate the foreign with logophobia by dramatizing the vulnerability of the domestic sphere, when, in all three films, the reporter's child views the cursed tape. *Ringu*, for example, depicts Reiko woken from her sleep by a vision of her dead niece. The room is dark with shadows that play across the paper walls. After the vision dissipates, Reiko rushes from her room to check on her son. She shrieks in horror when she finds him bathed in the blue light of the television, watching the last frames of the cursed video. She gathers him in her arms and covers his eyes, but she is too late. He viewed the tape and now bears the curse. *Ring Virus* and *The Ring* depict similar scenes, and in this manner all three films add intensity to their narratives.

As they dramatize a parent's efforts to protect a child from dangerous images, a domestic logophobia pervades all three films. The potential meaninglessness of the tape, making it a site of heterolingualism across the films, simultaneously takes on strong associations with the nondomestic and the exotic. The tape is not entirely meaningless, then, but rather represents the danger of uncontrolled foreign images entering and endangering the home. In this respect, *The Ring* Intertext presents a complex structure of logophobia; it demonstrates radical discursive heterogeneity within and across cultural formations and yet also maintains an abstract division between home and away. This makes the logophilic drive of the narratives an attempt to reconcile these zones, and indeed the protagonists journey far and wide as they search for answers. In their effort to delimit the force of the cursed tape and resolve its enigmas, the characters interconnect the domestic and the distant, making the exotic conform to the meanings of the local.

The polarity between logophilia and logophobia not only shapes *The Ring* Intertext and its transnational flow, but also strikingly characterizes the surrounding discursive and political-economic context. For instance,

Ring Virus indicates remarkable patterns of discourse between Japan and South Korea. Traditionally, these relations have been fraught by the history of Japanese imperialism on the Korean peninsula. As Michael Robinson notes, Japan's colonial project prompted the restriction of all forms of Korean culture, including bans on the Korean language (19–21; see Cumings 141). Conversely, South Korea prohibited the distribution or exhibition of Japanese cultural products following the Japanese defeat in World War II. Both these cases demonstrate the institutional deployment of logophobia with aims of national and cultural autonomy.

This changed in the late 1990s, and *Ring Virus* stands centrally within this transnational discursive shift. In 1998, South Korea began incorporating Japanese films into its market and Japanese capital into its domestic media industry (Chung and Diffrient 208 n. 5; Paquet "Japanese Films in Korea"). This process proceeded in stages from 1998 until 2004 and eventually South Korea eliminated the ban on Japanese cultural products. This coincided with *Ringu*'s overwhelming success in Japanese theaters. However, in 1998 institutional barriers remained that curtailed the direct distribution of *Ringu* in South Korea. Thus *Ringu* could only legitimately enter the country as a remake, and indeed, *Ring Virus* appeared a year after *Ringu* and succeeded in the South Korean domestic market ("1999"). Yet the production of *Ring Virus* reveals an even more complex picture of cultural migration. The Japanese company Omega Project, one of the firms that produced *Ringu*, cofinanced the film's production along with AFDF Korea and Hanmac films, making *Ring Virus* an international coproduction at the level of financing (Ichise; Paquet, email to author). However, the South Korean producers never paid for the remake rights for the film, making the film an *illegal* international coproduction (Ichise). In these ways, *Ring Virus* articulates changing conditions in Japanese–South Korean interactions. The film creates a cultural and discursive bridge between the nations and yet simultaneously demonstrates the lingering constraints on discursive exchange; it originates from a tension between logophilia and logophobia that conforms partially to national boundaries and yet also transforms and transcends them.

The Hollywood remake demonstrates a realignment of discursive flows that threatens to reinforce certain cultural boundaries and relations of power. The imbalanced trade in distribution rights versus remake rights makes this most apparent. Following the domestic success of *Ringu* in 1998, DreamWorks bought the film's remake rights in 2001 (Brodesser and Lyons). Notably, DreamWorks paid $1.3 million for these rights, which actually exceeded *Ringu*'s production budget of $1.2 million ("Project: *The Ring*"). This provided a valuable revenue stream for the Japanese producers, which is particularly important given the extreme difficulty "foreign" films have entering the US market. However, this contrasts dramatically with *The Ring*'s production budget of $48 million ("Project: *The Ring*"), and the film's eventual global earnings of $249 million (Brodesser). The Hollywood film quickly exceeded the earnings of *Ringu* in Japan (Xu; Friend). Furthermore, when DreamWorks bought the remake rights to *Ringu*, it also purchased its distribution rights for the US theatrical and video markets, as part of its deal for *all* worldwide rights (Brodesser and Lyons). Rather than releasing *Ringu* in theaters or on video, however, DreamWorks withheld the film while they produced their remake (Lee).[5] This exclusion caused some popular consternation; on the release of *The Ring*, American audiences who attempted to view *Ringu* were upset to find it unavailable in any format (Arnold). *Ringu* eventually reached the US market when DreamWorks simultaneously released *The Ring* and *Ringu* on video in early 2003 (Sporich; "Corrections").

This interaction articulates the asymmetrical relations of cultural power across the region. The remaking of *Ringu* as *The Ring* engendered a new pattern of discourse through the subsequent proliferation of Hollywood remakes of East Asian films. The exact expression of this transnational exchange accords with the economic imbalance among the players; Hollywood's economic superiority allows it to pay for remake rights in sums that exceed the budgets of Japanese film producers so extremely that they benefit from the influx of money. Gang Gary Xu signals the spatial component of this extreme disparity of power when he calls this phenomenon "Hollywood's way of outsourcing."

Furthermore, the case of *The Ring* demonstrates a transnationally imbalanced deployment of logophilia and logophobia, which maintains and augments these asymmetries of power. In some sense the transnational film remake is always overdetermined by its conflated articulation of logophilia and logophobia, as it disseminates through revision. *The Ring* makes this more conspicuous, however, by revealing the relative impenetrability of the US media market to non-Hollywood films as well as Hollywood's transnational mobility. This represents a severe trade imbalance in cultural goods and demonstrates how Hollywood strategically navigates national and transnational cultural arenas. Hollywood's selective association with the United States quite literally renders non-Hollywood films "foreign" within the US media market and thereby exerts a cultural logophobia along national lines. However, as it simultaneously dominates many media markets around the globe, Hollywood attempts to render its own films transnationally legible; in effect, Hollywood inscribes a transnational logophilia everywhere it can except the United States. Thus, the transnational operation of logophilia and logophobia in the political

economy of *The Ring* Intertext diverges from the heterolingualism found
in its narrative and aesthetic strategies, marking an important point of
contradiction between text and context.

Ø: Transnational Technologorrhea

Yet *The Ring* is not a circle but rather forms a spiral, tracing expansive
lines that move ever-outward. The similar narrative resolutions of *Ringu*,
Ring Virus, and *The Ring* insinuate the perpetual dissemination of the
cursed videotape. To curtail its effects, it must be duplicated and viewed
by others.[6] Here, the productive tension between logophilia and logophobia becomes overly productive, ceaselessly so, creating an endless flow of
discourse, a *logorrhea*. Yet this process is only possible through the powers
of duplication inherent in the VCR. In this respect, the films dramatize
tendencies particular to the media technology, suggesting the indivisibil-
ity of discourse and technology under the category of "communications
technologies." Thus *The Ring* Intertext presents a pattern of simulta-
neous, synergistic, and ceaseless proliferation of discourse—through a
technology of discourse—a *technologorrhea*.

In their depictions of continual yet constrained proliferations of
discourse, these films appear to give allegorical expression to their own
material conditions. The logophobia of the protagonists, who try to contain the spread of the cursed video only to later aid in its duplication
and distribution, matches that of DreamWorks, who halted the spread
of *Ringu* into the United States but later disseminated this text as *The
Ring*. Yet this equation has limited allegorical value. *The Ring* Intertext
depicts the spread of cursed images through *mechanical* reproduction,
not through a kind of textual repetition and revision comparable to cinematic remaking. Rather, the films evoke tensions around the remake's
disavowed "other," the dupe, the copy. The films thus recall Forrest's
elucidation of the close relation between cinematic remaking and film
distribution, categories distinguished as much by law as by their different
modes of repetition. In this regard, the films do connect to their objective
circumstances because DreamWorks coordinated their power over film
distribution with their remaking of *Ringu*, deftly navigating and exploiting conventional divisions between mechanical and textual reproduction
across a vast transnational space.

Yet the technologorrhea depicted in the films contrasts markedly
with this corporate consolidation of rights. They depict furtive, unsanc-
tioned, even illicit acts of dubbing and circulation, tainted by generic
trappings of horror. An underground, dangerous circuit of media distribution, this is a nightmare of media piracy. Shujen Wang, for one,

examines piracy in East Asia as the criminalized counterpart to legitimate media distribution. Facilitated and sustained by communications technologies such as VCRs, VCDs, DVDs, and personal computers, piracy networks disseminate media with speed and efficiency that largely circumvents, outperforms, and subverts Hollywood and other legitimate distributors (2). Wang suggests that piracy poses a resistance to legitimate distribution, a counterdistribution (187–88, 191); it constitutes a form of counterpower within the overall dynamic of technologorrhea. Viewed from this vantage, the allegory of piracy seen in *The Ring* Intertext duplicitously inverts the films' objective material conditions. A hegemonic expression of resistance, *The Ring* Intertext in fact opposes piracy; the transnational remake as counterpiracy.

The synergistic forces of media discourses and technologies propel these struggles for power according to a complex transnational geography, revealing a broader pattern of technologorrhea. Thus the Hollywood studios attempted to thwart Sony and Matsushita, themselves competitors, from distributing VCRs in the US market (Wasko, *Hollywood* 126–130; Wasser 83–85, 88–91). Yet as Harold Vogel notes, home video quickly became Hollywood's single largest source of revenue (103). Likewise, we have seen numerous interpenetrations among media technology manufacturers and cultural producers across the Pacific: Sony bought Columbia Pictures in 1989 in "the largest-ever Japanese takeover of a US company" (Castro et al. 70); Matsushita acquired MCA in 1990, only to resell it in 1995 (Pollack); South Korean *chaebol* Cheil Jedang invested $300 million in DreamWorks ("DreamWorks East"). Yet the same logic of mutual/perpetual technological dissemination drives global media piracy: Sony and Matsushita introduced and continue to distribute VCD players throughout Asia, helping to sustain an interdependent market for VCD manufacturers and media pirates in the region (Wang 50–51, 54–57). Here, technologorrhea drives a dynamic interaction between domination and resistance across the Pacific.

The Ring Intertext is remarkable for its complex relation with these forces. Comprised not only of a constellation of texts but also their industrial and cultural connections, it navigates disparate temporalities, spaces, and identities in a distinctly transnational formation. The films reveal tensions about technology and discourse, each of which fracture into technophilia and technophobia, logophilia and logophobia. These divisions occur throughout the films' narratives and aesthetic strategies and resonate with greater cultural struggles among Japan, South Korea, and the United States. Yet, these forces do not operate in a system of static binaries, but rather dialectically, producing new forms and conditions in a continual process of struggle and change. As a powerful component of globalization, communications technologies help to transform radically existing relations of geography, representation, and imagination, and *The Ring* Intertext is firmly enmeshed in this process. Seen in combination, in relation, and in their circulations, the films of *The Ring* Intertext draw lines of connection across apparent cultural divides and reveal the heterogeneous forces that pull these lines in a struggle for cultural power.

Notes

1. In this chapter, I refer to the English translation of the novel.

2. The following films have either been remade or are in some stage of production: *Addicted* (2003), *Antarctica* (1983), *Hi Dharma* (2001), *Infernal Affairs* (2002), *Ju-on* (2003), *My Sassy Girl* (2001), *One Missed Call* (2003), *Pulse* (2001), *Shall We Dance* (1996), and *A Tale of Two Sisters* (2003).

3. *Ringu* appears to have given new life to this convention, as it strikingly occurs in *A Tale of Two Sisters* and *Ju-on*.

4. In the novel, the curse is caused by a virus; the ghost literally infects a videotape, and this pseudoscientific ghostly/viral explanation also occurs in *Rasen* and is obliquely implicated in *Ring Virus*.

5. "Holdback provisions" are standard practice in deals for remaking films, which state that the original cannot enter a media market for a certain period before the release of its remake (Lee qtd. in Herbert 98).

6. In *Rasen* the curse of the videotape makes its way into a written account of the videotape's contents. The end of the film implies that this written description will be published and curse all the customers who buy and read this "novelization." *Cure* (1997), a film soon to be remade by Hollywood, also features a similarly generative conclusion. The film tracks a serial killer who compels others to murder by mesmerizing them through speech. At the end of the film, the investigating detective appears to have caught the antagonist's "condition," and he proceeds to compel other people to kill, continuing the cycle of murderous discourse.

10

Simon McEnteggart

Sequelizing the Superhero

Postmillennial Anxiety and Cultural "Need"

T HE RECENT RESURGENCE IN contemporary US cinema of the superhero film has indeed been prolific, featuring an extremely broad
range of heroic characters that not only battle "evil" but have
also been subjected to various spin-offs and sequels. Discussing the
notion of sequelization and its relation to the superhero is a particularly interesting prospect because the superhero is, essentially, a fantastical extension of the Western frontier hero. With the interplay of
the outsider-redeemer figure combined with themes of extralegal violence and the community under siege, the Westerner-come-superhero
thus embodies features of American cultural and religious heritage. Such
themes originated in the founding of the United States itself and are,
therefore, acutely ideologically and culturally specific. Indeed, "whereas
the classical monomyth seemed to reflect rites of initiation, the American
monomyth derives from tales of redemption" (Lawrence and Jewett 6).
As such, superhero narratives are concerned with the perpetuation of
American frontier cultural rhetoric, engaging in ideologically motivated
adventures to "tame" civilization with morality tales in conjunction with
righteous powers. Employed in this fashion, the appearance (and recur-
rence) of superhero films during periods of sociocultural destabilization

Figure 10.1. *Superman Returns* (Bryan Singer, 2006). Courtesy Warner Bros/
D.C. Comics/The Kobal Collection.

and unrest fulfill what can only be described as a cultural "need." Using
superhero films in this way assuages anxieties of identity and reassembles
cultural traditions and values that are seemingly under threat from external forces. Through the repetition sequelization induced, such fears are
continually allayed to indoctrinate a sense of sociocultural "calm" and
stability through patriotic confidence. The superhero sequel, therefore,
operates in several ideologically interwoven realms including identity,
repetition, memory, nostalgia, and cultural/religious frameworks that
function as an ideological support system, albeit an "ideological mystifi-
cation" allegorized in a fantastical context (Žižek 28).

This chapter explores, as Paul Budra and Betty A. Schellenberg
describe it: "the repetition-with-variation" (Introduction 17) within the
postmillennial superhero sequel, with particular reference to the Blade,
Spider-Man, Superman, and X-Men films. The saturation of superhero
narratives and sequels at the box office is unprecedented, encapsulating a
variety of ideologically motivated discourses in response to events involving and surrounding the millennium itself. Such discourses are inherent
within the postmodernist cultural conventions that permeate the narratives, and additionally highlight the ideological reassembly in the wake

of the attacks on the Twin Towers and the subsequent sociocultural upheaval that followed. The cinematic endeavors of the superhero sequel are ultimately constructed to incorporate and re-present such historical trauma, yet this postmodern philosophy is not without complexity.

Re-Presenting Historical Trauma

As Andreas Huyssen has acutely noted, "the past has become part of the present in ways simply unimaginable in earlier centuries. As a result, temporal boundaries have weakened" (1). This is particularly relevant with regard to the superhero on film because the figure functions as a form of "semipalimpsest" due to the adaptation process from page to screen. The origin of each superhero reflects a dimension of the socio-cultural destabilization of the era of inception (Wright 24), and because this is core to characterization cannot be compromised without rewriting the philosophies intrinsic to the hero. Yet while such previous historical anxieties are addressed through this function, the cinematic superhero must be continually adapted and modified to incorporate and exhibit reflections from the ever-evolving American cultural climate. Issues of memory and nostalgia are therefore immediately present, and indeed re-presented, within the challenges each respective hero must face and defeat, with victory further reinforced through the continual repetition of sequelization.

The X-Men trilogy—*X-Men* (Bryan Singer, 2000), *X-Men 2* (Bryan Singer, 2003), and *X-Men 3: The Last Stand* (Brett Ratner, 2006)—repeatedly re-presents such temporal transitions. The X-Men films collapse a variety of historical trauma within the narrative structures, which use notions of memory and nostalgia to engage with and represent cultural persecution in myriad forms. While the comic books themselves were produced during the civil rights era, with the philosophical dichotomy between Martin Luther King Jr. and Malcolm X allegorized through Professor Charles Xavier and Magneto, the sequels also continually reinforce the holocaust. The experiences of Magneto as a young Jewish boy re-present the horrific trauma of the concentration camp, and as an adult reference is repeatedly focused on his "brand" or tattoo that he received while imprisoned (Trushell). The historical trauma of both the holocaust and the civil rights movement are thus temporally amalgamated and reinforced throughout the X-Men sequels, serving to ideologically align the "otherness" enforced on mutants as akin to the trauma of prior atrocities. Through this alignment, the disgust and outrage at the ignorance of such areas of international history are channeled into the mutant discourses, thus enforcing a more penetrative resonance among spectators. Anti-Semitism and racism debates are therefore extended into the antimutant hysteria within the sequels, using memory simultaneously to broaden and deepen empathy with the plight—and potential future—of those with mutation.

Additionally, such usage casts Magneto not in a simplified context of "evil" but as a misguided antihero of sorts. The awareness of his horrific experiences, emphasized through re-presentation and the repetition of sequelization, contend that his intent and motivations are virtuous, but undermined through extremism. Similar to Malcolm X, Magneto rejects the peaceful coexistence Professor Xavier sought after for more proactive and extremist methods that ultimately result in a re-enactment of his fascist past. Indeed, Magneto is seemingly unaware that his trauma has fashioned him into a dictator figure, most starkly represented through his costume that employs motifs from Hitler and the Nazi military. In a more contemporary context, Magneto's threatening televisual broadcasts and incitement for mutant violence also displays connotations of Osama bin Laden and Al-Qaeda. His vehement belief and extremist actions in his goal for supremacy contribute to such a reading, and as a more recent re-presentation of historical trauma, invite outrage. Historical trauma is central to Magneto, with his victimization during the holocaust intrinsic to his morality. However, such trauma is countered by alternative memory politics exemplifying fascism and extremism that position him as a simultaneously misguided and ruthless villain.

Through the distinctly postmodern amalgamation of temporal space and memory politics, "the reflexive past of representation" informs cultural and ideological meanings ascribed within the superhero sequel (Deleuze, *Difference* 71). As such, the sequels employ a wealth of historical connotations that fundamentally permeate the narrative in order to address the ideological destabilization of the moment. With the postmillennial superhero sequel, the reassembly of national identity has been invoked by anxieties including the millennium itself, the events of 9/11 and the concept of terrorism. With both *X-Men* and *Blade* (Stephen Norrington, 1998), the confrontations that occur are internal conflicts between the heroes and villains that transpire within the United States. Yet the subsequent sequels, *X-Men 2* and *Blade II* (Guillermo del Toro, 2002), produced after 9/11, reveal an external ideological threat that forces both factions to set aside their differences to engage with a greater menace, a narrative trait emblematic of the cultural rhetoric following the attack on the Twin Towers. However, the superhero sequel does not merely reflect such contemporary (and seemingly controversial) cultural discourses, it actively engages with them: re-presenting motifs based on 9/11 itself with the superhero—the embodiment of traditional American cultural values—attempting to save the populace from an event that has already transpired. As Pam Cook argues, "rather than being seen as a reactionary, regressive condition imbued with sentimentality, it can be perceived as a way of coming to terms with the past. . . . In other words, while not necessarily progressive in itself, nostalgia can form part of a transition to progress and modernity" (4).

Superman Returns (Bryan Singer, 2006) incorporates nostalgia throughout the respective narrative, in particular through allegorized forms of 9/11, to achieve such a transition. In *Superman Returns*, during an inaugural flight mission that propels a space shuttle to launch via a plane, an accident occurs causing the craft to spiral out of control, falling toward an explosive finale on US soil. While no public monument resembling the Twin Towers as such exists, the plane is on a collision course with a baseball stadium, a venue associated with a beloved area of American cultural heritage. While a direct re-presentation of an aircraft colliding with a culturally iconic building (something like the Twin Towers) would have been an extremely controversial scenario (one viewed in poor taste), the postmillennial superhero sequel deftly avoids this through its selection and allegorical rendering of the target. *Superman Returns* can, therefore, incorporate the plane-as-missile circumstances of 9/11 yet allegorize the cultural importance of the target.

While "the death's head, that elusive sign of allegorical history" of 9/11 is re-presented in the postmillennial superhero sequel, the significant departure from historical fact, and subsequently memory of the event, is derived through the intervention of the superhero figure (Lowenstein 76). As the superhero functions as representative of traditional American religious and cultural values, his or her presence within the narrative informs the reassembly of national identity following 9/11. Thus when Superman halts the plane from colliding, anxiety is assuaged and identity restored, even if this restoration is illusory. The repetition of superheroic intervention, induced through sequelization, additionally contributes to such ideological reformation by repeatedly allaying distress and anguish. The re-presentation of the historical trauma of 9/11 uses memory of the event to heighten the intensity of the cinematic interpretation; yet with the intervention of the outsider-redeemer superhero, history is cinematically rewritten to allay the post-traumatic symptoms of the US populace. The postmillennial superhero sequel is ideologically concerned with reestablishing American national identity by allegorically re-presenting the historical trauma of 9/11 and adapting events that allow the superhero (and American cultural values) to triumph. Cultural victory is continually reaffirmed and perpetuated through the repetition of the patriotic images contained within each superhero film and each sequel.

The re-presentation of historical reality is an extremely postmodern dialectic, what Jean Baudrillard critically refers to as "substituting signs of the real for the real itself; that is, an operation to deter every real process by its operational double . . . which provides all the signs of the real and short-circuits all its vicissitudes" (*Simulacra* 4). In the symbolic re-presentation of historical trauma, the intentions of the superhero sequel are cultural compensation; just as *Rambo: First Blood Part II* (George P. Cosmatos, 1985) re-presented "victory" in the Vietnam War and *Rocky IV* (Sylvester Stallone, 1985) re-presented the cold war "triumph" allegorized in a boxing match, the superhero sequel ultimately achieves similar ideological ends. Such "prosthetic memories" thus inform cultural rehabilitation during social upheaval (Cook 2). As Ian Gordon states, "by tying popular memory to marketable figures, nostalgia has become a way of owning the past" (192). Yet it is the primary function of such an ownership through the superhero sequel that national identity crises are addressed and catered for, therefore performing a pivotal role in the reconstruction of a cinematic ideological consensus.

The postmillennial superhero sequel contributes to the reassembly of ideological stability not only through explicit 9/11 allegories, but also by using alternative representations of cultural conflict. In *Blade Trinity* (David S. Goyer, 2004), for example, the mythology surrounding Dracula is dramatically altered. The traditional history of the character Bram Stoker established is jettisoned, replacing Dracula's aristocratic European origins in Transylvania with warlord status and deity worship in the Middle East. Dracula's pyramid-like tomb is also located in Syria (with additional direct reference to Iraq), and Dracula is much more violent and bloodthirsty than his nineteenth-century counterpart. He was "born perfect" as the ultimate embodiment of pure evil without any weaknesses. Such a mythological overhaul ultimately posits the region as the origin of all evil because it was there that Dracula emerged as the source of vampirism. Without him, there would be no vampires at all, and thus no enemies for Blade to fight. That Dracula was worshipped in the Middle East thousands of years earlier also denounces religious beliefs from that region because to worship Dracula is to worship death and war. While *Blade Trinity* does not directly allegorize the events of 9/11 itself, the reassembly of US national identity is conveyed through cultural dichotomy and oppositional discourses. In this regard, the history and culture of the Middle East is re-presented as barbaric, violent, and fascist, as opposed to the civilization, peace, and freedom the United States represents. Notably, the dichotomy also incorporates religion within this framework. Because the Middle East is aligned with such negative traits and because Dracula was previously revered as a deity, Islamic faith is also by extension subjected to the same negative connotations. As such, Islamic faith is represented in opposition to the positive discourses aligned with the United States, and in this context, in opposition to Christianity. Employing this divisive ideological device in this manner is, as Ziauddin Sardar and Merryl Wyn Davies attest, "an adversarial vision of the world described in sharply moralist terms with clear imperial meaning" (143). The battle between Blade and Dracula is not simply a conflict of hero and villain, therefore, but of various ideological binary discourses:

Middle East	America
Barbarism	Civilization
Fascism	Democracy
Islam	Christianity
Vampire	Human
Bloodthirsty violence	Righteous violence
Hedonism	Restraint
Evil	Good
Dracula	Blade
"Them"	"Us"

In representing ideological conflict in this fashion, *Blade Trinity* emphasizes American cultural values as undoubtedly righteous ones. Furthermore, these binary divisions ensure that Blade—one of the few African-American superheroes, and something of a blaxploitation antihero—automatically adopts a position always available to his Caucasian counterparts. This ensures the triumph of American cultural values and the stabilization of identity, even while (as argued later) maintaining racial and religious points of demarcation.

X-Men 3: The Last Stand also exhibits such ideological traits, yet the fundamental source on which the narrative is predicated—notions of "otherness" and the acceptance thereof—allows for an interesting deviation. Rather than pure ideological reformation, the narrative simultaneously reinforces and criticizes post–9/11 US cultural rhetoric. While the long-established opposition of freedom versus fascism is prevalent through the confrontations between the X-Men and the extremist Brotherhood, the premise of a "mutant cure" is introduced that allows conformity with regular humans. The procedure is a choice, however the bigotry toward those with the mutant gene, combined with the weaponization of the "cure," insinuate otherwise. Of particular note is that the manufacturing of the drug is also located at the detention center on the island of Alcatraz where the mutants are held captive. Thus, with the

Figure 10.2. *X-Men: The Last Stand* (Brett Ratner, 2006). Courtesy 20th
Century Fox/The Kobal Collection.

themes of detention and conformity on an island close to the US mainland, allegories of Guantánamo Bay, where the suspected Islamic mili-
tants that are detained and questioned—perhaps indefinitely—arise and
find metaphoric characterization in the mutant detainees. The mutant,
code-named Leech, whose ability suppresses the mutant gene and is the
source of the "cure," is detained within a white padded cell, which is
monitored and subjected to experimentation. The information derived
from Leech halts the progress of the extremist Brotherhood, and as such
Leech adopts the position of a political prisoner, much in the same way
an Islamic informant may influence contemporary conflict. Leech's status
as a political prisoner, and the weaponization of his information, incites
the mutant population into violence via the Brotherhood, or alternatively
to seek sanctuary (and integration) with the X-Men. This philosophical
division allegorizes the contemporary Islamic religious division, and as
the X-Men emerge victorious, so too does co-existence and US values.
Interestingly, however, only through the extremist actions of the Brotherhood is Leech freed from his detention and the very concept of the
"cure" revoked. Because the focus of the narrative is concerned with the
extremist oppression of freedom, the sequel foregrounds the restoration
of US identity and cultural values through such ideological instigation.

The postmillennial superhero sequel re-presents revised historical events amalgamated with traditional American value systems, attempting, through the repetition of cinematic devices and the perpetual cycle of sequelization itself, to allay the sociopolitical concerns of the populace post–9/11. Gilles Deleuze explains: "repetition is essentially inscribed in need, since need rests upon an instance which essentially involves repetition: which forms the for-itself of repetition and the for-itself of a certain duration" (*Difference* 77). As such, superhero sequels operate a cultural need to reestablish identity through the repetition of a revised memory and nostalgia until an equilibrium has been restored. However, the anxiety and social malaise exhibited in post–9/11 US culture is intrinsically tied with theories of apocalypse, notions that had already incited fear at the turn of the millennium, fears that the superhero sequel also attempts to allay.

Halting the (Religious) Apocalypse

As Huyssen acknowledges: "at stake in the current history/memory debate is not only a disturbance of our notions of the past, but a fundamental crisis in our imagination of alternative futures" (2). Such bleak, dystopian visions of the future were heightened at the turn of the millennium, exemplified by films such as *Strange Days* (Kathryn Bigelow, 1995), *End of Days* (Peter Hyams, 1999), and *The Matrix* (Andy and Larry Wachowski, 1999). The events of 9/11, and the subsequent trauma, intensified the impending sense of angst, instigating additional apocalyptic premonitions throughout much of Western popular culture. The apocalyptic future is an ideological and theological concern due to its biblical origins, arousing both social anxiety as well as religious fundamentalism. Lee Quinby argues, "Americans have been taught to reside in apocalyptic terror and count on millennial perfection. For a substantial number, this is an intense Bible-based fundamentalism. For a larger majority, these fears and hopes are more nebulous, a loose blend of religious symbols and secular expression. In the United States, this imprecise yet overpowering belief system is a way of life" (5).

Apocalyptic visions, and the Judeo-Christian theology intrinsic in its prevalence, are repeatedly represented within the postmillennial superhero sequel, a form of cinematic "biblical sequelization." Religious allegories amalgamated with cultural rhetoric are frequently used, and incorporated with the intervention of the outsider-redeemer, in the reassembly of national identity. Although many texts regarding the religious philosophy are inherent within the superhero narrative, the dystopic visualization represented by the millennial superhero sequel(s) highlights contemporary ideological and theological upheaval (see Garrett; Oropeza; Skelton).

Superman Returns initially represents the apocalypse in miniaturized form, as Lex Luthor verifies his intentions of dominating real estate. In a fully functioning model village, Luthor experiments with a fragment of kryptonian crystal to assess the implications and potential benefits. The results destroy the model "capitalist" and "natural" landscapes within the village, devastate the highly intricate transport systems, explode oil rigs, and cause the "death" of scores of the population. This apocalyptic premonition exhibits the religious and cultural angst fundamental throughout US history, due to the biblical connotations ascribed to the very land itself. The utopian idealism and Christian fervor that existed during the "founding" of the United States extended into the land as paradise, as a substitute Eden. As this religious ideology has perpetuated through time, notions of apocalypse are inherently tied to the destruction of the United States/Eden. "The obvious model for this monomythic Eden," Lawrence and Jewett attest, "is the Midwestern small town as seen through the lens of pastoralism" (23). Superman's hometown of Smallville, and model village decimated in the apocalyptic portent, exemplify the Edenic landscape under threat, which Luthor intensifies through kryptonian experimentation. The experiment is also responsible for the occurrence (and re-presentation) of 9/11 allegories, insinuating that the two events are not mutually exclusive but inherently tied. In doing so, the link between 9/11 and the apocalypse is made explicit, serving to heighten doomsday anxieties and increase the need for superheroic, and messianic, intervention.

When Luthor attempts to administer his scheme and the apocalypse achieves fruition, the sequel uses memory and nostalgia from the Bible and prior Superman films to reconstitute national identity and alleviate anxiety. As the dystopic land mass rises from the depths threatening the Edenic landscape of the United States, Superman intervenes and removes the hellish terrain through his explicit Christ-like allegories and his alignment with Judeo-Christian themes of enlightenment. Thus Superman, as the messianic embodiment of US cultural and religious heritage, simultaneously fulfils the role of averting the apocalypse and the prophesized Second Coming, displacing anxiety with religious and national faith. "In a paradoxical sort of way," argues Capps, "religion produces fears that result in the anxieties that religion then seeks either to eliminate or assuage" (141). As an allegory of Christ, Superman adheres to the voice of his omniscient father, ascends to the (metaphoric) heavens, and knowingly "sacrifices" himself—in crucifixion posture—for the sins of the planet in preventing Judgment Day. Although the apocalyptic fears represented through the model town achieve (limited) fruition, the re-presented repetition of biblical narratives, amalgamated with the intervention of the redemptive superpowers of Superman, serve to allay apocalyptic and theological angst.

Similarly, *Spider-Man* (Sam Raimi, 2002) and its sequels—*Spider-Man 2* and *Spider-Man 3* (Sam Raimi, 2004, 2007)—contain such ideological reinforcement. Christian allegories abound, such as the Green Goblin and Spider-Man reenact scenes from the Bible and quote scripture during confrontations (Richardson). The Green Goblin even interrupts Aunt May's prayers to posit himself explicitly as the epitome of religious evil. In the sequel, Spider-Man saves a train of civilians while in a crucifixion posture, and he is then lifted and carried above the heads of those he has saved, with a prominent injury in his side evoking the wound caused by the Holy Spear. The entire event re-presents the biblical narrative surrounding Christ's crucifixion, as Spider-Man sacrifices himself, due to the greed and wrath of his enemies, to save innocent civilians. With Spider-Man's capture by Venom and the Sandman in the third installment, Spider-Man is again forced into the crucifixion posture while his proposed "sins" are recounted. The only way in which the hero escapes an untimely demise is through the continual reference to biblical themes of forgiveness and his benevolent use toward his enemies. Thus when representations of an apocalyptic nature arise, Spider-Man's alignment with Judeo-Christian morality plays connotes religious righteousness as he vanquishes his nemeses. As with Superman, such righteousness is represented as inherently American through the continual presence of the US flag and the iconography of Spider-Man's costume, with the monomythic Eden present in his suburban origins. As such, when the climatic battle with the Green Goblin occurs in an extremely dystopic, hazardous landscape, the Goblin melds with the mise-en-scène seamlessly, cementing his satanic association. Spider-Man protrudes from the dystopian milieu, rejecting alignment, and is tormented both physically and psychologically until his virtuous retaliation defeats his foe, removing the apocalyptic premonition from its potential fulfillment. Similarly, Dr. Octopus, in his attempts to create sustainable fusion, forges a hellish apocalyptic sphere that threatens to engulf New York City by assimilating and vaporizing the Edenic landscape. Again, Spider-Man's intervention halts the apocalypse therefore restoring religious and national identity once more.

The sequelization process uses the repetition of memory and nostalgia to allay religious anxieties, re-presenting Christian iconography and narrative devices in conjunction with national identity. This simultaneously alleviates fears of apocalypse and enforces Christian fundamentalism as a superior, righteous ideology. However, the repetition evokes postmodernist concerns regarding the dissolution of the "real" as divinity is reproduced through icons (Baudrillard, *Simulacra* 8). In this context, replicating biblical narratives with superhuman agencies dilutes the meanings pertaining to Christianity while still fulfilling the cultural "need." While *Superman Returns* and the *Spider-Man* trilogy exemplify the reproduction of the "real" through abilities of the body, *Fantastic Four: Rise of the Silver Surfer* (Tim Story, 2007) takes an alternative approach. The Silver Surfer traverses space acting as a herald for the cosmic entity known as Galactus, a being that absorbs, or rather consumes, the life energies from planets. biblical parallels are clear, with Earth as Eden, Galactus as (an unmerciful) God, and the Surfer as "created" son. Indeed, the Silver Surfer functions as celestial divinity by halting the apocalypse, and seemingly sacrificing himself for the people of Earth, despite the greed, wrath, and envy Dr. Doom exhibits. What differentiates the Messianic Surfer from other superheroes is the derivation of his powers. Cosmic energies are channeled through his surfboard and, as such, the source of his celestial divinity lies within the relation between them. The surfboard operates much like the crucifix, in that the crucifix and its relation with Jesus Christ is fundamental to Christian theology, and it is arguably the image on which the faith continually bases itself. The "real" icon of Christian divinity is Christ's crucifixion, where the resonance and power of the relation between Jesus and the crucifix, and the sacrifice made, are focused. In a postmodern dialectic, the Surfer's relation with his surfboard, and the power derived from their union, allegorizes the icon of divinity into an existentialist form. In doing so, the halting of the apocalypse and the sacrifice of the superhero extend beyond that of the more physical heroes into an acutely postmodern, celestial, and existentialist conception.

This redemptive function is, however, not available to all. As an African-American hero, the character of Blade is limited in the extent to which Christian allegorical meanings are produced. Like Superman and Spider-Man, the titular hero in *Blade* is forced to adopt the crucifixion posture, but in this case he is drained of blood for his nemesis Deacon Frost to inaugurate a "vampire apocalypse." Blade returns from the brink of death by drinking the blood of his love interest in a highly sexualized—and Oedipal—sequence, reborn not through the righteousness attributed his white peers but through "perverse" fleshly desires. The animalistic context in which Blade's rebirth occurs, in conjunction with the antihero/blaxploitation themes permeating the narrative, reduces the connotations derived from the religious allegories. In doing so, Blade has limited access to divine meanings, and is instead associated with fleshly sins and barbarism, and as such is denied Messianic status. Indeed, the vampire apocalypse is only possible due to the very existence of Blade, who becomes indirectly responsible for the atrocity. Additionally, Blade uses his redemptive abilities in extreme violence against his enemies, resulting in a variety of explicit fatalities, a feature inadmissible for his white counterparts. *Blade II* incorporates similar biblical and apocalyptic narrative devices as Blade is again graphically crucified and drained of life. Yet his subsequent rebirth in a waterfall of blood simultaneously rejuvenates and baptizes him, allowing his violent eradication of vampires to continue. The Blade trilogy incorporates severely restricted biblical allegories, allowing Blade's redemptive abilities to fulfill the cultural "need" during postmillennial anxiety, yet concurrently reinforcing racial stereotypes. Therefore, while Blade immobilizes one apocalypse after another, he is categorized as an antihero and a "lesser" superhero than his white peers. Blade, as an African-American superhero, is never allowed into the spiritual and sacrificial realm of allegorical meaning pertaining to Christ's crucifixion, allegories his white counterparts readily embody; he is continually reborn in a barbaric, animalistic context that is predicated on sexual and bodily indulgences of the flesh, which he subsequently articulates into extreme, fatal violence against his oppressors. While the Blade sequels adhere to reconstituting national and religious identity by averting the apocalypse and vanquishing the enemy, the films also arguably inform another cultural function of reestablishing the dominant social (and racial) hierarchy.

Despite increasing secularization, such apocalyptic anxieties and re-presented biblical narratives are still prevalent in Western popular culture. John Shelton Lawrence and Robert Jewett acknowledge that: "the connection of these superhero materials with the American religious heritage illustrates the displacement of the story of redemption. Only in a culture preoccupied for centuries with the question of salvation is the appearance of redemption through superheroes comprehensible" (44). Therefore the anxieties, as well as their allayment, are attributed to the nostalgia of biblical texts that are re-presented throughout the postmillennial superhero sequels. They perform a cultural function in alleviating sociocultural and theological concerns, by representing apocalyptic premonitions and using the superhero to halt the impending doom. This collapsing of temporal space and cultural narratives reflects the dissolution of postmodern boundaries that additionally contributes to postmillennial social unrest. Various motifs, and consequently the meanings derived from them, are intertwined to re-present alternative ideological interpretations and resolutions in support of American cultural rhetoric. These cinematic devices within the superhero sequel extend beyond the re-presented sociocultural events that reside within the narrative and into the very modernist boundaries of life and death, and psychology.

"Don't you people ever die?!"
—X-Men

The postmodern destabilization of the postmillennial superhero's—and villain's—body and mind is indicative of cultural uncertainty and anxiety, as once-previous thresholds, considered absolutes, dissipate. The pre-millennial superhero films (and sequels) witnessed the death or perma-nent removal of the vast majority of villains preventing their appearance in future sequels, the only notable deviation being Lex Luthor within the Superman series. Paul Budra argues that "a specifically postmodern unease is generated, not by encroaching threats, but by the perception that the world is increasingly one in which borders have collapsed, in which preconceptions, hierarchies, absolutes, and perhaps reason itself are being abandoned" (191). While in this context the superhero film rather obviously involves superpowers, the postmodern use of the body and mind, and the erosion of traditional notions of life and death, reflects contemporary ideological unrest.

The villains in the Spider-Man sequels are extremely postmodern creations, becoming even more culturally iconic through their fluctua-tions between various, and previously regarded stable, realms. When Norman Osborn volunteers as the preliminary test subject in experi-mental procedures he becomes the Green Goblin but is completely unaware of his transformation. As well as his augmented musculature and reflexes, Norman also develops a form of dual personality. As such, this allows him to traverse both the professional (capitalist) realm and the personal (Goblin) realm at ease in consolidating power and maintain-ing his empire. In doing so, the Freudian boundary between the id and the ego has become permeable, allowing Norman to at times adhere to patriarchal law, and at others subvert it completely, all at the discretion of his unconscious. Yet Norman's complete unawareness of his dual person-ality disorder insinuates that, although a questionable husband and father figure, he is not so much the "villain," but helpless to his neurosis. Nor-man does eventually understand and conflate both arenas in his desire for self-aggrandizement, conversing maniacally with himself in a mirror as he schemes against Spider-Man. This representation of mental illness, with two distinct personalities within one mind, incorporates postmodern anxiety as the sheer unpredictability of Norman's mental illness inspires fear, suspicion, and paranoia. Indeed, in the final confrontation between the Green Goblin and Spider-Man, Norman attempts to reconcile by attempting to explain his circumstances, yet the distrust, combined with the continual erosion of the id/ego boundary, ends in death. The dissolution of modernist boundaries, and the anxieties caused, requires allayment in the superhero film, and as such the resolution can only be achieved through Norman's removal; a psychiatric unit could unwittingly release him to menace society once more, thus death appears the permanent solution. Norman's death itself is of particular interest because it functions as a suicide, commonly associated with the mentally ill while also regarded by Christianity as a sin. What constructs the Green Goblin as distinctly villainous is not so much his physical empowerment, but a mental illness that has become increasingly renowned in contemporary popular culture, one that has the ability to afflict any individual and as such instigates social unrest.

This postmodern polemic continues in *Spider-Man 2* as Norman's son Harry, so embittered with a hatred for Spider-Man, actually witnesses and converses with his deceased father. Believing Spider-Man murdered Norman, and following the shock of revelation that his supposed enemy's true identity is his best friend, Peter Parker, Harry's mind succumbs to the same illness that ensnared his father. Harry's dual personality takes the form of Norman rather than an idealized maniacal version of himself; this simultaneously resumes the anxieties involving mental illness and emotional trauma, and additionally reveals that Norman can never truly "die" because he is incapable of death. Norman's physical body may be destroyed, but as a psychological condition he can live forever, and as such his villainous machinations will continue. As Harry also dons the mantle of the Goblin in *Spider-Man 3*, the sequelized repetition of dual personality mental disorder reinforces the anxieties involving the dissolution of the boundaries of death and the mind. In doing so, the films associate the danger and violence of the villains with the illnesses themselves, rather than purely on the basis of evil intent. Such themes are solidified further with the temporary amnesia Harry develops after battle because he is continually susceptible to personality alterations, and is therefore an unpredictable threat. Harry frequently changes between faithful ally and Machiavellian adversary, repetitively instigating conflict and distress with his almost-whimsical play with the traditional boundaries of the id and ego, and the conscious and unconscious. As with his father, only through death does Harry's torment end, and sociocultural apprehension is appeased; yet similarly, this is not to say that they or their goals will not resurface through other potential villains. Despite the interventions of Spider-Man, his actions are a temporary respite; mental illness has the ability to afflict any individual, and as such social unrest is perpetuated, with villains and their neuroses potentially recurring within any future sequels.

Spider-Man's other villains similarly disturb the boundaries of both body and mind. Dr. Octopus attaches four robotic limbs to his spinal column, and with the destruction of the neural inhibitor microchip also allows the artificial intelligence to become amalgamated with his mind. Dr. Octopus converts into a hybrid of man and machine, while also designated as an animal, blurring the boundaries between oppositional areas that have been a (post)modern paranoia in science fiction for decades, from *Metropolis* (Fritz Lang, 1927) to *The Matrix*. Octavius is seemingly punished for ambitiously defying scientific limitations and attempting self-exaltation to obtain, as he describes it, "the power of the sun in the palm of [his] hand." The Sandman meanwhile has the ability to alter his body into any size, shape, and mass, with his namesake derivative of not only his capabilities, but also the fairy-tale character that permits and enters dreams. Lastly, Venom is a hybrid of human and alien, with a sentient-yet-symbiotic costume that has duplicated Spider-Man's abilities. In each case, the villain is an amalgamation, or anthropomorphic, of a variety of generally oppositional discourses: science and nature, body and mind, human and alien, reality and mythology, and so forth. While Spider-Man himself permeates similar boundaries, his access to American religious and cultural heritage halts any potential anxiety involving his powers. As his nemeses reject such an alignment, they are construed as perverse violations of the natural order, and therefore monstrous.

The X-Men sequels disrupt postmodern boundaries in an alternative context due to the focus on "otherness" and cultural acceptance. "The mutant body is oxymoronic," argues Scott Bukatman, "rigidly protected but dangerously unstable. In its infinite malleability and over-determined adolescent iconography, the mutant superhero is a locus of bodily ritual" (96). Because mutation is genetic in nature rather than acquired, potentially anyone could be afflicted and develop superpowers, be cast as a mutant, and persecuted as "other." The more obvious allegory is that of pubescent angst, yet *X-Men 2* also aligns the victimization of mutants with homophobia, as Iceman amusingly "comes out" to his parents to which they rather ignorantly remark, "Have you tried not being a mutant?" The sequels repeatedly represent such prejudice at governmental and social levels. Because the alignment is with those persecuted however, the sequels attempt to allay the postmodern anxiety that potentially anyone could be a mutant, or different, from the dominant aspects of Western culture that could be construed as ideologically threatening.

Many of the characters also return from death. Jean Grey is killed in the finale of *X-Men 2* yet, "there is a definite allusion to a great leap forward in evolution beyond physical death," due to the response of Professor Xavier and the shadow of the Phoenix (Housel 85). Jean is reborn as the Phoenix in *X-Men 3* due to her telekinetic abilities in which she not only displays power of unlimited capacity but also has a dual personality disorder. This mental illness is again predicated on the dissolution between the id and ego, between restraint and abandon, and as such "good" and "evil" personalities. The abilities "Dark" Jean exhibits can alter matter at the molecular level and reshape reality at a whim, resulting in a massacre that includes the "death" of her mentor Professor Xavier. Jean dissolves postmodern boundaries of death, the mind, and more profoundly her evolved state, as each area is never an absolute; Jean is unlimited in her capacity to alter anything in reality, and in doing so destroys any and all preconceived boundaries of modernity. Even her "death" at the hands of Wolverine cannot be considered absolute because reality is susceptible only to her unbridled desires. Professor Xavier meanwhile is subsequently revealed to have survived his "death" as well, transplanting his consciousness into that of a comatose patient that simultaneously disrupts postmodern boundaries and opens debates regarding the ethical use of superpowers.

The premise of *X-Men 3* resides in the creation of a "cure" for the mutant gene that is gratuitously applied on the mutant population, most notably on the extremist Brotherhood coalition. By the end of the sequel, scores of mutants, including Magneto, have been "cured" of their abilities and thus the postmodern threat is alleviated. However, after the climatic battle on Alcatraz, Magneto demonstrates that the nullification of his abilities was temporary, and as such it is implied that every mutant affected should, in time, reacquire his or her abilities. Therefore the postmodern threats, and the option for further sequels, is a viable commodity as all the heroes and villains previously considered incapacitated can return to engage in further sociocultural re-presentations.

The sequelization of such postmodern themes in the Blade sequels uses different conventions due to the horror motifs within the narrative. Budra claims that in "postmodern horror films the interplay of meanings that has arisen from the postmodern rejection of certitude is itself presented . . . as a collective madness which is completely homicidal, monstrous, because it kills established orders and values, slashes moral certainties, and stomps on ontological assumptions" (191). In *Blade*, the vampires represented are in accordance with the cultural mythology in which they have become accustomed. Yet in *Blade II* a new "race" of vampires has been genetically designed. They drink blood not through fangs, but through a mandible jaw that horrifically separates and paralyses prey, while a "tongue" extracts blood and plasma to feed. The genetic modifications also create a new set of "rules" with regard to their destruction because the modified vampires are now immune to garlic and silver, and they have an impenetrable bone chassis around the heart. Additionally, their prey is the vampire because it provides lasting sustenance, rather than the traditional human opponent. As the mythology of the traditional vampire has become standardized in Western culture, the resurgence of such postmodern techniques intensifies the anxiety of the unknown vampiric monster, escalating anguish and horror. *Blade Trinity* destabilizes such boundaries even further with the introduction of a physically malleable Dracula and vampire dogs, both in the traditional form as well as genetically modified examples. In representing vampirism and genetic manipulation in such a fashion, the threat becomes more widespread, more imposing, and above all, more evil. When Blade defeats his new postmodern enemies, he restores the narrative to the traditional status of human and vampire. In doing so, he returns the equilibrium to the more culturally "known," and therefore removes the uncertainty and paranoia of those that ignore the boundaries of modernity. Yet even this premise is problematic because the traditional vampires are also deviant. They snort powdered blood in the fashion of cocaine, and they can be returned to human state with a viral detox once bitten. The nature of vampirism in the *Blade* series is constantly in flux and generates anxiety due to this refusal of stability.

The anxieties prevalent within the dissolution of postmodern boundaries are explicitly ideological, inscribed in the theological and cultural unrest throughout Western culture at the turn of the millennium. Postmillennial superhero sequels portray such paranoia, predominantly aligning the angst with the villains that perpetuate the narratives, serving to connote the erosions as evil. However this also provides an additional function. In associating postmodern motifs with the nemesis, the villains become iconic in status and can be continually used through further sequelization due to their popularity, and as such superheroes can repeatedly battle with the evolving sociocultural fears these threats embody. Superheroes are not subject to the same regulations as their counterparts: "whether [because of] a 'miraculous' return from seeming death, or a return to the right path, the values they embody are too strong to quell or kill" (Fingeroth 167). It is in embodying and re-presenting such traditional cultural and religious heritage that the cinematic superhero can never die or retire because he or she is continually sequelized to engage with the sociocultural unrest as valued by villainous nemeses.

Sequelizing the postmillennial superhero employs myriad postmodern techniques. As Michael Zeitlin attests, "postmodern sequels tend less to follow, serve, and continue than to select, incorporate, and transform their precursor texts" (161). The precursor texts in question not only include the previous comic book influences and cinematic interpretations, but also the cultural and political discourses that have evolved over time. The millennium and the events of 9/11 have ushered unprecedented levels of sociocultural anxiety, which are, in turn, reflected and re-presented. The postmillennial superhero sequel incorporates such unrest within the narrative in the attempted reassembly of national identity, eroding postmodern boundaries of memory and nostalgia, historical trauma, theological angst, and Cartesian discourses. In amalgamating such temporal, philosophical, and cultural themes, the postmillennial superhero sequel informs an ideological "need." Anxieties in the popular consciousness are repeatedly re-presented allegorically in order for the superhero, the embodiment of traditional American religious and cultural values, to vanquish such anguish from the public sphere. The "divergence between so-called reality and our distorted representation" (Žižek 28) is indeed problematic with regard to the use of signs as simulacra of the real, using re-presentations within the sequels to allay social unrest and simultaneously construct a new collective "memory" and by extension a new cultural equilibrium. The postmillennial superhero sequel is a highly complex cinematic text, predicated on the confrontation and alleviation of sociocultural anxieties that permeate American culture. As such, superheroes will continually re-emerge during periods of upheaval and unrest, to battle allegorically the evolving social, cultural, and theological threats that spread angst throughout the United States.

11

Nicholas Rombes

Before and After and Right Now

Sequels in the Digital Era

THIS CHAPTER ASKS QUESTIONS about the relation between sequels and digital media that, in its database structure, highlights and transforms the process of rearranging time to tell stories, a process that, always fundamental to cinema, was often concealed. Rather than unfold in a linear, analytical fashion, the chapter borrows from our contemporary understanding of the archive in the digital era, where information seems never to disappear, but remains stored in vast databases. As Jacques Derrida has reminded us, the "archivization produces as much as it records the event" (17), and this chapter is the product of a certain slant of thinking about digital archives, a slant of thinking no doubt infected by the very structures of archiving that it describes. Going on to think about the processes by which human presence is both perpetuated and rendered unnecessary by new digital effects, this chapter challenges conceptualizations of reality within this milieu of "before" and "after," and therefore to notions of originality.

As the ever-growing digital archive makes the past evermore accessible, how do we speak of "before" and "after" in cinema? Imagining the linear temporality that for so long characterized narrative cinema is increasingly difficult in part because the ubiquity of media and media

Figure 11.1. *Aliens* (James Cameron, 1986). Courtesy 20th Century Fox/The Kobal Collection.

interfaces means that stories are continually in a "present" state. During the classical cinema era—roughly from the 1930s through the 1950s—viewers had very little control over physical interaction with the screen. Sequels were released and viewed according to the economic imperatives of the studios. In the twenty-first century, however, what does releasing a sequel mean when audiences exercise a much greater degree of control over not only the film cycle that includes sequels, but over the temporal dimensions of individual films themselves? In what ways do the numerous bonus features, added material, and alternate endings and footage included on DVDs contribute to the conceptualization of the sequel in contemporary film production?

Temporal disorder is a key figure of the digital era, which is further characterized by what Fredric Jameson has called a "crisis in historicity" whereby the past, present, and future meld into a vaguely ahistorical, floating present ("Postmodernism" 118; see also Cubitt, Mulvey). And yet—at the same time—audiences are perhaps more literate about film and cinema history and the material conditions of film production than ever before. Sequels sit at the heart of this contradiction because they foreground some of the most complex gestures associated with the dissolution of temporal distinctness in the digital era.

The entire notion of sequels suggests a familiarity with the "original." For instance, *Aliens* (James Cameron)—the 1986 sequel to *Alien* (Ridley Scott, 1979)—assumes some knowledge of the basic *Alien* storyline, but reiterates the basic plot of the first movie during an early scene when Ripley is questioned by a Board of Inquiry about the circumstances that led her to destroy the ship in this exchange:

VAN LEUWEN

Look at it from our perspective. You freely admit to detonating the engines of, and thereby destroying, an M–Class star-freighter. A rather expensive piece of hardware. . . .

INSURANCE INVESTIGATOR (dryly)

Forty-two million in adjusted dollars. That's minus payload, of course.

VAN LEUWEN

The shuttle's flight recorder corroborates some elements of your account. That the Nostromo set down on LV–426, an unsurveyed planet, at that time. That repairs were made. That it resumed its course and was subsequently set for self-destruct. By you. For reasons unknown.

RIPLEY

Look, I told you. . . .

VAN LEUWEN

It did not, however, contain any entries concerning the hostile life form you allegedly picked up.

Traditionally, sequels have reminded viewers who may not have seen or may have forgotten plot details from the original movie, generally, as illustrated in the previous exchange, while advancing the plot of the sequel itself. In the *Aliens* example, we not only learn the basic plot contours of the original *Alien*, but also something about the film's anti-corporate ideological positioning.

Modern cinema emerged during an era when physics was challenging previous conceptions of time as constant, universal, and ceaselessly forward-moving. As Stephen Kern has noted, Albert Einstein's "general theory of relativity had the effect, figuratively, of placing a clock in every gravitational field in the universe, each moving at a rate determined by both the intensity of the gravitational field at that point and the relative motion of the object observed" (19). As cinema during the first decades of the twentieth-century developed parallel editing or cross-cutting that required viewers to follow enormous leaps across time (for example, flashbacks) and space (cross-cutting between two or more separate physical spaces), audiences began to internalize the logic of what was to become standard editing techniques. Scholars such as Anne Friedberg and Mary Ann Doane have suggested that viewers were prepared and conditioned for accepting such spatial leaps because they were increasingly immersed in everyday technologies that themselves cut across space. Doane suggests that "editing borrowed the authority of the telephone to rationalize the instantaneous movement from site to site effected by the cut" (*Emergence* 194).

In the twenty-first century, the question is not parallel editing within movies, but rather between them. And just as spectators were prepared for temporal shifts within movies during the early 1900s due, in part, to peripheral technologies such as the telegraph and telephones, today's spectators are prepared for temporal shifts between movies by the rapid splicing of time and space through digital-era technologies such as the web, cell phones, and MP3 players, which render the before and after of movies an anachronism. Lev Manovich has written, "contrary to popular images of computer media as collapsing all human culture into a single giant library (which implies the existence of some ordering system), or a single giant book (which implies a narrative progression), it is perhaps more accurate to think of the new media culture as an infinite flat surface where individual texts are placed in no particular order" (77). Movies are historical insomuch as they are made at a particular point in time, but for audiences viewing them they always unfold in the present tense.

On a smaller scale, this is evident in the bonus and supplementary materials routinely available on DVDs. DVD box sets for films such as the Lord of the Rings series (Peter Jackson, 2001, 2002, 2003) now offer the entire sequence of films in one package, both reinforcing and eroding the historical materialism of the films themselves. Viewer choice and time-shifting—introduced by the Sony home video recorder in the 1970s—now means that sequels are aesthetic, rather than temporal, matters. The "no particular order" that Manovich describes is indeed a feature of the digital era, when the past-ness of movies is flattened as they are digitally remastered and repacked for home viewing in ways that render them digital—and hence contemporary—narratives. Audiences have access to vast amounts of paratextual data. Features incorporated within such DVD packages provide an extensive source of information pertaining to production and the historical milieu of a film. In other words, at the same time that films become ahistorically ever-present, they also are deeply enmeshed in historical contexts.

So many sequels now are franchises that viewers are encouraged to see them as components of a greater whole, rather than as single units. Indeed, the very interface itself—such as the DVD menu—encourages what Roland Barthes called, in relation to reading, *tmesis*, a skimming or skipping around in the text: "a rhythm is established, casual, unconcerned with the *integrity* of the text; our very avidity for knowledge impels us to skim or skip certain passages (anticipated as 'boring') in order to get more quickly to the warmer parts of the anecdote..." (*Pleasure* 11). The migration of movies in the digital era onto multiple screens—televisions, computers, cell phones, and so on—sanctions a form of skimming that throws into question the very notion of a stable, primary, coherent text. How does one "watch" a DVD, for instance, with the ability to jump to specific chapters, or to navigate with ease forward and backward through a film? Against these larger technological changes, sequels are losing their historicity, their temporal status not so much because viewers no longer care which movie came "first," but rather because the entire paradigm of before and after is being supplanted with a continual present because archives are readily available for recall. And yet, paradoxically, *tmesis* is countered by an ever-deeper investigation of films, as the pause and step-frame function on many DVD player interfaces allows for an investigation of a film's images with unprecedented closeness for the lay viewer.

We are perhaps at the beginning of a period when historical media is ever present, available for recall after a few keystrokes. Consider the availability of a film such as *Citizen Kane* (Orson Welles, 1941), which in the 1950s and 1960s was available for viewing in limited venues, such as art-house revivals, museum showings, retrospectives, and perhaps occasionally on television. Today, a film is widely available—in fragments or in whole—within seconds at the earliest, or days at the latest. Clips of a production are readily and freely accessible online, while the film itself can be purchased in numerous retail outlets, or purchased or rented via the Internet (for example, Netflix, Amazon, and so on). In the near future, *Citizen Kane* might well be available as a pay-for-download file, streaming directly into a computer or a television. The availability of a film such as *Citizen Kane* across so many platforms and in so many mediums suggests that it exists not so much as an artifact from the past, but rather as something very much of the present.

The word "sequel" itself first appears in the fifteenth century, derived from the Latin *sequi*, "to follow," while the first use of the term to mean "story that follows or continues another" was recorded in 1513. These early meanings literally depended on a notion of a before and after. We should not be surprised, then, that cinema emerged as physics was coming to understand that, at least in theory, no reason exists why time unfolds in a sequential, one-way direction. Physicist Brian Greene has noted that "the laws of physics that have been articulated from Newton through Maxwell and Einstein, and up until today, show a *complete symmetry between past and future*. No where in any of these laws do we find a stipulation that they apply one way in time but not in the other" (144–45). In this light, the so-called flattening of history that is supposedly a marker of postmodernism is less an unfortunate dehistorisizing gesture than a confirmation of the deepest structures of the material world. Digital media and its randomly accessible archive is a metaphor for a universe that quantum physics is gradually revealing to be more fluid and uncertain than previously known. Physicist Michio Kaku reminds us that one of Einstein's great breakthroughs was to demonstrate that "time is not an absolute, as Newton once thought" (33). Of course, movies have always represented the passage of time in ways that were not purely linear, as in the standard flashback sequences, or by skipping ahead in the story by days, weeks, or even longer periods. However, the emergence of more openly self-conscious disruptions of linear time in movies such as *Pulp Fiction* (Quentin Tarantino, 1994), *Memento* (Christopher Nolan, 2000), or *Eternal Sunshine of the Spotless Mind* (Michel Gondry, 2004) occurred in the same historical period as the emergence of digital media with its binary codes and access interfaces that make concepts such as "before" and "after" seem arbitrary. One could say that the migration of temporally disruptive films from the avant-garde (for example, Maya Deren's *Meshes of the Afternoon* [1943], with its repeating loops of action) to the mainstream (for example, *Run Lola Run* [Tom Tykwer, 1998]) roughly coincided with the emergence of relatively affordable consumer digital cameras and desktop video editing systems, such as iMovie or Avid, and the availability of affordable non-linear editing systems in the 1990s.

Sequels are becoming ghosts in the digital era; in the increasingly globalized cinematic marketplace, films are remembered more for being "remakes of" rather than "sequels to." Like a virus, the binary code of the digital spreads, replicating itself, spreading new versions of itself in new languages. Sean Cubitt has written that the "digital corresponds so closely to the emergent loss of an ideological structure to social meaning because it no longer pretends to represent the world" (250). In the novel *Loop* (1998), Koji Suzuki's sequel to *Ring* and *Spiral*, we learn that the entire setting of the novel *Ring* might have been in a virtual reality loop: "*Ring* would be a book, then a movie, a video game, an Internet site—it would saturate the world through every branch of the media" (191). *Ring* was originally published in Japan as *Ringu* in 1991, followed by the Japanese film *Ringu* (Hideo Nakata) in 1998, and the American version, *The Ring* (Gore Verbinski) in 2002. The logic of *Ring*—both in terms of its plot and its various media manifestations—suggests a disruption of the linearity. The world of the *Ring* is an eternal loop, not a straight line. As in the digital era with its ever-increasing archive storage capacities and larger and larger memory, nothing ever really goes away. Instead, information (in the form of images, text, music, and so on) is recycled, sampled, mashed-up, and reformatted, until distinctions between past and future disappear.

This is reinforced on a material level where a viewer's experience with the interface of a film no longer provides even the illusion of linearity. Film has persistently suggested what we might term a "linear materialism": literally, the film has traditionally moved forward through the projector. As the story world of the film advances forward through time (with the exception of flashbacks and other conventional temporal disruptions), so too the film advances through the projector through time. Traditional projection methods involve a beginning (leader), middle, and end. During the analog era, videotape remediated this structure because movies on VHS tapes also had a materially identifiable beginning, middle, and end that required time to pass during the rewinding or fast-forwarding process. In the West, the temporal imaginary has time flowing from left to right (as in timelines), a structure echoed in audio and VHS tapes, which spooled forward from left to right. But in the digital era, the link between a film's internal, story time and its external, material time has been broken. DVDs—as physical objects—have no clear beginning, middle, or end. And downloaded movies that are stored as a series of ones and zeroes are even more abstracted from so-called real time. In which direction does time flow inside a computer? This has permeated the way that some movies are made as well. All three Lord of the Rings films were shot simultaneously, even though each of the films was released a year apart. In what sense is a film a sequel if it is produced at the same time as the "original"?

The proliferation of moving images today and their easy accessibility across many enormous archives suggests that the very flow of time that made distinctions between "original" and "sequel" possible is, in fact, impossible. As Manovich has noted, as "a cultural form, the data-base represents the world as a list of items, and it refuses to order this list" (225). We should, perhaps, not be surprised that we are attuned to movies that are temporally confused, such as *Pulp Fiction*, *Memento*, or *Eternal Sunshine of the Spotless Mind*. Films such as these, made at the dawn of the digital era, are artifacts of a way of thinking that renders strict notions of sequels obsolete: what would a sequel of *Memento* (a film whose narrative is revealed in reverse chronology) look like? In *Theory of Film*, Siegfried Kracauer wrote of the surrealist film *Entr'acte* (René Clair, 1924) that one of its more startling sequences "depicts a special mode of reality—reality as perceived by those who are moving at extreme speed" (183). Our own "special mode of reality" today suggests a flattening of time not necessarily because everything is accelerated, but rather because its instant availability suggests the illusion of speed. True, time passes between the making of movies—such as such as *Ter-minator* and *Terminator 2: Judgment Day* (James Cameron, 1984, 1991), or *Spider-Man*, *Spider-Man 2*, and *Spider-Man 3* (Sam Raimi, 2002, 2004, 2007)—but the ease with which they can be viewed (rented, purchased, and so on) renders the temporal distance between them as anachronis-tic. Furthermore, as subsequent "deluxe" or "special edition" film ver-sions are released—often with extra footage, cleaned-up transfers, and sometimes updated effects—the movies remain artifacts of the present. In other words, cleansed of the imperfections that characterized their original releases, rereleased films further erode the gaps that made differ-ences between "original" and "sequel" meaningful. When George Lucas digitally altered the DVD release of *Star Wars: A New Hope* (1977) to include computer-generated imagery (CGI)–enhanced scenes and bits of new footage woven into the film, he created something that was a prod-uct of 2004 rather than 1977. Such retrofitting effectively destroys the possibilities of prequels and sequels, as the depth of time collapses into the flatness of a continuous present. Even "old" films are "restored" not to their original state, but to a remastered, clean, enhanced state that bears all the visual markers of the present.

In "CivilWarLand in Bad Decline," a short story about an amuse-ment park that "re-creates" the American Civil War era, George Saun-ders wrote:

> When visitors first come in there's this cornball part where they sit in this kind of spaceship and supposedly get blasted into space and travel faster than the speed of light and end up in 1865. The unit's dated. The helmets we distribute look like bowls and all the paint's peeling off. I've argued and argued that we need to update.

But in the midst of a budget crunch one can't necessarily hang the moon. When the tape of space sounds is over and the walls stop shaking, we pass out the period costumes. We try not to offend anyone, liability law being what it is. We distribute the slave and Native American roles equitably among racial groups. Anyone is free to request a different identity at any time. (10)

The passage is both funny and scary, suggesting a mixing-up of time not unlike our own present. It is not that history itself has become a franchise, but rather that our reproduction of that history now takes the form of unprecedented spectacle, and that that spectacle is not bound by time. Instead, it is always already available for recall on our computer or cell phone screens.

The dissolution of sequels is part of a larger reconfiguration of traditional cinematic categories. Indeed, those responsible for some of the most radical images and sequences in films today are probably not readily familiar by name. Unlike the stars of the *auteur* theory, popularized in the United States by film critic Andrew Sarris in 1962, today's *auteur* experimentalists are not film directors. Instead, those most responsible for the relentless absurdity of images on the screen work for companies with names such as Lola Visual Effects, Persistence of Vision, Double Negative, Asylum Visual Effects, and Animal Logic. And although the demands of conventional genre films—action, science fiction, fantasy, natural disaster—give rise to these sequences, the sequences themselves frequently transcend these limits and enter the realm of Art.

In all likelihood these names are not familiar: Zareh Nalbandian, managing director and co-founder of Animal Logic; or Chris Godfrey, director of visual effects; or Andy Brown and Kirsty Millar, who were the visual effects supervisors for *House of Flying Daggers* (Zhang Yimou, 2004). Here—from the Animal Logic Web site—is a brief description of their work on *The Matrix Reloaded* (Andy and Larry Wachowski, 2003): "For *Reloaded* the team completed ten sequences, which included building entire 3D characters the Twins, who are able to fully interact with the live action stars when in their CG phasing states" (Animal Logic 3). What is astounding is not the sentence itself, but rather that we no longer find sentences like this astounding. The invisible hand of the CGI avant-gardists is everywhere. Persistence of Vision—which has worked on *Star Wars Episode II: Attack of the Clones* (George Lucas, 2002), *Titan A. E.* (Don Bluth and Gary Goldman, 2000), and others—describes its work this way: "POV works with the direction to conceive shots, solve story-telling problems, edit the sequence, and even add music, dialogue and sound effects. When complete, the animatic will communicate the composition, style, and elements of every frame in the sequence. It removes guesswork, aides in communication and budgeting, and, we've found, increases the morale of the crew before and during shooting" ("Pre-Visualization" 1). But is "guesswork" not fundamental to the messy nature of the creative process?

Lola Visual Effects: digital cosmetic enhancements, a visual effects company based in Santa Monica, California, specializes in making people look younger and fitter on the screen, digitally. This is not the "soft focus" filmmaking of Hitchcock's era; this is digital lies using cold binary logic of ones and zeros. If you happened to see the latest *X-Men* and wondered about the youthful Patrick Stewart—who looked younger and fresher than in movies he made when he actually was younger and fresher—it is because of companies such as Lola VFX. Here is what they do: "We remove scars, facial hair, pimples, wrinkles, dimples and blotches. We make bodies firmer, legs longer, faces younger, breasts fuller, cheekbones higher, eyes bluer, and skin smoother. We achieve this while ensuring that all the effects are realistic and convincing" ("Who We Are" 1). This is the image logic of the digital era, a form of self-reenactment. It is a system of radical filmmaking that goes largely unnoticed by scholars and theorists because film theory is still bound by a way of reading films that emerged in response to the classic era.

Consider this statement: "Our work has far-reaching implications from extending an actor's career for one more sequel to overall success at the box office. We allow actors and studios to create one more blockbuster sequel (with the actor's fan base) by making the actor look as good (or better) than they [*sic*] did in their [*sic*] first movie" ("What We Do" 1). What is there to say about such a brash and unapologetic thing as this statement? The statement was not written by Aldous Huxley, nor was it a darkly funny dystopian story by George Saunders. This is a real, true, and sincere statement by a company that digitally alters the faces and bodies of the actors we see on the screen, a special effect so seamless, so natural that its very surrealism lies in the fact that it disguises itself as reality. The corporate executives of the new "image realization" companies have become today's theorists of the image. Gareth Edwards, founder and chief technical officer at Image Metrics, has written that "human faces in games have rarely seemed 'authentic.' Authenticity is not just about the 'realism' of the base mesh—it is certainly possible to present a single image of a 3D head which looks great, but expression is more about detailed, subtle movements and tiny nuances" (1). And what is it that Image Metrics does? According to Andy Wood, the company's CEO, "Image Metrics's core technology automatically transfers a human being's facial performance onto a digitally-created character. We capture an actor's facial performance directly from a camera or an existing recording—there's no motion capture studio, no special equipment or metal markers. Whatever the actor does, the computer character does" (1).

What does it mean to be real in a movie in the digital era? What is a movie's historical place in time when it exists in numerous "restored" versions? What happens when a restored version of the original movie is released for home viewing *after* the sequel? What happens when we create a realism that outstrips the detail of reality itself, when we achieve and then go beyond a one-to-one correspondence with the real world? Jean Baudrillard has spoken and written about the pointlessness, the banality of Art ever since it "liberated" itself from its High Status as art and became coterminous with everyday reality. "At the end of this history," according to Baudrillard, "the banality of art is mixed up with the banality of the real world" (*Conspiracy* 90). In a cruel paradox, the deconstruction of Art was completely successful: it no longer exists. Movies, too, have always depended on a boundary, however fluid, between natural reality and our manipulations of that reality. In fact, our entire taxonomy of cinematic genres—science fiction, historical epic, comedy, thriller, mystery, avant-garde—depended not only on these distinctions, but on a sort of baseline realism against which they were measured. After all, fantasy is a genre, but is realism? What happens in the digital age when the very conditions of the realism against which not only genre, but aesthetics, are measured no longer exist?

"We could put Marilyn Monroe alongside Jack Nicholson, or Jack Black, or Jack White," says Andy Wood. "If we want John Wayne to act alongside Angelina Jolie, we can do that. We can directly mimic the performance of a human being on a model. We can create new scenes for old films, or old scenes for new films" (qtd. in Waxman, "Cyberface"). What is significant here is not that movies are devising new ways of compositing the real, but rather that the real itself is the product of this composition. What Andy Wood and others are doing is really an exercise in philosophy, forcing us to rethink not only our relation to reality, but also the fundamental nature of reality itself. And it seems—looking at these developments now, in the wake of postmodernism—perfectly natural that our cinematic technologies are finally fulfilling the promise and logic of deconstruction. Ironically, while the so-called postmodern rejection of capital "T" Truth and "Reality" itself used to be associated with the Radical Chic Professoriate, today its logic permeates popular culture and political discourse, even from the Right. Ron Suskind recalls being told by a senior advisor to George W. Bush in 2002:

> Guys like me [Suskind] were "in what we call the reality-based community," which he defined as people who "believe that solutions emerge from your judicious study of discernable reality. . . .

That's not the way the world really works any more. . . . We're
an empire now, and when we act, we create our own reality. And
while you're studying that reality—judiciously, as you will—we'll
act again, creating other new realities, which you can study too,
and that's how things will sort out."

You can imagine this sort of thing being said in a graduate seminar in
literary theory in 1988 and being understood as a statement of high
theory: reality is not "objective," out there waiting to be found, but
rather something that is constructed, the product of social, economic,
cultural, and political forces.

When, in the *New York Times* article, Andy Wood uses the phrase
"soul transference" to describe the process of a computer mapping an
actor's face "onto any character virtual or human, living or dead," and
then goes on to say that "the model has the actress's soul. It shows
through" (qtd. in Waxman, "Cyberface"), you know you have reached
the point where Philip K. Dick's paranoid fictions of the 1960s and
1970s no longer serve as prescient harbingers of the future, but rather
as bits of nostalgia for a time when such a future could be imagined.
"The Kalbfleisch simulacrum stopped," we read in Dick's 1964 novel
The Simulacra, a story about a president of the United States who is a
simulacrum. "Its arms stuck out, rigid in their final gesture, the withered
face vacuous. The simulacrum said nothing and automatically the TV
cameras also shut off, one by one; there was no longer anything for
them to transmit" (32).

In her pioneering book *How We Became Posthuman*, N. Katherine
Hayles noted that "one of the striking differences between researchers
who work with flesh and those who work with computers is how nuanced
the sense of the body's complexity is for those who are directly engaged
with it" (244). This human complexity is precisely what companies such
as Image Metrics (does this not sound like the name of a company out of
a Philip K. Dick novel?) hope to capture for the screen. Under the sign
of such companies, human beings become models for reality, mannequins
on which an even greater real is layered. "When people see what we can
do with this system—for example, making Marilyn Monroe say words
she never spoke—they see how they can use it to make better games and
films," Andy Wood has said. "Our technology will ensure we achieve our
goals . . . it can't fail to" ("Andy Wood Goes to Hollywood"). The place
of human beings in digital cinema is not secure; technologies that were
once used to create "special effects" now create human beings *as* special
effects. Companies such as Image Metrics are not interested in creating

realistic looking explosions, tidal waves, fires, and so on, but rather in creating human beings who look more real than we do.

And so we find ourselves as the subjects of our own vision machines, which we created to penetrate and capture reality. The reversal is nearly complete. In *Poltergeist* (Tobe Hooper, 1982), a girl with blonde hair stares into the eerie static of the television, listening to ghosts. In *The Ring* a girl with black hair—a ghost herself—crawls out of the television, across the floor, and toward another screen, the one that separates us from her. The virus at the heart of the Koji Suzuki novels that include *Ring* is not really the videotape, but rather the screens that make the display of the tape possible. In the same way, sequels during the classical era depended on boundaries, on the temporal distance between the release dates of movies. Sequels were defined as much by the inaccessibility of the original as by the sequel itself. But today, as the boundaries of space and time collapse, and as actors (such as Patrick Stewart) can be digitally modified so that they appear to age "correctly" from one sequel to another, the very limitations that made "before" and "after" meaningful have eroded. More significantly, the hypervisible digital archive—which makes increasingly greater amounts of data available on screens far from the actual physical embodiment of the archives—further erodes distinctions between before and after. The proliferation of "originals" and "sequels" in the digital era, and the easy navigation forward and backward through those texts suggests nothing more than a growing tyranny of the present.

12

CAROLYN JESS-COOKE

Sequelizing Spectatorship and Building Up the Kingdom

The Case of *Pirates of the Caribbean,* Or, How a Theme-Park Attraction Spawned a Multibillion-Dollar Film Franchise

"There's never a guarantee of coming back, but passing on—that's certain."

—Captain Hector Barbossa,
Pirates of the Caribbean: At World's End

AT THE BEGINNING OF *Pirates of the Caribbean: Dead Man's Chest* (Gore Verbinski, 2006), the action-adventure sequel to *Pirates of the Caribbean: The Curse of the Black Pearl* (Gore Verbinski, 2003), Pirate Captain Jack Sparrow (Johnny Depp) enters the story by shooting his way out of a coffin-at-sea. Literally returning from the dead, Sparrow soon gets caught up with the dilemmas of the afterlife as he is

Figure 12.1. *Pirates of the Caribbean: The Curse of the Black Pearl* (Gore Verbinski, 2003). Courtesy Walt Disney Pictures/The Kobal Collection.

forced to pay back a blood debt to another undead pirate captain (Davy Jones, played by Bill Nighy). Buoyed by Depp's charismatic performance as the incarnation of Rolling Stones' rocker Keith Richards's imagined pirate son, the film's soggy storyline and gimmicky gags nonetheless enjoyed the most successful opening weekend in box-office history, reaping in excess of $235 million worldwide in just ten days (*"Pirates of the Caribbean"*). A blitzkrieg of merchandizing, tie-ins, and associated events ensued, such as a world ocean race in a boat named *Black Pearl*; a real sunken treasure hunt; an updated version of the opera *Pirates of Penzance*; an entirely new musical, *The Pirate Queen*, by the creators of *Les Misérables*; a theatrical production, *The Last Pirate*, by Charles Way; several video games; a mobile phone game; high street fashion tie-ins; and revamped versions of the original theme park ride where the *Pirates* adventure originally began.

As the third (and purportedly final) *Pirates* film installment, *Pirates of the Caribbean: At World's End* (Gore Verbinski, 2007), hits the screens as I write in May 2007 to even greater box office success—$401 million worldwide in just six days (" 'Pirates 3' ")—and with an additional gamut of tie-ins and promotional activities, audience activity is apparently fast becoming redefined by such franchises and their associated events and commodities with significant investments in the concerns and processes of sequelization. This chapter argues that the synergistic activities propagated by film franchises use the structure of the sequel as a contextualizing framework by which spectators understand and participate with a film's range of associated products and events as continuations of a narrative and by which the spectatorial experience is continued across a variety of associated texts, products, and events. Although numerous franchises and "event movies" could provide effective case studies of global reception activities, the textual history of the Pirates of the Caribbean, in concert with its transposition of a spatial source to a textual "world" and commercial franchise, this franchise's reiteration of Disney values, and its mechanisms of rewriting and sequelization provoke more urgent consideration in an environment of escalating consumer participation and media synergy.

Throughout the Pirates of the Caribbean franchise, spectatorship is continually constructed as the starting point of a long list of interrelated, secondary spectatorial experiences, all of which involve repetition, immersion, familiarity, role-playing or secondary performance, memory, and interaction between generations. The trope of the sequel—already an important part of the franchise's structure, made up of a film sequel to a theme park ride and two sequels to that sequel—is considered in this light as a useful framework within which to begin to comprehend the ways in which spectatorship is (re)figured in the Pirates of the Caribbean franchise as an increasingly sequential activity across multiple media platforms.

As indicated earlier, the "original" on which the Pirates of the Caribbean franchise is based is not a text; it is a theme park ride, which Walt Disney personally devised and executed over the three years prior to his death in 1966. A cutting edge display of animation and technological prowess, the Pirates ride was among the first to use Audio-Animatronics in its creation of moving, life-size pirate figures. It was also markedly cinematic from the outset, guiding Disneyland "guests" on a boat through several "scenes" from a sequentially staged pirate narrative. One of Disneyland's most popular rides, the Pirates of the Caribbean attraction has been adapted numerous times before Verbinski's trilogy: for example, as an interactive theme park ride, Pirates of the Caribbean: Battle for Buccaneer Gold (2005), which allows up to five players to enter a virtual pirate reality and reenact the (loose) narrative established by the original Pirates ride. The emphasis of this game/ride is less on virtuality than recreating "real experiences" (Schell and Shochet 11). Designed to be an "immersive adventure," Pirates of the Caribbean: Battle for

Buccaneer Gold extends the original Pirates of the Caribbean ride by
building on the *experience* of that ride, and by creating a heightened
interactive environment in which participants not only view the story in
3-D, animatronic form, but also get to adopt the role of pirate (12).

Similarly, Gore Verbinski's film trilogy, commencing in 2003 with
the first installment, *Pirates of the Caribbean: The Curse of the Black Pearl*,
extends the original theme park "experience." In keeping with the values of that experience, the trilogy is predicated on nostalgia, memory,
and the concept of entering and participating with a fictional "world."
As the trilogy develops, the values underpinning the Pirates' experience
are reiterated and heightened. The meshing of film viewing, consumer
activities, and media events that surround the Pirates films underlines
spectatorship as experiential, but always in the sense that something is
being *re*experienced—or in other words, that the varied forms of interactivity consistently engage with a past that can be technologically revisited.
Just as Captain Jack Sparrow emerges from the "dead" at the beginning
of the second Pirates film and by the end of it is "alive" and well in the
afterlife, so too does the entire Pirates franchise organize spectatorial
engagement as a navigation of beginnings, endings, and aftermaths, all of
which are underlined and facilitated by interaction and participation.

By looking to some of the ways in which the Pirates franchise
spreads across multimedia platforms, generates "post-performance reception" activities (Bennett 164), and extends the diegesis to create a Pirates
"world," this chapter argues that the kind of relation that is forged
between consumers/spectators and the film franchise is a *sequelized* spectatorship, or a set of personalized spectatorial experiences and encounters in which repetition, reenactment, and collective memory-making are
organizing principles. A long list of buzzwords has recently emerged to
discuss similar ideas, such as virtual reality (VR), immersive aesthetics,
pervasive play, intertextual matrices, and convergence. Each one of these
terms and definitions identifies new kinds of relations that have evolved
between the spectator and screen media as more and more developing
technologies emerge. As Henry Jenkins urges us, convergence, or "the
flow of content across multiple media platforms, the cooperation between
multiple media industries, and the migratory behavior of media audiences
who will go almost anywhere in search of the kinds of entertainment
experiences they want" dramatically impacts "the relationship between
existing technologies, industries, markets, genres and audiences" (Jenkins,
Convergence Culture 2; "Cultural Logic" 34). What Jenkins makes clear,
and as the Pirates of the Caribbean franchise shows us, is that not just
technology is responsible for the creation of immersive and virtual spectatorial experiences, but also those methods of extending a film across

several mediums, commodities, texts, and cultural events that expand the narrative into a kind of "world," or hypertextual environment, within which spectators are invited to become active participants.

My discussion of sequelized spectatorship involves a consideration of three key conceptual areas: immersion, control, and merchandizing. Each of these areas describes a specific kind of relation between film and spectator, particularly one in which *affect* and *effect* are important. Sequelized spectatorship is identified specifically as the effects created by an affective environment, or the process by which spectators reengage with and continue a visual narrative throughout social and material spaces through a range of consumer and performative activities.

A starting point for such a study is immersive environments. Edwina Bartlem defines these in terms of the process by which "one is drawn into an intimate and embodied relationship with a virtual and physical architecture." Notably, immersive spectatorship not only creates an "intimate" relation between spectator and screen, but also involves elements of spectatorial control. In this regard, note Walt Disney's comments to his Disneyland developers: "I don't want the public to see the world they live in while they're in the park" (qtd. in Bryman 95). The dedication plaque at Disneyland suggests Disney's desire to cordon off both the real world and real *time*, as it reads: "Here you leave Today and enter the world of Yesterday, Tomorrow, and Fantasy." Allan Bryman also notes Disney's control spreading to linguistic reinventions within the parks, turning a simple "queue" into a "pre-entertainment area," while the area outside the park became "backstage" and the internal vicinity "onstage" (108). The tendency for control intensified after Walt Disney's death, evidenced by Team Disney's motto: "Talk tough, talk cheap, and keep total control" (qtd. in Lewis, "Disney" 94). As a completely immersive and meticulously controlled environment, Disneyland serves as a physical model for many of Disney's virtual and multimedia platforms, all of which control experience through immersive mechanisms. Consistently drawing on notions of territory, destination, and pilgrimage (for example, Magic Kingdom, Disney World, and Lafitte's Landing), Disney's clearly defined physical boundaries lends the Pirates ride, and subsequently the Pirates franchise, a distinctly touristic experience (see Adams 98; Bryman 95–98; Fjellman 10). More important is the *kind* of touristic experience that is offered; by consistently eclipsing physical, historical, textual, cultural, experiential, and interactive territories, the Disney "tourist" engages with the company's range of synergistic activities and outputs with the knowledge that each territory merges with the others and, therefore, that the Disney experience is a uniquely synergistic encounter. With this in mind, the Pirates franchise operates as a sequel to Disney's world-making activities by creating a massive range of methods of engagement, consumerism, and entertainment from a host of interrelated narratives. Close readings of the films evidence the sequel as an organizing, internal principle that establishes dialogues between the experience of the film franchise and the reception activities that have followed. The Pirates franchise is not simply aware of its own merchandizing and intertextualization, but is arguably a self-reflexive component of a larger Pirates "world." The stakes of this argument, therefore, lie in the effects of reconstituting the film text as its own paratext—or what Gérard Genette defines as the relation between a text and the "accessory messages and commentaries which come to surround the main body of text" (*Palimpsests* 86)—and how this affects our engagement with that text as, in essence, a sequel of itself.

Piracy's popularization through the channels of literary, filmic, and multimedia formats have contributed entirely to its symbolic reworking. From as far back as the thirteenth century BC, tales abound of notable historical figures that were purportedly captured by pirates—Julius Caesar and Saint Patrick among them—thus enlivening historical data with narratives of bravery, adventure and revenge. In 1724, the book *A General History of the Robberies and Murders of the Most Notorious Pyrates* by Captain Charles Johnson[1] helped to romanticize the pirate further by assembling several purportedly factual biographies of eighteenth-century rogues. Persistently embodying ideals of liberty, rebellion against bureaucracy, and masculine prowess, piracy gradually made its way onto the map of popular culture in the form of well-defined stereotypes—for instance, a bearded, middle-aged man with a black eye-patch, a wooden leg and/or hook prosthetic, parrot, and distinctive growl—and eventually in the form of a comic operetta (Gilbert and Sullivan's *Pirates of Penzance*, 1879), casinos (Las Vegas's Treasure Island Hotel and Casino), festivals, magazines, theme parties, fashion accessories, board and video games, online and mobile phone games, and a theme park ride at Disneyland (see Land).

Film played a key role in piracy's popularization. From cinema's early days a pirate "genre" emerged from a steady stream of pirate adventures, such as Robert Louis Stevenson's *Treasure Island* (1883) and its adaptations by Victor Fleming (1934) and Byron Haskin (1950), Sir J. M. Barrie's *Peter Pan* (1904) and its 1953 Disney animation directed by Clyde Geronimi, Wilfred Jackson, and Hamilton Luske, as well as *Captain Blood* (Michael Curtiz, 1935), *The Crimson Pirate* (Robert Siodmak, 1952), *Pirates of Penzance* (Wilford Leach, 1983) and, more recently, *Cutthroat Island* (Renny Harlin, 2002) and the animated *Treasure Planet* (Ron Clements and John Musker, 2002), all of which marked the conventions of the pirate genre and imagined the pirate as more comparable to a latter-day rock star than a scurvy early modern rogue.

Walt Disney's plans for his Pirates of the Caribbean theme park attraction built on piracy's retextualizations throughout popular culture and the ride was designed, like the rest of Disneyland, to be a "three-dimensional movie" (Watts 390). Pirates was the final attraction that Disney personally supervised from inception to installation, and plans for the ride evolved swiftly from original conceptions of a walk-through wax museum to an indoor boat ride through which Disneyland guests witness moving automatons in various tableaux that collectively construct a narrative (along with a soundtrack, "Yo Ho! [A Pirate's Life for Me!]")—a turning point in using cutting-edge technology to create lifelike animations. The ride was to be experienced as a portal through piracy's textual and social networks with which guests were most likely already familiar; likewise, the Pirates of the Caribbean film franchise offers more than the traditional film narrative, with critics finding it more "an experience rather than a story" (Stevens). The Pirates franchise operates as a rather proactive kind of rewriting of the original Pirates experience, symbolically implicated by the revision and updating of the theme-park ride to correspond with each new film installment. In other words, the Pirates films are not simply a remake of the original ride and the texts on which that ride was based, but they are part of a conversation between an "original" and sequel with which the spectator takes part. As spectators, this kind of rewriting is in terms of writing *ourselves* into the textual "world" that is organized by the franchise, at the same time as we are called on to negotiate and engage in a variety of rewriting activities throughout the series of extrafilmic events and multimedia tie-ins as extensions of the films' textuality.

The texts associated with piracy's popularization have contributed to a contemporary understanding of piracy as an intertextual event, and—as the original Pirates theme-park ride exploited to its advantage—participation with textual networks that usually culminated in an immersive readership, whether in the form of trying out versions of "Aaaargh!" during the "International Talk Like a Pirate Day,"[2] or as an active participant in a variety of adaptational methods proffered by the numerous interactive games and textual spin-offs that have emerged in the franchise's wake. Each of the associated Pirates features—the Jolly Roger flag, the song "Yo Ho! (A Pirates Life for Me!)," catchphrases such as "Drink up me hearties, yo ho!" or "Shiver me timbers!" as well as the drunken, witty, and cunning characteristics Captain Jack Sparrow embodies—find their way into the films from numerous textual sources. But rather than mark the spot of its textual origins, Pirates operates on the understanding that the franchise is part of a larger process of textual reception and that our engagement with the film is part of responding to and rewriting the Pirates narrative in complicity with the films' own forms of rewriting and response.

With these kinds of textual interactions the Pirates franchise defines our engagement with it as a spectatorial "sequel" to an "original" event. But not only through its source texts is this engagement constructed; indeed, the swathe of related Pirates merchandize and offshoots informs and shapes our engagement with the film to the point where sequelized spectatorship comes to mean the act of negotiating adaptation and rewriting processes of original texts *at the same time as* repeating, "rewriting," and reexperiencing a text that is constructed by its own reception and textualization.

From the outset the Pirates ride operated as an extension of the logic of Disneyland. Contextualized within the "totally controlled environment" of Disneyland in which visitors find "themselves immersed in a fantasy world where unique images and experiences evoked laughter, wonder, curiosity, and emotional warmth," the Pirates ride guides guests seated in a boat through an underground cavern featuring 3-D scenes—prescribing, therefore, the order and pace by which the scenes are experienced and preventing guests from straying into the sets (Watts 390, 389). Although the Pirates ride is organized as a sequential "ride," with one scene following on from the next, the "narrative" is not linear, but designed as a repetitively circular experience that one can repeat and enjoy as many times as desired. This is entirely in keeping with the Walt Disney Company's tendency to rerelease its films in cinemas and on television, video and DVD, which are, for the most part, remakes of fairy tales and narratives that had previously enjoyed circulation throughout popular culture (Brockus 198–99).[3] In both cases, repetition is a crucial aspect of the overall experience. Both activities reflect the dichotomy of repetition and circularity underscoring Disneyland. Although Walt Disney famously crafted what he termed "weenies," or attractions that lure the eye, then the feet, thereby guiding visitors in a carefully organized sequence of attractions, from one ride to the next, and so on, Disneyland is a maze of interconnecting sequences in which one can find a variety of journeys, destinations, and experiences (see Bryman 99). The ways in which such sequences are interconnected precisely establishes such journeys and experiences as collaborative, synergistic, and necessarily collective, thereby perpetuating the sense of a "world" in which the textual meets the spatial and in which participation, appropriation, and the circulation of meanings across fan communities are central dynamics.

The "world" of the Pirates franchise is constructed primarily by retextualizations of Captain Jack Sparrow. Popularized by a gamut of fan endorsements and, subsequently, commercial and media tie-ins, Sparrow operates across the franchise as a source of (inter)textual unity across the films *and* as a paratextual agent beyond the filmic narrative. As a film character, Sparrow invokes Paul Budra's notion of the "charismatic" sequel protagonist, who, usually the subject of horror films, enables and sustains numerous sequels precisely because he or she frequently evades death. In the Pirates films, Sparrow avoids death because he is already dead, and his charisma is largely the result of Depp's quirky and rigorously researched performance, which originally caused studio execs to lament, "He's ruining the film!" (qtd. in Williams, "Interview"). Sparrow also sustains the Pirates sequels *and* the sequelization of the franchise in the forms of Sparrow merchandize, media tie-ins, and cultural events because of character traits that specifically endorse his celebrity. Repeatedly referring to his own infamy, part of Sparrow's filmic characterization is to construct his own mythology and to add to and comment on his reputation. Insistent on being addressed as "Captain" Jack Sparrow, one of Sparrow's characterizations is this repeated salute: "You will always remember this as the day you almost caught Captain Jack Sparrow"—a

Figure 12.2 *Pirates of the Caribbean: At World's End* (Gore Verbinski, 2007). Courtesy Walt Disney/The Kobal Collection/Mountain, Peter.

notable refrain across all three films and the subject of repeated comedy. Another characterizing refrain is the repeated scene of Sparrow (or his messengers) being slapped across the face by a (different) scorned former lover, suggesting his promiscuity and, perhaps more important, his notoriety. Surprisingly chuffed by Captain Norrington's (Jack Davenport) comment that Sparrow is "the worst pirate I have ever heard of," Sparrow retorts proudly, "but you have heard of me." Both the first and last film installment show Sparrow dreaming of being "the *immortal* Captain Jack Sparrow."

His charismatic characterization notwithstanding, Sparrow is not the films' main character. According to the screenwriters, Ted Elliott and Terry Rossio, Elizabeth (Kiera Knightly) is the protagonist (Holleran). Yet a massive public response to the first film saw Sparrow highlighted as the most popular character for audience interaction and participation, and apparently the person most children want to be when they grow up (see Land 169). Betty Jo Tucker, for instance, declared Depp's character one of "filmdom's most memorable rogues" ("Keeping an Eye"), and Emanuel Levy hailed Sparrow as "the only truly iconic screen character to have yet come out of this new millennium." Notably, Depp's performance kept critics and audiences in hot anticipation of the sequels. In her review of *Pirates of the Caribbean: Dead Man's Chest*, Tessa Strasser minces no words: "Few sequels are ever quite as good as the original, but if Depp's role in the third *Pirates* movie is any bit as large as it was in this, there are only good things on the horizon." At the very least, film reviews applauded Depp's performance for keeping the franchise afloat (Catsoulis; Rechtshaffen). Film execs felt the same way; gushed producer Jerry Bruckheimer at the release of *Pirates of the Caribbean: Dead Man's Chest*, "None of us would be back if Johnny Depp had not wanted to play this character again" (qtd. in Tucker, "How to Steal a Movie").

Sparrow's popularization has perceivably impacted his characterization in the two *Pirates* sequels. Chosen by critics and fans as a key figure of popular culture—and apparently the most popular Halloween costume in the United States in 2006—Sparrow quickly garnered his own MySpace profile ("Captain Jack Sparrow"), a dedicated fan-listing Web site called *Savvy?* ("Captain Jack Sparrow Fan Listed"), a Wikipedia entry ("Jack Sparrow"), and a parodic recharacterization as Captain Jack Swallows (Darrell Hammond) in metaparody *Epic Movie* (Jason Friedberg and Aaron Seltzer, 2007; McConahay). The discourse surrounding the Sparrow character perceivably creates a community of participation, at the same time as the sheer scale of interactive contexts tailored for Sparrow rewrites the character as an "intertextual commodity" (Marshall). In other words, Sparrow's numerous retextualizations used the character as an organizing textual framework for a variety of community events and collective experiences, and this framework inevitably corresponded to and magnified the overarching Pirates "world."

Sparrow's community of response found its way into the final *Pirates* installment in the form of a community of Sparrows. Here, Sparrow is depicted in Davy Jones's Locker as on the receiving end of a postmortem punishment in the form of multiple hallucinations. In full self-reflexive mode, these hallucinations are Sparrow's narcissistic multiplications of himself—that is, Sparrow imagines himself as both captain and crew members of the Black Pearl (including a goat and hen), reminiscent of the identical Agent Smiths that multiplied in *Matrix Reloaded* and *Matrix Revolutions* (Andy and Larry Wachowski, both 2003). Effectively rewriting himself in a variety of imagined contexts, Sparrow registers the discourse surrounding this character (and, more generally, the Pirates franchise) as paratextual, or what Genette describes as a text's "secondary signal" (*Palimpsests* 3). As a method of reading and engaging with the franchise, Sparrow's textual secondariness underscores the ways in which the franchise responds to its own reception—for example, allowing players to perform the character of Captain Jack Sparrow in the Pirates of the Caribbean MMORPG (or massively multiplayer online role-playing game) that features Depp's voice or updating the original Disneyland Pirates ride by installing a new Sparrow automaton in Depp's likeness in replacement of the "original" Sparrow. Our engagement with Sparrow as a film character and throughout each of the related media tie-ins involves navigating Sparrow's intertexts and his rewriting as the paratext of Pirates' larger textual domain. The result of this is that the *Pirates* franchise becomes an "original" or source, insofar as Sparrow's relation to the franchise becomes defined as a secondary textualization of an originating work.

Sparrow's retextualization persistently expands the Pirates "world" in terms of the discursive activity surrounding this character, which is continually and necessarily collaborative. As spectators of the Pirates films, we never engage with a "source" text, or within an isolated diegetic terrain, but rather with what Matt Hills refers to as a "hyperdiegesis," a "vast and detailed narrative space" in which "only a fraction [. . .] is ever directly seen or encountered" within a given text, "but which nevertheless appears to operate according to principles of internal logic and extension" (137). This extension is facilitated by the strictly collaborative exercises generated by Sparrow's rewriting and the Pirates "experience." These exercises involve discussing the film with friends, family, and strangers in online chat rooms and web blogs, engaging in Volvo's online hunt for a treasure chest filled with $50,000 in gold doubloons and keys to a brand spanking new Volvo XC90 by answering online weekly Pirates-related riddles, and, as other Disney films have engineered, engaging in a memorable experience by which family and cultural relationships can be defined, strengthened, and continually recalled through the Pirates of the Caribbean. Like the Disney "world" from which it departs, the Pirates "world" is founded on a concept instead of a narrative, using the structure of the sequel as a strategy that underlines the crossover between media. As Espen Aarseth notes of recent developments in multimedia concepts—citing *Death Jr.* as a primary example—"concept licenses, rather than content, move between media platforms" (204; see also "Death Jr."). In the case of the Pirates franchise, this move between platforms extends into the realm of audience engagement, as suggested by the advertising slogan for the MMORPG: "The most notorious pirate in the Caribbean . . . is you" (see "Pirate's Legend").

Such community-building exercises not only expand the Pirates "world" but inevitably lead back to its source texts. Piracy's textual history furnished the Pirates ride with the values of teamwork and community building. In many historical accounts piracy emerges as the construction of a new social order that, despite the violence and danger that faced every pirate, was purportedly desirable to many "legitimate" seafarers in terms of the forms of belonging, trust, and self-governance on which piracy was predicated (see Land 174–80). Such descriptions of piracy's social organization bear striking parallels to Disney's corporate structure. Markus Rediker describes the typical pirate ship as "a little kingdom" (206), whereas Chris Land observes that piracy during its "golden age" operates as a "transnational brotherhood" (179). Such descriptions would sit equally well within most of Disney's ventures. Note the following examples: "Team Disney" is the term given to Disney's management team, and the name "Imagineer"—with its evocations of Alexandre Dumas' band-of-brothers novel, *The Three Musketeers*, which features the motto "One for all, and all for one"—is attributed to every Disney employee involved in research and development. Even the employees who enact Disney characters in full costume at Disneyland bear the job description "Teamster," being part of the International Brotherhood of Teamsters. By reconstructing piracy's textual history as a ride at Disneyland, Walt Disney couched the social resonances of piracy within the physical, commercial, and ideological boundaries of his corporate domain. Effectively acting as a paratext to the Walt Disney Company, the Pirates ride substantiated the particular emphases on community, belonging, and synergy that underscore the Disney ethos.

Portraits of community and teamwork abound in the Pirates films, but for different purposes than those outlined earlier. In *Pirates of the*

Caribbean: *At World's End*, the opening scene features a portrait of the kind of mass hangings that Captain Charles Johnson detailed in his book, during which a young boy sings a pirate "anthem" immediately before his execution, but not before the whole siege of convicts has joined in. Not only does the song spread quickly throughout the execution court but also, the film informs us, resonates through the pieces of eight that are held by all nine lords of the Pirate World, who must then gather at Brethren Court. In addition, Brethren Court is the *fourth* Brethren Court, and is thus underscored by its serial nature. The film's opening scene quickly marks the interconnectivity and scale of a "world" comprising smaller collectives, communities, and codes. The film's structure is accordingly composed of interconnected narratives and communities, and as such the spectatorial engagement involves a negotiation of collectives and codes that deliberately facilitates and provokes engagement with extrafilmic collectives and codes, such as the Pirates of the Caribbean MMORPG, which, as its name suggests, is a specifically collaborative game, designed to connect players with "thousands of other players" with whom the player can "forge alliances."[4] The diegesis, in other words, is composed of "real" opponents and figures. As Larry Shapiro, executive vice president of the Walt Disney Internet Group's business development and operations, observed, the Pirates mobile phone game "allows players to interact across multiple carriers" (qtd. in Marchetti). Describing the game as "an exciting new universe," Shapiro's words are echoed by franchise contributors, who are at pains to call each separate textual offshoot a "world" or, at the very least, a means by which "players" and participants can enter the Pirates "world." Such ventures in world creation involve patterns of continuation and end-deferral within a community context. By operating within an interactive community, the narrative is continually extended across the interactions and contributions of its players. And of course, these interactions and contributions extend far beyond the game: a Pirates of the Caribbean MMORPG web forum is available at www.plundertheport.com, the express purpose of which is to facilitate discussions with other players.

By creating numerous "worlds" and communities that—more important—are connected to and interactive with a larger textual domain, the Pirates franchise generates an immersive landscape that attempts to make *everything* related to the Pirates text. Indeed, the chief imperative of immersive media is to make everything—even the most arbitrary aspects of the quotidian—a part of media reality. As Jane McGonigal writes of gaming, "a good immersive game will show you game patterns in non-game places; those patterns reveal opportunities for interaction and intervention." At once immersive and prescriptive with regard to the kind of experience one is to expect and enjoy while inside that "world," worlds such as Magic Kingdom, Disney World, Tokyo Disneyland, and Disneyland Paris construct consumer experiences that reach far beyond their time inside the park's walls. Suggesting cinema as an early "immersive art form," McGonigal describes immersive gaming as a subgenre of the larger activity of *pervasive play*, which "consists of 'mixed reality' games that use mobile, ubiquitous and embedded digital technologies to create virtual playing fields in everyday spaces." The distinction between immersive gaming and pervasive play, she claims, is made by a rhetorical element of the subgenre that appears to underscore the franchise ethos in contemporary cinema: "This is not a game." This disclaimer operates somewhat antithetically to its initial presupposition: it operates to eschew the game-status of an actual game and, thus, embed the concept of gaming into every reality. Among the outcomes of McGonigal's research in this area is the suggestion that both pervasive play and immersive gaming involve extending the game play. In effect, pervasive play becomes an experience of sequelization and convergence, in that the gaming reality is not only transferred to every scenario, but that every scenario becomes an opportunity for the game *to continue*, and therefore defer any kind of ending.

Sequelized spectatorship is comparable to the type of gaming outlined in McGonigal's thesis. The Pirates franchise included, such immersive "worlds" are nothing more than perpetually deferred narratives. More specifically, participation and interaction within immersive environments is predicated on and contributes to the continuation of a narrative beyond its cinematic encounter. Notably, the structure of the sequel is reiterated throughout such continuations. Drawing on the spectator-consumers' knowledge of its textual predecessor, the "sequel"— whether in the form of a mobile phone game, online game, merchandize, or any of the cultural events noted earlier—rewards that knowledge by offering spectator-consumers' rewriting capabilities or the ability to use their memories, knowledge, and engagements with a textual predecessor in the creation of their own "personal" sequel. The sense of "community" that Disney increasingly constructs among its fan base, and which is reinstated by the Pirates franchise, is a territory within which social interaction is defined by sequelization.

The list of merchandizing tactics and gimmicks generated from the Pirates franchise underlines and (of course) capitalizes upon this idea. Here an observation by Steve McBeth, vice president of consumer products for Disney, is significant: the policy of providing "movie mementoes," he states, "extends the entertainment experience [. . .]—it's a way of letting the fun of the movie continue" (qtd. in Twitchell 142). Like their media intertexts, the morass of Pirates merchandize enables the experience of the movie to continue in the form of toys, fake pirate flags, plastic pieces of eight, and so on. Merchandizing also operates as an important "memory-making" tool (see Brockus 198), whereby the experience of the film and its media events and tie-ins can be recalled and reexperienced through a physical object. But in the case of the Pirates films, merchandize not only continues and recalls the Pirates narrative, but also remediates the vast range of intertexts beneath the Disney umbrella.

Importantly, we should note briefly just how big this range is. Dubbed "the foremost merchandizing company in Hollywood" (Wasko, *Understanding* 50), Disney was among the first transnational media corporations to identify the importance of merchandizing, and it remains at the forefront of synergistic innovations between media and commercial vehicles. When *Snow White and the Seven Dwarfs* was released in 1937, Disney had followed the trend of film serials in cinema's early years by creating a literary tie-in in the form of serial comics, produced weekly, two months before the film's release. With the comic serial reaching the point of the story at which the dwarfs are returning home to find an unexpected guest, marketing executives intended the film as an extension of the comic, with readers rushing to cinemas to find out what happened next. In the early 1980s, Disney formed an alliance with fast-food empire McDonalds resulting in the McDonald's Happy Meal venture, which included small toys based on characters from Disney films. In May 1996, a contract was signed that allowed McDonald's exclusive rights to produce fluffy toy figurines of Disney characters to accompany its Happy Meals. Such toys contributed enormously to the success of Happy Meals, which, by 2002, made up 20 percent of the annual sales of McDonald's, totaling approximately $3.5 billion. With Pirates, celebrated by the company as "our biggest cross-platform franchise ever," Disney has reached a merchandizing apex (see "Walt Disney Q3 2006"). As reported in Disney's Earnings Conference Call Transcript for the third quarter of 2006, the Disney Consumer Products division's income increased by 70 percent over the previous year to $105 million, much of which was due to sales of Pirates-themed merchandize (see "CARU Asks Disney to Stop").

Contextualized within the specifically interactive and experiential "world" of the Pirates franchise, Pirates merchandize offers more than recall and continuation; like the textualization, popularization, and rampant performance of the Captain Jack Sparrow character, Pirates merchandize for the most part operates as a paratextual "tool" by which the "original" can be rewritten and "reread" by fans. This is not to suggest, however, that memory-making does not figure in Pirates merchandize. More exactly, the forms of memory-making at large across

Disney merchandizing involve forms of collaboration and community
building additional to those created by the strategies outlined earlier.
Indeed, Disney's merchandizing creates *generational* communities, perpetuating experiences and memories not just across geographical locations,
but also from one generation to another, so that the act of engaging in
a Disney film or venture becomes heavily invested with emotional ties.
For instance, I have distinct (and especially fond) memories of watching the 1983 rerelease of *The Sword in the Stone* (Wolfgang Reitherman,
1963) at age five with my mother at our local cinema; I now own this
film in DVD format and look forward to enjoying it with my daughter
when she is old enough specifically because of the memories it contains
of me and my mother enjoying time together. Such emotional investment
additionally makes my endorsing any products associated with this film
much more likely. As Susan Brockus states, "Disney's dedication to the
production of family-friendly entertainment means that such selection
may be inextricably entwined with perceptions of family and the creation
and retention of family memories" (199).

The persistent rerelease of Disney's films facilitates generational
memory-making and transference, at the same time as each rerelease
generates memories in the form of additional features, merchandizing
gimmicks, and continual citations of the film's heritage. In the case of
the Pirates franchise, the act of rereleasing the films is replaced by the
structure of the sequel—of which there are two—and, as I suggested
earlier, by framing all related Pirates products and activities through
the notion of *creating* a sequel in the form of an experience that may
be shared by scores of other participants. But the importance of such
sharing across generations creates a loyalty and much more emotional
participation with the franchise that, essentially, contributes beyond any
other strategy to the construction of an immersive "world."

Disney's status as cultural heritage brings to our engagement with
the Pirates franchise a connection not only with the vast number of
intertexts and paratexts generated by its synergistic textualizations, but
also a connection to the family experience and, beyond that, to the particular culture to which Disney has subscribed as a souvenir and signifier. This is a key component of the Pirates franchise in terms of the
specifically "souvenir" kinds of merchandize (pirate weapons, flags, maps,
and outfits), which evoke a sense of heritage and retrieving history, and
also in terms of the specifically generational nature of piracy embedded
within the films. With Keith Richards making headlines in a cameo role
as Sparrow's father—and all the connotations this brings to Sparrow's
retextualization in popular culture—the film franchise also grapples with
the issue of Will Turner's father in terms of his emotional debt to "Boot-

strap" Bill Turner (Stellan Skarsgård) and Will's (vain) wish to escape the family tradition of piracy. The franchise ends on the suggestion of a continuation of the adventure in the form of a second generation, featuring an after-credits shot of Will's son (Dominic Scott Kay) waiting for him on the horizon. In its double exploitation of souvenirs and generational ties—both of which are Disney hallmarks—the franchise concludes with the sentiment that, to paraphrase Barbossa (Geoffrey Rush), passing on the Pirates cultural heritage is certain if the "worlds" propagated by Disney are to survive.

Each of the paratexts and paratextual activities noted earlier evidence what Toby Miller et al. describe as "marketing modules," which "serve more than an economic function, for when they penetrate public space, they also affect the aesthetic experience of filmgoing" (264). Similarly, sequelized spectatorship involves the *affect* of the sequel as an organizing framework through which the franchise can be experienced, while the commercial imperatives of the sequel are part of the overall *effect*. The types of affect and effect outlined in this chapter are complicit with models of interactivity and participation explored elsewhere,[5] particularly in terms of the suggestion that, in immersive environments and VR scenarios, the spectator directs his or her own experience. As my discussion of sequelized spectatorship indicates, such agency always subscribes to a carefully mapped geography of control. Yet describing this encounter as passive is not enough; as a Pirates spectator, for instance, I witness and participate with my own spectatorial encounter. Part of that encounter is the construction, or rewriting, of the Pirates franchise as a sequel to my reception. The rather reflexive correspondences between writing and rewriting, as well as paratext and source text, underscore the notion of sequelized spectatorship. At the same time as it proffers various scenarios and systems of "secondariness" as an informing ingredient for our engagement with the films, the Pirates franchise is constructed as its own paratext, its own reception, or its own system of sequelization. In addition, the host of products and experiences comprising the franchise suggest that the concepts of "original" and "sequel" are in place, but not fixed: it is the spectator that generates the sequelization of a conceptual "original."

In its creation of synergistic modes, activities, and "worlds," the Pirates franchise reworks the traditional original-sequel trajectory into a horizontal pattern of participation. What is the result for the Walt Disney Company? More money, of course; as box-office figures show, audiences are not simply keen on familiarity but on cross-media activities and tie-ins deriving from a source-text. Another outcome is that, following the Pirates franchise, Disney is trimming the fat off its film production output to less than half (from 18 films a year to approximately

8), with a specific focus on Disney-branded productions instead of films produced by subsidiary studios (Ryssdal). The idea behind this move is to concentrate on spending more money on films with merchandizing and franchise value, and arguably on building up the Disney "kingdom" so that each new venture recalls and continues the cultural heritage that the Walt Disney Company has come to evoke. But beyond these industrial measures, the specific methods of spectatorial sequelization created by film franchises perpetuate and will no doubt continue to perpetuate such a cultural heritage and propel Disney's momentum.

In closing, I draw on a scene from *Pirates of the Caribbean: At World's End* as a final metaphor for the kind of spectator-franchise relation for which I have been arguing. Stranded on his ship in the barren desert of the afterlife, Captain Jack Sparrow resorts to single-handedly pulling the *Black Pearl* back to the ocean by a rope through the sand—getting, of course, absolutely nowhere. Aided by one, two, and finally millions of Tia Dalma's (Naomie Harries) crabs, Sparrow and his ship are carouseled over the dunes to open waters, back to the land of the living. The sequelizing mechanisms surrounding the Pirates films operate in a manner similar to Dalma's crabs, carrying the *concept* of the Pirates of the Caribbean to the vast, interactive spaces afforded by the Internet, mobile phones, and indeed the range of innovative tie-ins launched by the franchise. What this means for me, the single spectator, is that my engagement with the film is inherently collaborative, mediated, and part of a process of exchange and continuation: from the subject of conversation with friends and family to playing the mobile phone game during long commutes. And, just maybe, sharing the film's rerelease with future generations.

Notes

1. According to John Robert Moore, this is a pseudonym for Daniel Defoe, but like much of the historical data surrounding piracy, Moore's claim is impossible to verify. See Moore, and also Furbank and Owens for a counterargument to this claim.

2. Yes, this exists. See <http://www.talklikeapirate.com/>. N.d. Accessed 17 May 2007.

3. For instance, *Snow White and the Seven Dwarfs* was released in 1937 after a three-year production period, costing upward of $1.5 million. Earning $8 million on its release, the film has been released no less than nine times, continuing to earn $40 million in less than eight weeks on its relaunch fifty years after its original release (see Wasko, *Understanding* 129).

4. See <http://disney.go.com/disneymobile/mdisney/pirates/about.html>. Accessed 14 June 2007.

5. Matt Hills describes affect as "the attachments, emotions and passions of those who self-identify as 'fans,' but who may also contest the description" (xi), whereas Henry Jenkins talks about "impressions" and "expressions" in terms of how audiences react and respond to content (*Convergence Culture* 63). Hills also talks about "the serialisation of the audience" in similar yet clearly distinct terms to my argument in this chapter, and his comments are helpful and provocative for further study: focusing on "online fandoms," Hill considers fan activities as synthesizing with a text to the point where the text "perform[s] its fan audience-hood, knowing that other fans will act as a readership for speculations, observations and commentaries" (177). The forms of rewriting, reperformance, and retextualization outlined in his work complement the investigations of affect and effect in the context of sequelized spectatorship raised in this chapter.

Works Cited

Aarseth, Espen. "The Culture and Business of Cross-Media Productions." *Journal of Popular Communication* 4.3 (2006): 203–11. Print.

Adams, Judith A. *The American Amusement Park Industry: A History of Technology and Thrills*. New York: Twayne, 1991. Print.

Allen, Graham. *Intertextuality*. New York: Routledge, 2000. Print.

Anderson, Kurt. "American Roulette." *New Yorker Magazine* 8 Jan. 2007. Web. 16 Aug. 2007. <http://nymag.com/news/imperialcity/26014/index.html>.

Anderton, Frances, and John Chase. *Las Vegas: The Success of Excess*. London: Ellipsis, 1997. Print.

"Animal Logic: About Us." 1999. Web. 10 Oct. 2007. <http://www.animallogic. com/about/keypeople.html>.

Appadurai, Arjun. *Modernity at Large: Cultural Dimensions of Globalization*. Minneapolis: U of Minnesota P, 1996. Print.

"Archive of the General Discussions Forum." Fireflyfans.net Message Board. 15 Apr. 2007. Web. 7 Mar. 2007. <http://fireflyfans.net/threadlist.asp?b=2 &a=1>.

Aristotle. *Aristotle's Theory of Poetry and Fine Art*. 1911. Trans. S. H. Butcher. 4th ed. New York: Dover, 1951. Print.

Arnold, Thomas K. " 'Ringu' calls 'Ring' fans to video stores: To their horror, Japanese version is difficult to find." *USA Today* 25 Oct. 2002: D16. Print.

Aumont, Jacques. *The Image*. Trans. Claire Pajackowska. London: BFI, 1997. Print.

"Auraptor." "FFF.net I've Seen Serenity Thread." Fireflyfans.net Message Board. 24 June 2005. Web. 7 Mar. 2007. <http://www.fireflyfans.net/thread. asp?b=2&t=10997>.

Balio, Tino. *Grand Design: Hollywood as a Modern Business Enterprise, 1930–1939*. Berkeley: U of California P, 1993. Print.

———, ed. *The American Film Industry*. Rev. ed. Madison: U of Wisconsin P, 1985. Print.

Barthes, Roland. "The Death of the Author." *Image—Music—Text*. Trans. Stephen Heath. London: Fontana, 1977. Print.

————. *Empire of Signs*. Trans. Richard Howard. New York: Hill and Wang, 1982. Print.

————. *The Pleasure of the Text*. Trans. Richard Miller. New York: Noonday P, 1975. Print.

Bartlem, Edwina. "Reshaping Spectatorship: Immersive and Distributed Aesthetics." *FibreCulture* Dec. 2005. Web. 19 May 2007. <http://journal.fibreculture.org/issue7/issue7_bartlem.html>.

Batchen, Geoffrey. *Burning with Desire: The Conception of Photography*. Cambridge, MA: MIT Press, 1997. Print.

Baudrillard, Jean. *The Conspiracy of Art*. Ed. Sylvere Lotringer. Trans. Ames Hodges. New York: Semiotext(e), 2005. Print.

————. *Simulacra and Simulation*. Trans. Sheila Glaser. Ann Arbor: U of Michigan P, 1994. Print.

Beard, Steve. "No Particular Place to Go." *Sight and Sound* 5.4 (1993): 30–31. Print.

Benjamin, Walter. *Das Passagen-werk*. Gesammelte Schriften. Ed. Rolf Tiedermann. Vol. 2. Main: Surkamp, 1982. Print.

Bennett, Susan. *Theatre Audiences: A Theory of Production and Reception*. 2nd ed. London: Routledge, 1997. Print.

Berliner, Todd. "The Pleasures of Disappointment: Sequels and *The Godfather, Part II*." *Journal of Popular Film and Video* 53.2–3 (2001): 107–23. Print.

Biodrowski, Steve. "*The Return of the Living Dead*." *Cinefantastique* 15.4 (Oct. 1985): 16–18, 21–24, 26–28. Print.

"Biography for Kevin Costner." Internet Movie Database. N.d. Web. 22 Dec. 2006. <http://www.imdb.com/name/nm0000126/bio>.

Bishop, Kyle. "Raising the Dead: Unearthing the Non-literary Origins of Zombie Cinema." *Journal of Popular Film and Television* 33.4 (Winter 2006): 196–205. Print.

Biskind, Peter. *Down and Dirty Pictures: Miramax, Sundance, and the Rise of Independent Film*. New York: Simon, 2004. Print.

————. *The Godfather Companion*. New York: Harper, 1990. Print.

Bradshaw, Peter. "*Die Hard 4.0*." *Guardian Unlimited Arts*. 29 June 2007. Web. 22 July 2007. <http://arts.guardian.co.uk/filmandmusic/story/0,,2114084,00.html>.

Brockus, Susan. "Where Magic Lives: Disney's Cultivation, Co-Creation, and Control of America's Cultural Objects." *Journal of Popular Communication* 2.4 (2004): 191–211. Print.

Brodesser, Claude. "Vertigo Spins with U, Focus." *Variety.com* 19 Aug. 2004. Web. 27 Nov. 2008. <http://www.variety.com/article/VR1117909306?categoryid=1237&cs=1>.

Brodesser, Claude, and Charles Lyons. " 'Ring' Fits D'Works Digits." *Variety.com*. 1 Feb. 2001. Web. 27 Nov. 2008. <http://www.variety.com/article/VR1117793066?categoryid=13&cs=1>.

Brooker, Will. "Batman: One Life, Many Faces." *Adaptations: From Text to Screen, Screen to Text*. Ed. Deborah Cartmell and Imelda Whelehan. London: Routledge, 1999. 185–98. Print.

Browne, Nick. "Fearful A-Symmetries: Violence as History in the *Godfather* Films." Browne 1–22.

———, ed. *Francis Ford Coppola's* The Godfather Trilogy. Cambridge, UK: Cambridge UP, 2000. Print.

Bryman, Allan. *Disney and His Worlds.* London: Routledge, 1995. Print.

Budra, Paul. "Recurrent Monsters: Why Freddy, Michael, and Jason Keep Coming Back." Budra and Schellenberg 189–99.

Budra, Paul, and Betty A. Schellenberg. Introduction. Budra and Schellenberg 1–18.

———, eds. *Part Two: Reflections on the Sequel.* Toronto: U of Toronto P, 1998. Print.

Bukatman, Scott. "X-Bodies (The Torment of the Mutant Superhero)." *Uncontrollable Bodies: Testimonies of Identity and Culture.* Ed. Rodney Sappington and Tyler Stallings. Seattle: Bay Press, 1994. Print.

Burch, Noël. *To the Distant Observer: Form and Meaning in Japanese Cinema.* Berkeley: U of California P, 1979. Print.

Burrow, J. A. "Poems without Contexts: The Rawlinson Lyrics." *Essays in Criticism* 29 (1979): 1–19. Print.

Capps, Donald. "Childhood Fears, Adult Anxieties, and the Longing for Inner Peace: Erik H. Erikson's Psychoanalytic Psychology of Religion." *Religion, Society, and Psychoanalysis: Readings in Contemporary Theory.* Ed. Janet Liebman Jacobs and Donald Capps. Boulder, CO: Westview, 1997. Print.

"Captain Jack Sparrow." N.d. Web. 12 June 2007. <http://profile.myspace.com/index.cfm?fuseaction=user.viewprofile&friendid=130415021>.

"Captain Jack Sparrow Fan Listed, The." N.d. Web. 4 June 2007. <http://captain.saranya.net/>.

Caputi, Jane. "Films of the Nuclear Age." *Journal of Popular Film and Television* 16.3 (Fall 1988): 100–7. Print.

"CARU Asks Disney to Stop Advertising 'Pirates of the Caribbean' to Kids." N.d. Web. 2 June 2007. <http://www.assistantdirectors.com/News/?m=200609>.

Castle, Terry. *Masquerade and Civilization: The Carnivalesque in Eighteenth-Century English Culture and Fiction.* London: Methuen, 1986. Print.

Castro, Janice, Kanice Seiichi, and Elaine Lafferty. "From Walkman to Showman." *Time* 9 Oct. 1989: 70–71. Print.

Catsoulis, Jeannette. "Back to the Bounding Main." *New York Times* 24 May 2007. Web. 8 June 2007. <http://movies2.nytimes.com/2007/05/24/movies/24pira.html>.

Cattrysse, Patrick. *Pour une théorie de l'adaptation filmique.* Berne: Lang, 1992. Print.

Cazdyn, Eric. *The Flash of Capital: Film and Geopolitics in Japan.* Durham, NC: Duke UP, 2002. Print.

Chang, Justin. "New Zombie Zeitgeist." *Variety* 27 June–10 July 2005: 58, 68. Print.

Chung, Hye Seung, and David Scott Diffrient. "Interethnic Romance and Political Reconciliation in *Asako in Ruby Shoes.*" *New Korean Cinema.* Ed. Chi-Yun Shin and Julian Stringer. New York: New York UP, 2005. 193–209. Print.

Cieply, Michael. "It's Not a Sequel, but It Might Seem like One after the Ads." *New York Times* 24 Apr. 2007. Web. 23 July 2007. <http://www.nytimes. com/2007/04/24/movies/24orig.html?ex=1335067200&en=34c654466333c f3d&ei=5088&partner=rssnyt&emc=rss>.

Coates, Ryan. "Lack of Creativity in Hollywood? What Happened to Original- ity?" *Associated Content.* 20 July 2005. Web. 23 July 2007. <http://www.asso- ciatedcontent.com/article/5947/lack_of_creativity_in_hollywood.html>.

Conrich, Ian. "Metal-Morphosis: Post-Industrial Crisis and the Tormented Body in the *Tetsuo* Films." *Japanese Horror Cinema.* Ed. Jay McRoy. Honolulu: U of Hawaii P, 2005. Print.

Cook, Pam. *Screening the Past: Memory and Nostalgia in Cinema.* London: Rout- ledge, 2005. Print.

Corliss, Richard. "The Year of the 3quel." *Time* 4 Jan. 2007. Web. 7 Mar. 2007. <http://www.time.com/time/magazine/article/0,9171,1574141,00.html>.

"Corrections." *Hollywood Reporter* 13 Feb. 2003: 20. Print.

Crowther, Bosley. "The Lemps Again." *New York Times* 11 Jan. 1941. Web. 17 Dec. 2006. <http://movies2.nytimes.com/mem/movies/review.html?res=9A 05E5D9123DE33BBC4952DFB766838A659EDE>.

———. *The Lion's Share: The Story of an Entertainment Empire.* 1957. New York: Garland, 1985. Print.

Cubitt, Sean. *The Cinema Effect.* Cambridge, MA: MIT Press, 2004. Print.

Cumings, Bruce. *Korea's Place in the Sun: A Modern History.* New York: Norton, 1997. Print.

D'Agnolo-Vallan, Giulia. "Let Them Eat Flesh." *Film Comment* 41.4 (July–Aug. 2005): 23–24. Print.

"Death Jr." N.d. Web. 17 May 2007. <www.deathjr.com>.

DeCandido, Keith R. A. " 'The Train Job' Didn't Do the Job." *Finding Serenity: Anti-Heroes, Lost Shepherds and Space Hookers in Joss Whedon's* Firefly. Ed. Jane Espenson. Dallas: Benbella, 2004: 55–62. Print.

DeCroix, Rick. " 'Once Upon a Time in Idealized America . . .': Simulated Uto- pia and the Hardy Family Series." *Cultural Power/Cultural Literacy: Selected Papers from the Fourteenth Annual Florida State University Conference on Lit- erature and Film.* Ed. Bonnie Braendlin. Gainesville: UP of Florida, 1991. 152–66. Print.

Deleuze, Gilles. *Cinema 1: The Movement Image.* Trans. Hugh Tomlinson and Barbara Habberjam. London: Athlone, 1992. Print.

———. *Difference and Repetition.* Trans. Paul Patton. London: Athlone, 1994. Print.

Denby, David. "Family Matters." *New Yorker* 14 Oct. 2005. Web. 20 Sep. 2006. <http://www.newyorker.com/archive/2005/10/24/051024crci_cinema>.

Derrida, Jacques. *Archive Fever.* Trans. Eric Prenowitz. Chicago: U of Chicago P, 1996. Print.

Dick, Philip K. *The Simulacra.* 1964. New York: Vintage, 2002. Print.

Dillard, R. H. W. "*Night of the Living Dead*: It's Not like Just a Wind that's Passing Through." *American Horrors: Essays on the Modern American Horror Film.* Ed. Gregory A. Waller. Urbana: U of Illinois P, 1987. Print.

Doane, Mary Ann. *The Emergence of Cinematic Time: Modernity, Contingency, the Archive*. Cambridge, MA: Harvard UP, 2002. Print.

———. "Technology's Body: Cinematic Vision in Modernity." *differences* 5.2 (1993): 1–23. Print.

Doherty, Thomas. "*Night of the Living Dead*: The Original." *Cinefantastique* 21.3 (Dec. 1990): 20–21, 60. Print.

Doyle, Sir Arthur Conan. *The New Annotated Sherlock Holmes*. Ed. Leslie S. Klinger. 3 vols. New York: Norton, 2005–6. Print.

"Dreamworks East." *Fortune* 28 Oct. 1996: 158. Print.

"Drew." "Cancelled Shows that Need Closure." Ex Isle Message Board. 31 Dec. 2006. Web. 7 Mar. 2007. <http://www.exisle.net/mb/index.php?show topic=42949>.

Drew, Bernard A. *Motion Picture Series and Sequels: A Reference Guide*. New York: Garland, 1990. Print.

Dryer, Jennifer. "Meaning in the Mundane: Andy Warhol's Theory of Repetition." *Travelling Concepts II: Meaning, Frame and Metaphor*. Ed. Joyce Goggin and Michael Burk. Amsterdam: ASCAP, 2002. 77–92. Print.

du Gay, Paul, Stuart Hall, Linda Janes, Hugh Mackay, and Keith Negus. *Doing Cultural Studies: The Story of the Sony Walkman*. London: Sage, 1997. Print.

Eco, Umberto. "Innovation and Repetition: Between Modern and Post-Modern Aesthetics." *Daedalus* 114.4 (Fall 1985): 161–84. Revised and rpt. as "Interpreting Serials" in *The Limits of Interpretation*. Bloomington: Indiana UP, 1990. Print.

Edwards, Gareth. "Next-gen games need to face facts." 7 July 2006. Web. 11 Nov. 2007. <http://www.image-metrics.com/news/im_news4_march24_2006.pdf>.

"11th Hour." "Guerilla [*sic*] Marketing Brainstorming Thread." Fireflyfans.net Message Board. 22 Aug. 2006. Web. 7 Mar. 2007. <http://fireflyfans.net/thread.asp?b=20&t=23296>.

Elsaesser, Thomas. "The Pathos of Failure: American Films in the 1970s: Notes on the Unmotivated Hero." Elsaesser et al. 279–92.

———. "Tales of Sound and Fury: Observations on the Family Melodrama." *Home Is Where the Heart Is: Studies in Melodrama and the Woman's Film*. Ed. Christine Gledhill. London: BFI, 1987. 43–70. Print.

Elsaesser, Thomas, Alexander Horwath, and Noel King, eds. *The Last Great American Picture Show: New Hollywood Cinema in the 1970s*. Amsterdam: Amsterdam UP, 2004. Print.

Esquenazi, Jean-Pierre. *Film, Perception et Mémoire*. Paris: L'Harmattan, 1994. Print.

Fielding, Helen. "*Bridget Jones's Diary*." *The Independent*, 1995–97. *The Daily Telegraph*, 1997–98. *The Independent*, 2005–6. Web. 20 Dec. 2006. <http://bridgetarchive.altervista.org/index1995.htm>.

———. *Bridget Jones's Diary*. 1996. Harmondsworth: Penguin, 2001. Print.

———. *Bridget Jones: The Edge of Reason*. 1999. Harmondsworth: Penguin, 2004. Print.

———. "Bridget Jones: This Time I Really Have Changed." 2001. Web. 20 Dec. 2006. <http://bridgetarchive.altervista.org/bridget_jones_changed.htm>.

Fingeroth, Danny. *Superman on the Couch: What Superheroes Tell Us about Ourselves and Society.* New York: Continuum International, 2004. Print.

Firat, A Fuat. "The Meanings and Messages of Las Vegas: The Present of our Future." *M@n@gement* 4.3 (2001): 101–20. Print.

"Firefly Season 2: On Demand—Seeking Independence from the Network Alliance." 15 Apr. 2007. Web. 7 Mar. 2007. <http://www.fireflyseason2.com/index.asp>.

Fischer, Dennis. *Horror Film Directors, 1931–1990.* Jefferson, NC: McFarland, 1990. Print.

Fjellman, Stephen M. *Vinyl Leaves: Walt Disney World and America.* Boulder, CO: Westview, 1992. Print.

Forrest, Jennifer. "The 'Personal' Touch: The Original, the Remake, and the Dupe in Early Cinema." Forrest and Koos 89–126. Print.

Forrest, Jennifer, and Leonard R. Koos, eds. *Dead Ringers: The Remake in Theory and Practice.* Albany: SUNY P, 2002. Print.

———. "Reviewing Remakes: An Introduction." Forrest and Koos 1–36. Print.

Forster, E. M. *Aspects of the Novel.* New York: Harcourt, Brace and World, 1927. Print.

Foucault, Michel. "The Discourse on Language." Trans. Rupert Swyer. *The Archaeology of Knowledge and the Discourse on Language.* Trans. A. M. Sheridan Smith. New York: Pantheon, 1972. Print.

Foundas, Scott. Rev. of *Resident Evil. Variety* 18–24 Mar. 2002: 24. Print.

Frasher, Michael. "Night of the Living Dead [1990]." *Cinefantastique* 21.3 (Dec. 1990): 16–22. Print.

Freud, Sigmund. "Beyond the Pleasure Principle." *The Standard Edition of the Complete Psychological Works of Sigmund Freud.* Ed. James Strachey and Anna Freud. Vol. XVIII. New York: Norton, 1978. 1–64. Print.

———. "Mourning and Melancholia." *On Murder, Mourning and Melancholia.* Trans. Shaun Whiteside. London: Penguin, 2005. 201–18. Print.

Friedberg, Anne. *Window Shopping: Cinema and the Postmodern.* Berkeley: U of California P, 1993. Print.

Friend, Tad. "Copy Cats." *New Yorker* 14 Sept. 1998: 51–57. Print.

———. "Remake Man: Roy Lee Brings Asia to Hollywood, and Finds Some Enemies Along the Way." *New Yorker* 2 June 2003. Web. 25 Nov. 2008. <http://www.newyorker.com/archive/2003/06/02/030602fa_fact>.

Furbank, P. N., and W. R. Owens. *The Canonisation of Daniel Defoe.* New Haven, CT: Yale UP, 1988. Print.

Gagne, Paul R. *The Zombies that Ate Pittsburgh: The Films of George A. Romero.* New York: Dodd, Mead, 1987. Print.

Garite, Matt. "The Ideology of Interactivity (Or, Video Games and the Taylorization of Leisure)." *Level Up.* Ed. Marinka Copier and Joost Raessens. Utrecht, The Netherlands: Universiteit Utrecht P, 2003. DVD.

Garrett, Greg. *Holy Superheroes! Exploring Faith & Spirituality in Comic Books.* Boulder, CO: Piñon, 2005. Print.

Genette, Gérard. *The Architext: An Introduction.* Trans. Jane E. Lewin. Berkeley: U of California P, 1992. Print.

———. *Palimpsestes: la littérature au second degree.* Paris: Seuil, 1982. Print.

———. *Palimpsests: Litereature in the Second Degree.* Trans. Channa Newman and Claude Doubinsky. Lincoln: U of Nebraska P, 1997. Print.

Giesz, Ludwig. *Phänomenologie des Kitsches.* Munich: Wilhelm Fink Verlag, 1971. Print.

Glaessner, Verina. Rev. of *The Living Dead at the Manchester Morgue. Monthly Film Bulletin* 42.495 (Apr. 1975): 78. Print.

Goggin, Joyce. "Casinos and Sure Bets: *Ocean's Eleven* and Cinematic Money." *Money and Culture.* Ed. Fiona Cox and Hans Schmidt Hannisa. Berne: Lang, 2008. 253–64. Print.

———. "Gaming/Gambling: Addiction and the Video Game Experience." *The Pleasures of Computer Gaming: Essays on Cultural History, Theory and Aesthetics.* Ed. Melanie Swalwell and Jason Wilson. Jefferson, NC: McFarland, 2008. Print.

———. "Making Meaning Happen at the High End of Low-Life." *Travelling Concepts II: Meaning Frame and Metaphor.* Ed. Joyce Goggin and Michael Burke. Amsterdam: ASCA P, 2002. 43–62. Print.

———. " 'Nigella's Deep-Frying a Bounty Bar!': *The Gilmore Girls* and Addiction as a Social Construct." *Screwball Television:* The Gilmore Girls. Ed. David Scott Diffrient and David Lavery, forthcoming. Print.

Gomery, Douglas. *The Hollywood Studio System.* New York: St. Martin's P, 1986. Print.

Gordon, Ian. "Nostalgia, Myth, and Ideology: Visions of Superman at the End of the 'American Century.' " *Comics and Ideology.* Ed. Matthew P. McAllister, Edward H. Sewell Jr., and Ian Gordon. New York: Lang, 2001. Print.

Gottdiener, Mark, Claudia C. Collins, and David R. Dickens. *Las Vegas: The Social Production of an All-American City.* Oxford, UK: Blackwell, 1999. Print.

Grant, Barry Keith. "Taking Back *The Night of the Living Dead*: George Romero, Feminism and the Horror Film." *Wide Angle* 14.1 (Jan. 1992): 64–76. Print. Rpt. in *The Dread of Difference: Gender and the Horror Film.* Ed. Barry Keith Grant. Austin: U. of Texas P, 1996. Print.

Greenberg, Harvey Roy. "Raiders of the Lost Text: Remaking as Contested Homage in *Always*." *Journal of Popular Film and Television* 18.4 (1991): 164–71. Print.

Greene, Brian. *The Fabric of the Cosmos: Space, Time, and the Texture of Reality.* New York: Vintage, 2004. Print.

Grove, David. "Christian Bale: Being Batman." *Film Review* 55 (2005): 198–202. Print.

———. "What the Butler Saw." *Film Review* 55 (2005): 208. Print.

———. "Writing Batman." *Film Review* 55 (2005): 204–6. Print.

"Haken." "Joss Post on Cancellation." Fireflyfans.net Message Board. 13 Dec. 2002. Web. 7 Mar. 2007. <http://fireflyfans.net/thread.asp?b=2&t=1161>.

Hark, Ina Rae. "The Wrath of the Original Cast: Translating Embodied Television Characters to Other Media." *Adaptations: From Text to Screen, Screen to Text*. Ed. Deborah Cartmell and Imelda Whelehan. London: Routledge, 1999. 172–84. Print.

Harvey, David. *The Condition of Postmodernity*. Oxford, UK: Blackwell, 1990. Print.

Hayles, N. Katherine. *How We became Posthuman: Virtual Bodies in Cybernetics, Literature, and Informatics*. Chicago: U of Chicago P, 1999. Print.

Hendrix, Grady. "Attack of the Threequel." *Vulture* 3 May 2007. Web. 22 July 2007. <http://nymag.com/daily/entertainment/2007/05/attack_of_the_threequel.html>.

Herbert, Daniel. "Remaking Transnational Hollywood: An Interview with Roy Lee." *Spectator* 27. 2 (Fall 2007): 94–100. Print.

Hickenlooper, George. "George Romero: I Am Legend." *Reel Conversations: Candid Interviews with Film's Foremost Directors and Critics*. New York: Citadel, 1991. Print.

Higashi, Sumiko. *Night of the Living Dead*: A Horror Film about the Horrors of the Vietnam Era." *From Hanoi to Hollywood: The Vietnam War in American Film*. Ed. Linda Dittmar and Gene Michaud. New Brunswick, NJ: Rutgers UP, 1990. Print.

Hillier, Jim. *The New Hollywood*. London: Studio Vista, 1993. Print.

Hills, Matt. *Fan Cultures*. London: Routledge, 2002. Print.

Hoberman, J. "Ten Years that Shook the World." *American Film* 10 (June 1985): 34–59. Print.

Holleran, Scott. "Interview with Ted Elliott and Terry Rossio." *Box Office Mojo*. 31 May 2007. Web. 1 June 2007. <http://www.boxofficemojo.com/features/?id=2323&pagenum=all&p=.htm>.

Horkheimer, Max, and Theodor W. Adorno. *The Dialectic of Enlightenment Philosophical Fragments*. Ed. Gunzlin Schmid Moerr. Trans. Edmund Jephcott. Stanford, CA: Stanford UP, 2002. Print.

Horwath, Alexander. "The Impure Cinema: New Hollywood 1967–1976." Elsaesser et al. 9–18. Print.

Housel, Rebecca. "Myth, Morality and the Women of the X-Men." *Superheroes and Philosophy: Truth, Justice, and the Socratic Way*. Ed. Tom Morris and Matt Morris. Chicago: Open Court, 2005. Print.

Hughes, Linda K., and Michael Lund. *The Victorian Serial*. Charlottesville: U of Virginia P, 1991. Print.

Husband, Janet. *Sequels: An Annotated Guide to Novels in Series*. Chicago: American Library Assn., 1982. Print.

Hutcheon, Linda. *A Theory of Adaptation*. New York: Routledge, 2006. Print.

Huyssen, Andreas. *Present Pasts: Urban Palimpsests and the Politics of Memory*. Stanford, CA: Stanford UP, 2003. Print.

Iaccino, James F. *Psychological Reflections on Cinematic Terror: Jungian Archetypes in Horror Films*. Westport, CT: Praeger, 1994. Print.

Ichise, Takashige. Personal interview. Trans. Chiho Asada. 4 Oct. 2006.

"International Talk Like a Pirate Day." N.d. Web. 3 June 2007. <http://www.talklikeapirate.com>.

Israel, Jonathan. *The Dutch Republic: Its Rise, Greatness, and Fall: 1477–1806*. Oxford, UK: Oxford UP, 1998. Print.

Iwabuchi, Koichi. *Recentering Globalization: Popular Culture and Japanese Transnationalism*. Durham, NC: Duke UP, 2002. Print.

"Jack Sparrow." *Wikipedia*. N.d. Web. 12 June 2007. <http://en.wikipedia.org/wiki/Jack_Sparrow>.

James, Henry. "The Art of Fiction." James, *Literary Criticism* 44–65.

———. "The Science of Criticism." James, *Literary Criticism* 95–99.

———. *Literary Criticism: Essays on Literature, American Writers, English Writers*. New York: Library of America, 1984. Print.

Jameson, Fredric. "Postmodernism and Consumer Society." *Postmodern Culture*. Ed. Hal Foster. London: Pluto, 1985. 111–25. Print.

Jenkins, Henry. *Convergence Culture: Where Old and New Media Collide*. New York: New York UP, 2006. Print.

———. "The Cultural Logic of Media Convergence." *International Journal of Cultural Studies* 7.1 (2004): 33–43. Print.

Jess-Cooke, Carolyn. *Film Sequels: Theory and Practice from Hollywood to Bollywood*. Edinburgh: Edinburgh UP, 2008. Print.

Johnson, Charles. *A General History of the Robberies and Murders of the Most Notorious Pyrates from Their First Rise and Settlement of the Island of Providence to the Present Year*. 4th ed. London: Routledge, 1926. Print.

Jones, Alan. "Dan O'Bannon on Directing." *Cinefantastique* 15.4 (Oct. 1985): 19–20, 54. Print.

———. "Dead Reckoning." *Film Review* 662 (Oct. 2005): 64–66. Print.

———. "A New Dawn." *Cinefantastique* 36.1 (Feb.–Mar. 2004): 34–37, 41–43. Print.

Jordan, Sean, and Edward Gross. "A Knight in Gotham." *Cinefantastique* 37.4 (2005): 22–35. Print.

Kaku, Michio. *Parallel Worlds*. New York: Anchor, 2005. Print.

Kakutani, Michiko. "The Idea Was Not to Have One." *New York Times* 29 Dec. 2002, sec. 2: 1ff. Print.

Katz, Ephraim. *The Film Encyclopedia: The Complete Guide to Film and Film Industry*. 6th ed. New York: Collins, 2008. Print.

Keathley, Christian. "Trapped in the Affection Image: Hollywood's Post-traumatic Cycle (1970–1976)." Elsaesser et al. 293–308. Print.

Kempster, Grant. "Batman Genesis." *Film Review* 55 (2005): 214–16. Print.

Kern, Stephen. *The Culture of Time and Space: 1880–1918*. Cambridge, MA: Harvard UP, 1983. Print.

Kernan, Alvin B. "The Henriad: Shakespeare's Major History Plays." *Modern Shakespearean Criticism: Essays on Style, Dramaturgy, and the Major Plays*. New York: Harcourt, Brace and World, 1970. Print.

King, Noel. " 'The Last Good Time We Ever Had': Remembering the New Hollywood Cinema." Elsaesser et al. 19–36. Print.

Klaprat, Cathy. "The Star as Market Strategy: Bette Davis in Another Light." *The American Film Industry*. Ed. Tino Balio. 2nd ed. Madison: U of Wisconsin P, 1985. Print.

Kofman, Sarah. *L'Enfance de l'art: Une interprétation de l'esthétique freudienne*. Paris: Galilée, 1985. Print.

Kolker, Robert Phillip. *A Cinema of Loneliness: Penn, Kubrick, Coppola, Scorsese, Altman*. Oxford, UK: Oxford UP, 1980. Print.

Kracauer, Siegfried. *Theory of Film: The Redemption of Physical Reality*. Princeton, NJ: Princeton UP, 1997. Print.

Kübler-Ross, Elisabeth. *On Death and Dying*. New York: Macmillan, 1969.

Land, Chris. "Flying the Black Flag: Revolt, Revolution and the Social Organization of Piracy in the 'Golden Age.' " *Management & Organizational History* 2.2 (2007): 169–92. Print.

Laplanche, Jean. *Essays on Otherness*. London: Routledge, 1999. Print.

Lawrence, John Shelton, and Robert Jewett. *The Myth of the American Superhero*. Grand Rapids, MI: Eerdmans, 2002. Print.

Lawrenson, Edward. Rev. of *Batman Begins*. *Sight and Sound* 15.6 (2005): 40–41. Print.

Lee, Roy. Personal interview. 9 Sept. 2006.

Lefebvre, Martin. "On Memory and Imagination in the Cinema." *New Literary History* 30.2 (1999): 479–98. Print.

Leitch, Thomas. "Twice-Told Tales: Disavowal and the Rhetoric of the Remake." Forrest and Koos 37–62.

Levy, Emanuel. "Pirates Dead Man's Chest: Depp's Iconic Role." *Emanuel Levy*. N.d. Web. 1 June 2007. <http://www.emanuellevy.com/article.php?articleID=2688>.

Lewis, Jon. "Disney after Disney: Family Business and the Business of Family." *Disney Discourse: Producing the Magic Kingdom*. Ed. E. Smoodin. New York: Routledge, 1994. 87–105. Print.

———. "If History Has Taught Us Anything . . . ." Browne 23–56.

Lightning, Robert K. "Interracial Tensions in *Night of the Living Dead*." *CineAction!* 53 (Nov. 2000): 22–29. Print.

Limbacher, James L. *Haven't I Seen You Somewhere Before? Remakes, Sequels, and Series in Motion Pictures and Television, 1896–1978*. 1979. Ann Arbor, MI: Pieriean, 1991. Print.

Long, Tom. "Energized 'Serenity' screams franchise." *Detroit News* 30 Sept. 2005. Web. 7 Mar. 2007. <http://www.detnews.com/2005/screens/0509/30/F04-332298.htm>.

Longworth, Karina. Rev. of *The Squid and the Whale*. 10 Oct. 2005. Web. 20 Sept. 2006. <www.cinematical.com/2005/10/06/review-the-squid-and-the-whale>.

Lopate, Phillip. "A Conversation with Noah Baumbach." *The Squid and the Whale*. Sony Classics, 2006. DVD.

Lowenstein, Adam. "Cinema, Benjamin, and the Allegorical Representation of September 11." *Critical Quarterly* 45.1–2 (July 2004): 73–84. Print.

Lowry, Ed, and Louis Black. "Cinema of Apocalypse." *Take One* 7.6 (1979): 17–18. Print.

Lucas, Tim. "Dawns of the Dead." *Video Watchdog* 38 (1997): 40–49. Print.

Lycett, Andrew. *The Man Who Created Sherlock Holmes: The Life and Times of Sir Arthur Conan Doyle*. New York: Free, 2007. Print.

Macgowan, Kenneth. *Behind the Screen: The History and Technique of the Motion Picture.* New York: Dell, 1965. Print.

Man, Glenn. "Ideology and Genre in the *Godfather* Films." Browne 109–132.

Manders, Stanley. "A New Dawn: Dead Reckoning." *Cinefantastique* (Feb.–Mar. 2004): 38–41. Print.

Manovich, Lev. *The Language of New Media.* Cambridge, MA: MIT Press, 2001. Print.

Marchetti, Nino. "Disney Developing 'Pirates' Mobile Game." *Digital Trends* 27 Apr. 2007. Web. 5 June 2007. <http://news.digitaltrends.com/news/story/10230/disney_developing_pirates_mobile_game>.

Marcus, Walter. "Five Anchor Bay Releases." *Video Watchdog* 54 (Nov. 1999): 22–34. Print.

Marshall, P. David. "The New Intertextual Commodity." *The New Media Book.* Ed. Dan Harries. London: BFI, 2002. 69–81. Print.

Martin, Adrian. "Zombies Pack Political Punch." *Age* 4 Aug. 2005: 19. Print.

"MartinT." "Save *Firefly*." Fireflyfans.net Message Board. 13 Apr. 2007. Web. 7 Mar. 2007. <http://fireflyfans.net/thread.asp?b=2&t=28149>.

Mazdon, Lucy. "Rewriting and Remakes: Questions of Originality and Authenticity." *On Translating French Literature and Film.* Ed. Geoffrey T. Harris. Amsterdam: Rodopi, 1996. 47–63. Print.

McCarthy, Guy. "Chris Marker: Marking Time." *Film West* 37 (1999): 20–22. Print.

McCarty, John. *Splatter Movies: Breaking the Last Taboo of the Screen.* New York: St. Martin's P, 1984. Print.

McConahay, Shari. "Captain Jack Sparrow Top Pick for 2006 Most Popular Halloween Costume." *Annies Costumes.* N.d. Web. 9 June 2007. <http://www.anniescostumes.com/popularhalloweencostumes2006.htm>.

McGonigal, Jane. "A Real Little Game: The Performance of Belief in Pervasive Play." N.d. Web. 2 June 2007. <http://www.avantgame.com/MCGONIGAL%20A%20Real%20Little%20Game%20DiGRA%202003.pdf>.

Miller, Toby, Nitin Govil, John McMurria, Richard Maxwell, and Ting Wang. *Global Hollywood 2.* London: BFI, 2002. Print.

Moore, John. *Defoe in the Pillory and Other Studies.* Bloomington: Indiana UP, 1939. Print.

Morley, David, and Kevin Robins. *Spaces of Identity: Global Media, Electronic Landscapes and Cultural Boundaries.* London: Routledge, 1995. Print.

Mottram, James. *The Sundance Kids: How the Mavericks Took Back Hollywood.* London: Faber, 2006. Print.

Mugleston, Robert. "Dynamic Duos." *Scriptwriter* 24 (2005): 48–51. Print.

Mulvey, Laura. *Death 24x a Second: Stillness and the Moving Image.* London: Reaktion, 2006. Print.

Neale, Steve. " 'The Last Good Time We Ever Had?' Revising the Hollywood Renaissance." *Contemporary American Cinema.* Ed. Linda Ruth Williams and Michael Hammond. Maidenhead, UK: Open UP/McGraw, 2006. 90–108. Print.

Nelson, David. "Movie Sequels through the Years." 7 May 2006. Web. 22 July 2007. <http://www.pointsincase.com/columns/david/5-7-06.htm>.

Newman, Kim. "Cape Fear." *Sight and Sound* 15.6 (2005): 18–21. Print.

———. *Nightmare Movies: A Critical History of the Horror Film 1968–88*. Rev. ed. London: Bloomsbury, 1988. Print.

———. Rev. of *Batman Begins*. *Empire* 194 (2005): 28. Print.

———. Rev. of *Day of the Dead*. *Monthly Film Bulletin* 53.632 (Sept. 1986): 266–67. Print.

———. Rev. of *Land of the Dead*. *Sight and Sound* 15.10 (Oct. 2005): 76–78. Print.

"1999." *Koreanfilm.org*. N.d. Web. 27 Nov. 2008. <http://koreanfilm.org/kfilm99.html>.

Nowlan, Robert A., and Gwendolyn Wright Nowlan. *Cinema Sequels and Remakes, 1903–1987*. Jefferson, NC: McFarland, 1989. Print.

Nugent Frank S. " 'Four Wives,' the Warner Sequel to 'Four Daughters,' Opens at the Strand—'Katia' at Little Carnegie." *New York Times* 23 Dec. 1939. Web. 23 Jan. 2007. <http://movies2.nytimes.com/mem/movies/review.html?res=9A05EED9153EE432A25750C2A9649D946894D6CF>.

———. "Strand's 'Daughters Courageous' Faces the Problem of the Prodigal Father—Miss Temple at the Roxy at the Roxy [*sic*] at the 86th Street Casino." *New York Times* 24 June 1939. Web. 23 Jan. 2007. <http://movies2.nytimes.com/mem/movies/review.html?res=9B07E0D7173BE033A25757C2A9609C946894D6CF>.

Oropeza, B. J., ed. *The Gospel According to Superheroes: Religion and Popular Culture*. New York: Lang, 2005. Print.

Osborne, Peter. *The Politics of Time: Modernity and Avant-Garde*. London: Verso. 1995. Print.

Palmer, R. Barton. "*Blood Simple*: Defining the Commercial/Independent Text." *Persistence of Vision* 6 (Summer 1988): 5–19. Print.

Paquet, Darcy. "Japanese Films in Korea." *Koreanfilm.org*. N.d. Web. 27 Nov. 2008. <http://koreanfilm.org/japanfilm.html>.

———. Message to the author. 23 July 2006. E-mail.

Patten, Robert L. "Serialized Retrospection in *The Pickwick Papers*." *Literature in the Marketplace: Nineteenth-Century British Publishing and Reading Practices*. Ed. John O. Jordan and Robert L. Patten. Cambridge, UK: Cambridge UP, 1995. 122–42. Print.

Peachment, Chris. "Dead Funny." *Time Out* 813 (Mar. 19, 1986): 19–20. Print.

Percesepe, Gary. "Introduction to the Politics 2004 Issue." *MississippiReview.com* <http://www.mississippireview.com/2004/Vol10No1-Jan04/1001-0104-00-percesepe-intro.html>.

Perez, Dan. Rev. of *Night of the Living Dead* [1990]. *Cinefantastique* 21.5 (Apr. 1991): 58–59. Print.

Perkins, Claire. "Remaking and the Film Trilogy: Whit Stillman's Authorial Triptych." *Velvet Light Trap* 61 (Spring 2008): 14–25. Print.

"Pirate's Legend." N.d. Web. 29 May 2009. <www.pirateslegend.com>.

"*Pirates of the Caribbean: At World's End.*" *Box Office Mojo.* N.d. Web. 2 June 2007. <http://www.boxofficemojo.com/movies/?id=piratesofthecaribbean3.htm>.

" 'Pirates 3' breaks opening box office record worldwide." *People's Daily Online* 29 May 2007. Web. 4 June 2007. <http://english.people.com.cn/200705/29/eng20070529_378756.html>.

Pitts, Michael R. *Famous Movie Detectives.* Metuchen, NJ: Scarecrow, 1979. Print.

Pollack, Andrew. "Matsushita Tells Why It Decided to Abandon Hollywood." *New York Times* 12 Apr. 1995: D10. Print.

"Pre-Visualization." *Persistence of Vision.* N.d. Web. 1 Dec. 2008 <http://persistenceofvision.com>.

"Project: *The Ring.*" *Variety.com* 18 Oct. 2002. Web. 24 Nov. 2008. <http://www.variety.com/studiosystems/index.asp?layout=studiosystems&ss_view=s_s_project&mode=allcredits&project_id=129010>.

Quaresima, Leonardo. "Loving Texts Two as a Time: The Film Remake." *Cinémas* 12.3 (2002): 73–84. Print.

Quinby, Lee. *Millennial Seduction: A Skeptic Confronts Apocalyptic Culture.* Ithaca, NY: Cornell UP, 1999. Print.

Radstone, Susan. "Screening Trauma: *Forrest Gump,* Film and Memory." *Memory and Methodology.* Ed. Susan Radstone. London: Berg, 2000. 79–110. Print.

Rae, Graham. "Dead Reckoning." *Cinefantastique* 37.4 (July 2005): 45–46, 50–51, 70. Print.

Rechtshaffen, Michael. "Pirates of Caribbean: At World's End: Bottom Line: Avast—As in a Vast Improvement over the Soggy Previous Installment." *Hollywood Reporter* 24 May 2007. Web. 10 June 2007. <http://www.hollywoodreporter.com/hr/film/reviews/article_display.jsp?&rid=9270>.

Rediker, Markus. *Villains of All Nations: Atlantic Pirates in the Golden Age.* London: Verso, 2004. Print.

Reith, Gerda. *The Age of Chance: Gambling and Western Culture.* London: Routledge, 1999. Print.

Rev. of *Zombie* [aka *Zombi 2*]. *Video Watchdog* 46 (1998): 74–75.

Richardson, Niall. "The Gospel According to Spider-Man." *Journal of Popular Culture* 37.4 (2004): 694–703. Print.

Roberts, Barrie. "Priscilla Lane, All American." *Classic Images* 284 (Feb. 1999). Web. 12 Jan. 2007. <http://www.classicimages.com/1999/february99/lane.html>.

Robinson, Michael. "Contemporary Cultural Production in South Korea." *New Korean Cinema.* Ed. Chi-Yun Shin and Julian Stringer. New York: New York UP, 2005. 15–31. Print.

Rotman, Brian. *Signifying Nothing: The Semiotics of Zero.* London: Macmillan, 1987. Print.

Rowe, Michael. "*Land of the Dead,* Home of the Brave." *Fangoria* 244 (June 2005): 50–55, 97. Print.

———. "Man of 1,000 Zombies." *Fangoria* 245 (Aug. 2005): 65–69. Print.

Russell, Jamie. *Book of the Dead: The Complete History of Zombie Cinema*. Godalming, Surrey: FAB Press, 2005. Print.

Russo, Tom. "Caped Fear." *Premiere* 18.9 (2005): 68–72, 135. Print.

Ryssdal, Kai. "Disney Slashing Movie Production: Interview with Michael Speier, *Daily Variety* Managing Editor." *Marketplace* 12 July 2006. Web. 3 June 2007. <http://marketplace.publicradio.org/shows/2006/07/12/PM200607126.html>.

Sakai, Naoki. *Translation and Subjectivity: On "Japan" and Cultural Nationalism*. Minneapolis: U of Minnesota P, 1997. Print.

Sardar, Ziauddin, and Merryl Wyn Davies. *American Dream, Global Nightmare*. Cambridge, UK: Icon Books, 2004. Print.

Saunders, George. *CivilWarLand in Bad Decline: Stories and a Novella*. New York: Riverhead Books, 1996. Print.

Schatz, Thomas. "The New Hollywood." *Film Theory Goes to the Movies*. Ed. Jim Collins, Hilary Radner, and Ava Preacher Collins. New York: Routledge, 1993. 8–36. Print.

Schell, Jesse, and Joe Shochet. "Designing Interactive Theme Park Rides: Lessons Learned Creating Disney's *Pirates of the Caribbean—Battle for the Buccaneer Gold*." *IEEE Computer Graphics and Applications* 21.4 (July–August 2001): 11–13. Print.

Schwartz, Hillel. *The Culture of the Copy: Striking Likenesses, Unreasonable Facsimiles*. New York: Zone Books, 1996. Print.

Sciretta, Peter. "Bruce Willis Says *Live Free or Die Hard* Is BETTER than *Die Hard*." *Slash Film* 4 May 2007. Web. 22 July 2007. <http://www.slashfilm.com/2007/05/04/bruce-willis-says-live-free-or-die-hard-is-better-than-die-hard/>.

Sconce, Jeffrey. *Haunted Media: Electronic Presence from Telegraphy to Television*. Durham, NC: Duke UP, 2000. Print.

———. "Irony, Nihilism and the New American 'Smart' Film." *Screen* 43.4 (2002): 349–69. Print.

Scott, A. O. "Growing Up Bohemian and Absurd in Brooklyn." *New York Times* 5 Oct. 2005. Print.

"ScottEVill." "Straight-to-DVD Movies of Cancelled (and Living) TV Shows." ExIsle Message Board. 14 Jan. 2007. Web. 7 Mar. 2007. <http://www.exisle.net/mb/index.php?showtopic=43283>.

Shaviro, Steven. *The Cinematic Body*. Minneapolis: U of Minnesota P, 1993. Print.

Shell, Marc. *Art & Money*. Chicago: U of Chicago P, 1995. Print.

"Sidaris." "Can't More Be Done? It Cannot Die." Fireflyfans.net Message Board. 22 July 2004. Web. 7 Mar. 2007. <http://fireflyfans.net/thread.asp?b=2&t=6351>.

Silverman, Stephen M. "Hollywood Cloning: Sequels, Prequels, Remakes, and Spin-Offs." *American Film* 3.9 (July–August 1978): 24–30. Print.

Simmel, Georg. *The Philosophy of Money*. Trans. Tom Bottomore and David Frisby. London: Routledge, 1990. Print.

Simonet, Thomas. "Conglomerates and Content: Remakes, Sequels, and Series in the New Hollywood." *Current Research in Film: Audiences, Economics, and Law.* Vol. 3. Ed. Bruce A. Austin. Norwood, NJ: Ablex, 1987. 154–62. Print.

Simpson, Jeff. "Next DI Implosion Planned." *Las Vegas Sun* 27 Apr. 2004. Web. 16 Aug. 2007. <http://www.lasvegassun.com/sunbin/stories/business/2004/apr/27/516758770.html>.

Simpson, M. J. "Dead Reckoning." *SFX* 25 (May 1997): 59–60. Print.

Skelton, Stephen. *The Gospel according to the World's Greatest Superhero.* Eugene, OR: Harvest House, 2006. Print.

Skurnick, Lizzie. "Chick Lit, The Sequel: Yummy Mummy." *New York Times* 17 Dec. 2006. Section 9: 1–2. Print.

Spencer, Liese. Rev. of *Ocean's Twelve. Sight and Sound* 15.2 (February 2005): 62–64. Print.

Sporich, Brett. "DHE 'Ring' Set to Bring Viewers into Inner Circle." *Hollywood Reporter* 23 Jan. 2003: 58. Print.

Stevens, Dana. "Booty Nights: The Jolly Swashbucklers of *Pirates of the Caribbean: At World's End*." *Slate.* 24 May 2007. Web. 2 June 2007. <http://www.slate.com/id/2166977/>.

Strange, Susan. *Casino Capitalism.* New York: St. Martin's P, 1997. Print.

Strasser, Tessa. "Movie Review: Depp Charms with New 'Pirates' Movie." *New York Times.* 12 July 2006 Web. 1 June 2007. <http://movies2.nytimes.com/2007/05/24/movies/24pira.html>.

Sullivan, Emmet. "Just Say 'Sequel': How Dangerous Is Hollywood's Remake Obsession? *Daily Northwestern.* 20 Apr. 2006. Web. 23 July 2007. <http://media.www.dailynorthwestern.com/media/storage/paper853/news/2006/04/20/Play/Just-Say.sequel-1921686.shtml>.

Suskind, Ron. "Without a Doubt." *New York Times Magazine.* 17 Oct. 2004. Web. 2 Oct. 2008. <http://cscs.umich.edu/~crshalizi/sloth/2004–10–16b.html>.

Sutherland, Meghan. "Rigor/Mortis: The Industrial Life of Style in American Zombie Cinema." *Framework* 48.1 (Spring 2007): 64–78. Print.

Sutton, Paul. "Afterwardsness in Film." *Journal for Cultural Research* 8.3 (2004): 385–405. Print.

———. "Afterwardsness in Film: Patrice Leconte's *Le Mari de la Coiffeuse*." *French Studies* 53.3 (1999): 307–17. Print.

———. "Cinematic Spectatorship as Procrastinatory Practice." *Parallax* 5.1 (1999): 80–82. Print.

———. "Remaking the Remake: Olivier Assayas' *Irma Vep* (1996)." *French Cinema in the 1990s: Continuity and Difference.* Ed. Phil Powrie. Oxford, UK: Oxford UP, 1999. 69–80. Print.

Suzuki, Koji. *Loop.* 1998. Trans. Glynne Walley. New York: Vertical, 2003. Print.

———. *Ring.* 1998. Trans. Robert B. Rohmer and Glynne Walley. New York: Vertical, 2005. Print.

Szebin, Frederick C. "*Night of the Living Dead*: The Remake." *Cinefantastique* 21.2 (Sept. 1990): 8–9. Print.

Taylor, Mark C. *Confidence Games: Money and Markets in a World without Redemption*. Chicago: U of Chicago P, 2004. Print.

Thompson, Anne. "Whedon Flock Ready for 'Firefly' Resurrection." *Hollywood Reporter* 22 July 2005. Web. 7 Mar. 2007. <http://www.hollywoodreporter.com/hr/search/article_display.jsp?vnu_content_id=1000989704>.

Thonen, John. "Sequels that Wouldn't Die." *Imagi-Movies* 3.1 (Fall 1995): 10–12, 17, 19, 21. Print.

Tomashevsky, Boris. "Thematics." *Russian Formalist Criticism: Four Essays*. Trans. Lee T. Lemon and Marion J. Reis. Lincoln: U of Nebraska P, 1965. 61–95. Print.

Trushell, John M. "American Dreams of Mutants: The X-Men—'Pulp' Fiction, Science Fiction, and Superheroes." *Journal of Popular Culture* 38.1 (2004): 149–68. Print.

T. S. " 'Ringside Maisie' Takes Up Quarters at the Capitol Theatre—'Adventure in Washington' with Herbert Marshall Arrives at Loew's State." *New York Times*. 1 Aug. 1941. Web. 5 Jan. 2007. <http://movies2.nytimes.com/mem/movies/review.html?res=9401EFD6123FE13BBC4953DFBE66838A659EDE>.

Tucker, Betty Jo. "Keeping an Eye on Jack Sparrow." *ReelTalk*. N.d. Web. 1 June 2007. <http://www.reeltalkreviews.com/browse/viewitem.asp?type=review&id=2181>.

———. "How to Steal a Movie: Part II." *ReelTalk*. N.d. Web. 1 June 2007. <http://www.reeltalkreviews.com/browse/viewitem.asp?type=review&id=1767>.

Twitchell, James. *Carnival Culture: The Trashing of Taste in America*. New York: Columbia UP, 1992. Print.

Venturi, Robert, Denise Scott Brown, and Steven Izenour. *Learning from Las Vegas: The Forgotten Symbolism of Architectural Form*. Cambridge, MA: MIT Press, 1996. Print.

Verevis, Constantine. *Film Remakes*. Edinburgh: Edinburgh UP, 2006. Print.

Vogel, Harold. *Entertainment Industry Economics: A Guide for Financial Analysis*. 6th ed. Cambridge, UK: Cambridge UP, 2004. Print.

Waller, Gregory A. *The Living and the Undead: From Stoker's* Dracula *to Romero's* Dawn of the Dead. Urbana: U of Illinois P, 1986. Print.

"Walt Disney Q3 2006 Earnings Conference Call Transcript." N.d. Web. 2 June 2007. <http://media.seekingalpha.com/article/15265>.

Wang, Shujen. *Framing Piracy: Globalization and Film Distribution in Greater China*. Lanham, MD: Rowman and Littlefield, 2003. Print.

Wasko, Janet. *Hollywood in the Information Age: Beyond the Silver Screen*. Austin: U of Texas P, 1995. Print.

———. *Understanding Disney: The Manufacture of Fantasy*. London: Polity P, 2001.

Wasser, Frederick. *Veni Vidi, Video: The Hollywood Empire and the VCR*. Austin: U of Texas P, 2001. Print.

Watt, Ian. *The Rise of the Novel: Studies in Defoe, Richardson and Fielding*. Berkeley: U of California P, 1957. Print.

Watts, Steven. *The Magic Kingdom: Walt Disney and the American Way of Life*. Boston: Houghton, 1997. Print.

Waxman, Sharon. "Cyberface: New Technology that Captures the Soul." *New York Times*. 15 Oct. 2006. Web. 9 Jan. 2007. <http://www.nytimes.com/2006/10/15/movies/15waxm.html>.

———. *Rebels on the Backlot: Six Maverick Directors and How They Conquered the Hollywood Studio System*. New York: Harper Perennial, 2006. Print.

"What We Do." *Lola Visual Effects*. N.d. Web. 10 Oct. 2007. <http://www.lolavfx.com/what/php>.

Wheaton, Mark. "Waking the Dead." *Starburst* 62 (Feb. 2004): 112–13, 115–18. Print.

Whedon, Joss. "Relighting the Firefly." *Serenity*. Universal Home Video, 2005. DVD.

"Who We Are." *Lola Visual Effects*. N.d. Web. 10 Oct. 2007. <http://www.lolavfx.com/who.php>.

Williams, David E. "A Real Scream." *Cinefantastique* 36.5 (Oct.–Nov. 2004): 3, 5, 7–8. Print.

Williams, Kam. "Interview with Johnny Depp." *The Black Collegian* Online. May 2007. Web. 2 June 2007. <http://www.black-collegian.com/extracurricular/kam/kam_johnny_depp_0507.htm>.

Williams, Tony. *Knight of the Living Dead: The Cinema of George A. Romero*. London: Wallflower, 2003. Print.

Wood, Andy. "Andy Wood Goes to Hollywood: The MCV Interview." 7 July 2006. Web. N.d. <http://www.image-metrics.com/news/im_news4_march24_2006.pdf>.

Wood, Robin. "Apocalypse Now: Notes on the Living Dead." *American Nightmare: Essays on the Horror Film*. Ed. Andrew Britton et al. Toronto: Festival of Festivals, 1979. Print.

———. "The Woman's Nightmare: Masculinity in *Day of the Dead*." *CineAction!* 6 (Summer–Fall 1986): 45–49. Print.

Wright, Bradford W. *Comic Book Nation: The Transformation of Youth Culture in America*. Baltimore, MD: Johns Hopkins UP, 2001. Print.

Xu, Gang Gary. "Remaking East Asia, Outsourcing Hollywood." *Senses of Cinema* 34 (Jan.–Mar. 2005). Web. 25 Nov. 2008. <http://www.sensesofcinema.com/contents/05/34/remaking_east_asia.html>.

Yakir, Dan. "Morning becomes Romero." Interview with George Romero. *Film Comment* 15.3 (May–June 1979): 60–65. Print.

Young, Paul. *The Cinema Dreams Its Rivals: Media Fantasy Films from Radio to the Internet*. Minneapolis: U of Minnesota P, 2006. Print.

Zeitlin, Michael. "Donald Barthelme and the Postmodern Sequel." Budra and Schellenberg 160–73.

Žižek, Slavoj. *The Sublime Object of Ideology*. London: Verso, 1989. Print.

Contributors

Jennifer Forrest is professor of French at Texas State University, San Marcos. She is the editor of *The Legend Returns and Dies Harder Another Day: Essays on Film Series* (McFarland, 2008), the coeditor of *Dead Ringers: The Remake in Theory and Practice* (SUNY Press, 2002), and author of articles on late-nineteenth-century French literature and popular culture. She is working on a book-length study of the late-nineteenth-century circus in French literature, art, and popular culture.

Joyce Goggin is associate professor at the University of Amsterdam, with an interdisciplinary appointment in literature, film, and new media. She is also head of studies for the humanities and computing at Amsterdam University College. Her recent publications include "Gaming/Gambling: Addiction and the Videogame Experience," "Jane Austen Reloaded: Portraits and Adaptations," and "Architectural Space, Cyber Bodies and the Literary Text: A Voyage through Neuromancer." She has also published articles on gambling, money, play, and magic and is currently editing a book on comics and graphic novels.

Ina Rae Hark is distinguished professor emerita of English and Film Studies at the University of South Carolina. She is the author of the volume on Star Trek in the BFI Television Classics series and the editor or coeditor of *Screening the Male, The Road Movie Book, Exhibition: the Film Reader,* and *American Cinema of the 1930s: Themes and Variations.* She has published more than thirty articles and chapters on film and media studies, concentrating in recent years on the films of Alfred Hitchcock and on science-fiction films and television.

Daniel Herbert is assistant professor in Screen Arts and Cultures at the University of Michigan. His essays appear in several edited collections and journals, including *Film Quarterly, Millennium Film Journal,* and *Quarterly Review of Film and Video.*

Carolyn Jess-Cooke is senior lecturer in Film Studies at the University of Sunderland. She is author of *Shakespeare on Film: Such Things as Dreams Are Made Of* (Wallflower Press, 2007), *Film Sequels: Theory and Practice from Hollywood to Bollywood* (Edinburgh University Press, 2008), and coeditor with Melissa Croteau of *Apocalyptic Shakespeares* (McFarland, 2009). She is also an award-winning poet.

Thomas Leitch teaches English and directs the Film Studies program at the University of Delaware. His most recent books are *Perry Mason* (Wayne State UP, 2005) and *Film Adaptation and Its Discontents* (Johns Hopkins UP, 2007).

Simon McEnteggart teaches at the Media and Culture Department at the University of Sunderland. His research interests include the superhero film and questions of ideology and the body in film.

R. Barton Palmer is Calhoun Lemon Professor of Literature at Clemson University. He has published extensively on literature and film. Recently published and forthcoming books include *Joel and Ethan Coen* (U of Illinois P, 2004); with Linda Badley, *Traditions in World Cinema* (Edinburgh UP 2005); *Hollywood's Dark Cinema*, 2nd rev. ed (U of Illinois P); with Linda Badley, *American Commercial-Independent Cinema* (Edinburgh UP); with David Boyd, *After Hitchcock: Imitation, Influence, Intertextuality* (U of Texas P), *David Cronenberg* (U of Illinois P).

Claire Perkins is assistant lecturer in Film and Television Studies at Monash University, Melbourne. Her book on US "smart" cinema is forthcoming from Edinburgh University Press.

Paul Sutton is principal lecturer in Film at Roehampton University in London. He has interests in Italian and French cinema, film theory, and critical theory, and he has written extensively on the idea of afterwardsness in film. He has published articles in journals such as *Screen*, *Parallax*, *Angelaki*, and the *Journal for Cultural Research* as well as book chapters on a range of subjects, including the remake and film directors Nanni Moretti and Olivier Assayas. He is currently writing the book *Remaking Film: In History, In Theory* (Blackwell, forthcoming).

Constantine Verevis teaches Film and Television Studies in the School of English, Communications & Performance Studies at Monash University, Melbourne. He is the author of *Film Remakes* (Edinburgh UP, 2006).

Index